The History of
Bowling Green State University

by

JAMES ROBERT OVERMAN

PUBLISHED BY

Bowling Green University Press

BOWLING GREEN, OHIO

©

BOWLING GREEN UNIVERSITY PRESS
Library of Congress Card Number
67-31442

Printed in the United States of America
Bowling Green, Ohio
1967

Table of Contents

Preface

SEVERAL YEARS AGO I overheard the remark that Bowling Green State University is an institution with a great future but no past. I am confident that the first part of this statement is true but know the second part is false. For Bowling Green State University does have an interesting past of which alumni, students, faculty, administrative officers and the people of Ohio can all be very proud. It is the knowledge of this past that furnishes the best evidence that the future will be even brighter than anyone can foresee at the present time. It was in the hope of being able to do something toward preserving a knowledge of this past (which seems to be in grave danger of being forgotten) that I decided to undertake the task of writing a history of the first 53 years of Bowling Green State University.

My chief qualification for the task I have undertaken is the fact that I have been connected with the University since it first opened its doors to students in September, 1914, and have been an interested observer of and, for most of the period, an active participant in its development. I have, therefore, attempted to clothe the cold facts with something of the human interest that accompanied the struggles of a young institution, and to show the spirit which always looked forward to a glorious future. I hope that this account of the early years will help the reader join with me in saying:

We are proud of Bowling Green State University. We are proud of its past. We are proud of its present. We are proud of the future that lies ahead.

I wish to acknowledge my debt to all who have helped in the preparation of this history. Particular thanks are due to President William T. Jerome III, whose interest and support have made its preparation and publication possible; to Ivan E. Lake, who furnished much information concerning the early days; to Kenneth H. McFall, whose doctor's dissertation *From Normal College to State University*, has been a constant help; to Ervin J. Kreischer, Treasurer Emeritus; and to many others who have either supplied or verified facts given in this history.

James Robert Overman
Dean—Emeritus

Bowling Green, Ohio
1967

CHAPTER ONE

A Brief History of Teacher Training in Ohio from the Beginning to 1910

ANY ACCOUNT of the history of the institution now known as Bowling Green State University must start with a consideration of teacher training in Ohio, since this school was created to provide such training for the teachers of the northwestern portion of the state. Although Ohio was among the earliest of the states admitted to the Union, it was one of the last to provide training for teachers in state-supported schools. In fact, it was almost a century after its admission as a state, in 1803, before legislation was passed providing for the first state support of teacher-training.

Reasons for the Late Start

Ohio's long delay in entering this field was not due to a lack of interest in the education of its citizens, but to a number of other causes. The first of these, both in time and importance, was the character and background of the early settlers. They were hardy pioneers and, as such, were independent, self-reliant, and highly distrustful of any attempts at centralized control. Dr. Alonzo Myers in his *Contributions to Education, No. 266, Columbia University Press,* states:

> Ohio was from the beginning opposed to centralization of government authority. . . . Nowhere is this prejudice against centralized administration better illustrated than in the various phases of educational legislation.

The early settlers were thrifty as well as independent. These two traits resulted in a willingness on the part of the General Assembly to encourage local enterprise and initiative in matters of education, as long as the state was not asked to furnish support or assume control.

4

The early settlers of Ohio, in the main, shared these characteristics of self-reliance and thrift, but differed widely in most other respects as different parts of the state were settled by people having widely diverse racial, religious, educational, political, and social backgrounds. Furthermore, for many years, the means of transportation and communication were poor, or non-existent. As a result each section provided its own educational facilities according to its own ideas. Samuel Lewis, State School Superintendent, stated in his annual report for 1838:

> The people have not heretofore followed any particular system (of education). The directors of each district have done that which was right in their own eyes, and generally adopted as far as they could the particular system of the state from whence they came.

First Certification of Teachers

There were no legal requirements for teaching in the early days. *A History of Education in the State of Ohio,* published in 1876 by the authority of the General Assembly, contains the following statement:

> The teachers of the pioneer schools in Ohio were selected more on account of their unfitness to perform manual labor than by reason of their intellectual worth . . . The capacity of a teacher to teach was never a reason for employing him, but the fact that he could do nothing else was a satisfactory one.

However, as early as 1825 there was considerable public sentiment for better teachers and, in that year, a law was passed requiring that teachers be certified. The certification authority was vested in a local board of three appointed by the Court of Common Pleas. A candidate seeking a teaching position appeared before this board, and had to convince the members that he had sufficient knowledge of subject matter and good moral character. The standards of the board members with respect to knowledge of subject matter were usually not very high, since they were, of necessity, based on the knowledge they themselves possessed. In 1831 the law was amended to require an examination in reading, writing, and arithmetic.

Local control of certification continued until 1864, when a law was enacted providing for a state board of examiners. This board conducted examinations and issued certificates that were good for the life of the holder.

The Establishment of Private Schools

The enactment of legislation requiring certification of teachers based on some knowledge of subject matter resulted in the establishment of a number of private normal schools. From 1830 to 1880, the number of such institutions increased very rapidly, until, at the end of this period, Ohio had more private normal schools, and institutions having normal departments, than any other state. These schools arose to meet a need, and for many years rendered valuable service to the people of Ohio. In the end, however, they proved inadequate, and became serious obstacles to the development of state-supported facilities for the training of teachers.

Many of these private schools were discontinued before the establishment of the first state normal school. Some of the stronger schools survived and were strongly opposed to the creation of new institutions with state support. Much of this opposition arose from an honest belief that the existing schools were meeting all the needs for teacher training and that no new institutions were needed. Some of the opposition, however, was due to the fear that the private schools would be driven out of business by the creation of new, state-supported institutions. Since many of the members of the legislature had received at least part of their education in these private schools, they naturally shared in these loyalties and fears.

The first normal school in Ohio was established at Marietta in 1832, as Marietta Collegiate Institute and Western Teacher's Seminary. Three years later, it was rechartered as Marietta College. In 1877, I. W. Andrews, who was then president of this college, addressed the State Teachers Association. After speaking of the excellent work being done at Miami University, he continued:

> I am equally sincere in the expression of the hope that no legislature of Ohio will make appropriations for the support of that institution whether in land or money. It is possible that the necessity exists somewhere that a state should provide funds from its treasury to support one or more colleges, but there is no such necessity in Ohio.

It should be remembered in this connection that, prior to 1902, neither Miami nor Ohio University received any regular financial support from the state.

Private Schools Inadequate

For many years before any action was taken to correct the situation, many educational leaders, educational associations, and state officials recognized the inadequacy of the existing institutions for the training of teachers. Several private colleges were doing excellent work in the preparation of high school teachers as far as knowledge of subject matter was concerned, but little or no consideration was given to the problems of teaching. This was partly due to lack of material of college grade for such courses, but even more to the unsympathetic or hostile attitude of most faculty members. As late as 1917, after the state Department of Education had set up professional requirements for a high school certificate, one professor of mathematics in a well-known Ohio college was giving his students a course in advanced mathematics and entering it on the records as *Methods of Teaching High School Mathematics*. He defended his action by stating that the mathematics course would do them more good, and that methods courses were a waste of time.

The situation with respect to the preparation of elementary teachers was much more serious. Such preparation was largely in the hands of private academies and normal schools. These were poorly equipped and were staffed, in many cases, by teachers with insufficient preparation. Furthermore, their entrance requirements were too low to permit work on the college level. The usual requirements for admission were a tolerably fair knowledge of the common branches, correct habits and good character. In an article published in the *Ohio Educational Monthly* of September, 1879, John Ogara wrote:

> Time and experience have demonstrated that it will not do to intrust this matter of the training of teachers to private institutions. Under this management they soon develop into mere catch-penny concerns. It is safe to say that today there are fifty institutions of various grades in Ohio that claim to be normal schools or to have normal departments—and it is equally safe to say that not one in ten of them has the slightest claim to the title outside of the name.

The private schools were not only deficient (in most cases) in the quality of their work, but they were also failing to provide an adequate supply of teachers. In 1860, Anson Smyth, State Commissioner of Common Schools, stated in his annual report:

> For the preparation of teachers for our schools, the state has never yet appropriated a dollar. The normal schools of the state are private enterprises and with their limited means can accomplish but little towards supplying 20,000 teachers.

Agitation for State Support

Dissatisfaction with existing facilities for the preparation of teachers led to early and repeated suggestions that the state enter this field. These recommendations came from prominent educators, teachers organizations, and state officials. As early as 1871, Gov. Thomas Worthington recommended to the General Assembly the establishment of a state school at Columbus for the training of teachers. The office of State Superintendent of Schools was created in 1837, and in 1838 Samuel Lewis, the first incumbent of the office, made several recommendations to the Assembly with respect to facilities for teacher education. These included the recommendation for the organization of a normal school at Columbus, and the appropriation of $5,000 for this purpose. The Assembly took no action. Similar recommendations were made in 1844, 1845, and 1846 by Samuel Galloway, Secretary of State, who assumed the duties of superintendent of schools after that office was abolished in 1840. Again the General Assembly failed to act.

In 1851, under the new constitution, the office of State Superintendent of Schools was revived under the title of State Commissioner of Schools. In 1865, E. E. White, who then held this office, was requested by the legislature to study the best normal schools in the country, and to recommend a plan for organizing one or more such schools in Ohio. His report was submitted to the Assembly in 1866. It recommended the establishment of county teachers' institutes, a normal institute in each of nine judicial districts, and a state normal school. This report probably set back the cause of state-supported teacher-training by many years, as it aroused strong opposition from two quarters. Many educators seriously doubted the value of the teachers' institutes and were opposed to state support for such a program. As always, the private schools and their friends in the legislature opposed the establishment of a state-supported normal school. As a result, no action was taken at this time or for over 30 years to follow. However, the agitation continued. In 1899, Lewis D. Bonebrake, State Commissioner of Schools, pointed out:

> Of all the states and territories of the American Union, Ohio, Arkansas, Delaware, New Mexico and Alaska are the only ones not attempting to provide special normal training for teachers.

Many Ohioans did not like this company, but three more years were to pass before the General Assembly took the first steps to remedy the situation.

Beginning of State Support

In the closing years of the nineteenth century, the movement for the professional training of teachers gained greater momentum throughout the country, and educational bodies in Ohio continued their agitation for state provision and control of such training. This resulted in the establishment of a pedagogical department at Ohio State University in 1897. The work of this department, and of similar departments in a number of private colleges, was planned for administrators and high school teachers, so the agitation for some state provision for the training of elementary teachers continued and increased.

In 1899, Charles F. Seese of Summit County introduced a bill in the General Assembly covering the whole field of teacher training. It met with the usual opposition from the private colleges and schools, and was defeated. However, Rep. Seese continued his interest in teacher training, and gave numerous talks before groups of teachers and citizens. Since the private schools and colleges opposed the establishment of new institutions on the grounds that Ohio already had too many, the original Seese bill was rewritten to provide for the organization of state-supported normal schools in connection with two old institutions—Miami University and Ohio University. This change, together with increased public sentiment, resulted in the successful passage of the new bill, on March 12, 1902, and the first victory was won in the long fight to secure state provision for teacher training.

The Normal School Commission of 1902

In addition to establishing normal schools at Ohio and Miami universities, the Seese bill provided for the establishment of a normal school commission to:

> Make an investigation of the need and advisability of the future establishment of one or more additional state normal schools and to consider how private institutions can become more active and effective in training teachers.

This commission was appointed by Gov. George K. Nash, and made its report in 1903. Its chief recommendation was for the establishment of a state Board of Education to:

> Have full charge of all normal schools and to have power to enter into contract or affiliation with private colleges and universities within the state to provide for teacher training.

It neatly evaded the troublesome question of the establishment of new normal schools by recommending that this problem be worked out by the state Board of Education. Possibly the recommendations of the commission were influenced by the fact that three of its four members were from existing colleges.

Agitation for New Schools

No action was taken on the report of Gov. Nash's commission and the agitation for new schools continued. This was especially true in northern Ohio. In 1904, Edmund E. Jones, State School Commissioner, stated in his report:

> I am satisfied that some provision should be made as early as possible for the teachers in the northern half of the state. I do not believe a large number of normal schools is necessary in Ohio. In my opinion, two additional schools conveniently located in the northern half of the state, with a higher department that might be known as a teacher's college, centrally located, would meet the needs of our state in this direction for many years to come.

Mr. Jones made similar recommendations in 1905, 1906, and 1907, but no action was taken by the General Assembly.

First Professional Training of Teachers

Local certification of teachers, as we have seen, came in Ohio in 1825, and state certification in 1864. The next significant change did not come until 1914, when legislation was passed requiring, for the first time, professional as well as academic training for the securing of a teaching certificate. Although this legislation was not passed until after the creation of the Bowling Green and Kent institutions, educators had been advocating such a move for some time, and everyone felt it would come within a few years at most. This feeling was an important factor in the establishment of the new state-supported schools in northern Ohio.

CHAPTER TWO

The Establishment of State Normal Schools in Northern Ohio, 1910

AFTER THE PASSAGE of the Seese bill in 1902, it was evident that some provision would have to be made for more and better teacher-training facilities in the northern half of the state. The only questions were when, where, and in what form.

Early Attempts

Existing colleges were still strongly opposed to the establishment of new institutions and hoped to secure state support for the training of teachers. Several bills were introduced in the General Assembly with this end in view. Among these was Senate Bill 87, introduced in 1906, which recommended state financial assistance to normal schools in connection with established colleges. Although this bill was supported by the friends of the private institutions, it failed to pass the House of Representatives. Other similar proposals also failed.

Although the private colleges never ceased their opposition to the establishment of new institutions, the sentiment in favor of such a move was gradually gaining strength. Two influences were largely responsible for this growth. First, the rapidly growing movement throughout the country for the professional preparation of teachers, and the opposition to this movement by colleges of liberal arts, led many educational leaders and public school administrators to the conclusion that the private colleges could not do a satisfactory job in this field. This point of view was expressed, in 1909, by John W. Zeller, State Commissioner of Common Schools. In his annual report he stated that private colleges could not give satisfactory training because:

(1) Their aim is academic and collegiate; their courses of study are academic and collegiate; their spirit is academic and collegiate. (2) They are not equipped for thorough and adequate work in this field, and have no funds to become so equipped. (3) Our colleges have a college atmosphere and college equipments and cannot, in the very nature of the case, do this work.

It is interesting to note that, in 1915, Mr. Zeller became instructor in history at the new institution in Bowling Green.

A second force was at work in favor of the establishment of new schools. This was the strong desire on the part of each of a number of towns in northern Ohio to secure a normal school for their community. This desire was based on the belief that such a school would bring many cultural as well as financial benefits to the community. Bowling Green was one of these towns and, in 1907, a group of influential citizens started a vigorous campaign to secure such a school for their city. Prominent in this group were B. F. James, an attorney, and R. A. Beattie, state senator from Wood County. In 1908, Sen. Beattie introduced a bill in the Senate providing for the establishment of a normal school at Bowling Green. In support of this bill, the citizens' group published a booklet setting forth the advantages of Wood County and Bowling Green as the location for a normal school. This booklet contained a map of northwestern Ohio and 28 full-page illustrations of Bowling Green buildings and street scenes and of the tract of rolling ground covered with native oak, hickory and other trees, known as the City Park. This tract was offered to the state as a site for the new school.

The Lowry Bill of 1910

Sen. Beattie's bill received little support, but the citizens of Bowling Green continued their efforts. Other towns of northwestern Ohio were also interested in securing the normal school, which all thought must soon be established. Among these, mention should be made of Napoleon, Ohio, because of the part two of its citizens were to play in the history of the new school. These were D. C. Brown, prominent merchant, and J. Hamilton Lowry, representative from Henry County. Mr. Lowry introduced the bill passed in 1910, and Mr. Brown was a member of the first Board of Trustees of Bowling Green State Normal School. Both men wanted the school for Napoleon, but both became loyal friends and supporters of the new school at Bowling Green.

The long fight for adequate teacher-training facilities for the state of Ohio finally reached a successful conclusion on May 19, 1910, when Gov. Harmon signed the bill sponsored by Rep. Lowry. This bill had been passed by both houses of the Legislature on May 10. It had been opposed (as usual) by the friends of existing colleges, but received strong support from school men, the representatives from the northern half of the state, and from Commissioner Zeller. The bitterness of the fight between the two factions was shown by the fact that the friends of the private schools accused Commissioner Zeller of employing too much pressure in favor of the bill.

The Lowry bill provided:

1. That the normal school system of the state of Ohio . . . be extended by the creation and establishment of two additional state normal schools, one in northeastern Ohio and one in northwestern Ohio, to be so located as to afford the best opportunity possible for all the people to obtain the benefits and advantages to be derived from teachers trained both theoretically and practically. Neither of such schools shall be located in any city or village which now has a college located therein.

2. Within thirty days after the passage of this act the governor shall appoint a commission composed of five persons . . . with full power and authority to select suitable locations, lands, or lands and buildings and secure options on the same as said commission shall find necessary for the establishment of said normal schools and upon such terms and conditions as said commission may deem to be for the best interests of the state and submit a report of their proceedings to the governor for his approval.

The Normal School Commission of 1910

On June 24, 1910, Gov. Harmon appointed the commission provided for in the Lowry bill. To avoid the possibility of bias toward any particular location, the members were all chosen from the central and southern parts of the state. The members were W. H. Johnson, Granville, instructor at Denison University; A. J. Catrow, Miamisburg, retired banker; J. S. Hummell, Wilmington, newspaper man; L. D. York, Portsmouth, retired businessman; C. L. Martzolff, Athens, instructor at Ohio University.

Choosing the Location

The commission met in July, and agreed upon the questions to be considered in selecting the location for the new school. These were (1) population within a 25 mile radius, (2) railroad and other transportation facilities, (3) moral atmosphere of community, (4) health situation in community, and (5) suitability of sites offered. On August 23, the commission announced that 16 communities had requested that they be considered as the location for the new school in northwestern Ohio. These were Arcadia, Bowling Green, Carey, Columbus Grove, Delphos, Findlay, Fostoria, Fremont, Grand Rapids, Leipsic, Lima, Napoleon, Perrysburg, Upper Sandusky, Van Wert, and Wauseon. Kenton was later added to the list of candidates. Findlay was eliminated, since it was the location of Findlay College. Toledo (not eligible as it was the site of the University of Toledo) and Findlay then strongly supported the candidacy of Bowling Green.

The citizens of Bowling Green lost no time in planning their campaign. A preliminary meeting of prominent citizens was called on August 17, 1910, by E. D. Bloom. Mr. Bloom was an attorney, state senator from Wood County and later lieutenant governor of Ohio. After considering the criteria set up by the commission, the group decided to call a meeting of citizens on August 29. At this meeting, a committee was appointed with Mr. Bloom as chairman. B. F. James reported on the work already done, and remarks and suggestions were made by a number of citizens. The chairman also announced that the commission would visit Bowling Green in September.

After the commission had visited all of the towns under consideration, the competition was narrowed to three candidates—Bowling Green, Fremont and Van Wert. Napoleon offered a beautiful site on the Maumee river and for a time had been a strong contender due to the powerful support of Rep. Lowry, the sponsor of the normal school bill, D. C. Brown, and other influential citizens. Napoleon was eliminated, however, because at that time it had a large number of saloons. This, in those days, evidently spoiled the moral atmosphere of the community in the eyes of the commission. Bowling Green at that time was dry under local option. Napoleon now gave its support to Bowling Green.

For a time, Fremont seemed to be the favored candidate. It offered the use of Spiegel Grove (former home of President Hayes) as part of the school campus and free use of the Hayes Memorial Library and Museum. This property could not be purchased by the state, and the commission found that the cost of purchasing adjacent property was prohibitive. The Hayes Memorial Commission insisted, if the Fremont offer were accepted, that it become the governing board for the new school or, at least, be represented on that board. These two conditions resulted in the elimination of Fremont, and the competition narrowed to Bowling Green and Van Wert.

Bowling Green Site

The commission arrived in Bowling Green on September 22, 1910, and was entertained at the home of B. F. James, who had been a college classmate of Prof. C. L. Martzolff, a member of the commission. After touring the city, the commissioners inspected the four sites which the citizens committee had suggested as possible locations for the new school. One of these was the tract east of town including the city park; a second was north of town, east of the Dixie Highway (Main Street) and north of the Poe Road; a third site was a mile south of town, south of Gypsy Lane Road and west of the Dixie Highway; and a fourth was the present site of Wood County Hospital. The commissioners were favorably impressed by the beautiful grove of trees in the city park. The story is told that Prof. Martzoff stood on a spot west of the present location of the University Union and, with a sweep of his arm to the east, said, "This, gentlemen, is where the new normal school should be located."

Although no official decision was made at that time, the commissioners advised that options be secured on all four sites. Such options were obtained on three of these tracts, 82½ acres including the city park, 185 acres south of town known as the Munn farm, and 100 acres north of the city.

At a meeting of the commission on November 10, Bowling Green was officially chosen as the location for the proposed school. Mr. Hummell was unable to attend the meeting and wired his proxy to Prof. Martzolff. With Prof. Martzolff casting two votes for Bowling Green, the vote was Bowling Green 3, Van Wert 2. The commission also selected the tract of land including the old city park as the site for the new institution.

Prof. Martzolff's friendship with his classmate, B. F. James, may have influenced him in favor of Bowling Green, but several other factors were probably more powerful. Foremost among these were the interest and the untiring efforts of a number of its citizens. Sen. Beattie, E. D. Bloom, and B. F. James have already been mentioned. Others of whose efforts we have a record were R. J. Eberly, J. N. Easley, B. F. Harding, Dr. J. C. Lincoln, J. H. Lincoln, E. E. Rogers, N. R. Harrington, F. P. Riegle; and S. A. Canary. There is evidence that the commissioners were favorably impressed by the attitude shown by the citizens of Bowling Green and felt that the community would give loyal support to the new school.

A second factor that should not be forgotten was the strong backing given Bowling Green by representatives and leading citizens of Findlay, Napoleon, and Toledo. Bowling Green was the choice of each, since they could not secure the school for their own community. Bowling Green's central location in northwestern Ohio, and its excellent transportation facilities were also in its favor. With two north-south railroads, and north-south and east-west electric interurbans and highways, it was easily reached from all directions. The fact that the city was dry was very strongly in its favor.

Origin of Bowling Green

The first home in Bowling Green was built in 1833, west of the present location of the Conneaut School, and the first post office was established the next year. The name of Bowling Green was suggested by Joseph Gordon, who carried mail through the new settlement on his route from Bellefontaine to Perrysburg. According to tradition, he suggested the name in honor of his old home, Bowling Green, Kentucky.

Bowling Green is the county seat of Wood County which, in 1910 and today, is one of the richest farming regions in the state. Until 1853, when a major system of irrigation ditches was constructed, much of the county was a marsh, known as the Black Swamp. Following the discovery of oil and natural gas in 1886, Bowling Green and the other towns of the region grew rapidly for a time. Glass factories were attracted by the gas, and added to the boom. There were once five glass factories in the county but, by 1914, when the new school opened, the oil and gas were almost exhausted and all of the glass factories were gone from Bowling Green. The town had returned to what it had been before, a small, residential city without any large industries, and dependent on farming for its prosperity. In 1914, the population was approximately 6,000, and many of these were retired farmers.

Probably most people would agree today that the choice of Bowling Green as the location of the new school was a satisfactory one. Problems and controversies have arisen between the town and the University from time to time but, in the end, satisfactory solutions have been found. In general, relations have been both pleasant and cooperative. However, the selection of the site was not so fortunate. The beautiful grove which attracted the commissioners is now mostly gone and the presence of rock near the surface has made construction both difficult and expensive. The nearness of the cemetery also has become an obstacle to the expansion of the campus.

Purchase of the Site

Having been officially selected as the location for the new school, Bowling Green's next problem was to buy the site chosen by the commission. The city moved as rapidly as possible in the purchase of the several parcels of land adjacent to the city park to complete the 82½ acres that had been offered to the state. In order to finance these purchases the city council at a meeting on December 5, 1910, decided that a bond issue not to exceed $50,000 would be needed. This proposal was voted on by the citizens in an election held on January 10, 1911, and was approved by a vote of 947 for to 11 against. On April 3, 1911, the council authorized a bond issue of $40,000 and on April 24 authorized the purchase of the real estate.

It was anticipated that title to all land included in the proposed site would be secured in a short time, but this did not prove to be the case. In some cases, the owners asked more for their property than the city was willing to pay, and in others clear titles could not be obtained. These and other difficulties caused so many delays that rumors were started (apparently by a Toledo newspaper) that the newly appointed Board of Trustees was seriously considering asking for authority to move the school to another town, and Fremont again became a candidate. A spokesman for the trustees told a reporter of the *Sentinel-Tribune* (the Bowling Green newspaper) that the Board had no serious intention of moving the new school elsewhere, providing all obstacles could be removed in a reasonable time. However, the trustees did secure permission from Gov. Harmon to move the school from Bowling Green, if it became necessary.

Finally, all difficulties but one were overcome. After completing the purchase of the various parcels of land needed to complete the 82½ acres of the proposed site, the Bowling Green city council had planned to donate the entire tract, including the old city park, to the state. Some questions were raised, however, concerning the legality of this procedure, so it was decided to sell the tract to a private citizen who would then sell it to the state for a nominal sum. Therefore, on October 26, 1911, the land was sold at public auction held on the site, to J. N. Easley, for the sum of 10 dollars. Mr. Easley immediately transferred the title to the state of Ohio for one dollar.

Although the vote on the proposed bond issue had been passed by an overwhelming majority, there was still some opposition. This was led by one member of the city council who succeeded in blocking the purchase by the city of the parcels needed to complete the site. He finally ceased his active opposition but continued to vote no on all normal school issues. The group opposed to the new school was small but vocal. Rumors were rife that an attempt would be made to defeat the plan for the transfer of the land to the state by outbidding the representative of the city at the public auction. When the time arrived, a crowd gathered at the spot where they expected the sale to be held. This was near the present location of Shatzel Hall. While the crowd was waiting, the auctioneer and J. N. Easley went to the opposite corner of the park (where Hayes Hall now stands) and the tract was quickly sold to the lone bidder.

CHAPTER THREE

Preliminary Planning
1911-1914

THE ACT OF 1910, creating the two new normal schools, contained the following provisions:

> As soon thereafter as the general assembly shall appropriate a sufficient amount of money for the purchase of said sites and the erection of suitable buildings thereon, the Governor shall appoint with the advice and consent of the senate five competent persons who shall constitute a board of trustees for the proposed normal school in the northeastern portion of Ohio and five other competent persons who shall constitute a board of trustees for the proposed normal school in the northwestern portion of Ohio.

> Each board of trustees shall organize immediately after the appointment by the election from its members of a president, secretary and a treasurer . . .

> Before adopting plans for the buildings of said normal schools each board shall elect a president of known ability for the school under its control, who shall have advisory power in determining said plans . . .

> The board of trustees in connection with the presidents of the normal schools shall select and appoint an able and efficient corps of instructors for the said schools, provide a suitable course of study for the theoretical and practical training of students who desire to prepare themselves for the work of teaching . . .

The First Board of Trustees

Pursuing the above provisions, Gov. Harmon on May 17, 1911, appointed the following to the Board of Trustees for the Bowling Green school: D. C. Brown, Napoleon, dry goods merchant; John Begg, Columbus Grove, farmer;

20

D. T. Davis, Findlay, banker; J. E. Collins, Fremont, Superintendent of Schools; and Frank P. Donnewirth, Bucyrus. Mr. Donnewirth declined the appointment and, on July 3, J. D. McDonel, Fostoria, clothing merchant, was appointed in his place. The members of the Board were all from northwestern Ohio, and one was engaged in public school work. A second member, John Begg, had been a teacher, and later returned to the educational field. A similar pattern was followed for a number of years, and emphasized the early purpose and character of the school as an institution to train teachers for the schools of northwestern Ohio. The Board visited Bowling Green for the first time on June 30, 1911, and organized by electing J. E. Collins, President; John Begg, Vice President; D. C. Brown, Secretary; and D. T. Davis, Treasurer.

The members of the Board of Trustees, throughout the entire history of the Bowling Green institution, have shown a sincere and deep interest in the development of the institution, and have given generously of their time and energy. With few exceptions, they have been above all selfish interests and politicial influence.

The members of the Board are appointed by the Governor of Ohio, with the consent of the State Senate. From 1911 to 1961, the Board consisted of five members each appointed for a term of five years, except the members of the first Board, who were appointed for one- to five-year terms. The state director of education was an ex officio member, but seldom met with the Board.

Two members of the original Board deserve special mention. The first of these is J. E. Collins who was the first president of the Board and was devoted to the duties of this office. At the time of his appointment, Mr. Collins was superintendent of the Fremont Schools, and later in his term held the same position in Lima.

Probably the member of the first Board who contributed the most was D. C. Brown, merchant and postmaster of Napoleon, Ohio. Mr. Brown was not only a member of the first Board (1911-14), but served again from 1918 to 1936. He was active in the movement to secure a normal school for northwestern Ohio, and was influential in the starting of an athletic program at the new school. In addition, he was the man, above all others, to whom, in the early days, Dr. Homer B. Williams, the school's first President, turned to for help and advice.

The First President

After organizing, the trustees considered the selection of a president for the new institution, but no action was taken at the first meeting. The choice of a president aroused a great deal of interest in Bowling Green, and throughout northwestern Ohio. By many the position was regarded as a political plum, and for weeks the newspapers of the area speculated as to whom the lucky man would be. There were many active candidates for the job, including school men, ministers, and prominent citizens in other professions. Many of these had strong backing from political and other groups.

Fortunately, the trustees refused to yield to these pressures. At their meeting on July 10, 1911, they announced that personal solicitation and wire-pulling would avail nothing, and that merit would decide this appointment. In spite of this announcement, the pressures continued and became even stronger. Several candidates claimed to have the support of Gov. Harmon; so, early in September, the trustees thought it advisable to have a conference with the Governor. They asked if he had a choice for the position and received an unqualified no in answer. He asked them to continue searching for the best-qualified man.

On February 16, 1912, the Board offered the presidency to Homer B. Williams, who had not been an active candidate, although his name had been prominently mentioned in the newspapers. Dr. Williams took the offer under consideration. He attended all Board meetings until May 23, 1912, when he formally accepted the presidency for an indefinite period.

At the time of his election, Dr. Williams was superintendent of schools at Sandusky, Ohio. His selection proved to be a most happy one. He was well qualified for the task of starting and developing a new school for the training of teachers. He held baccalaureate degrees from Ohio Northern and Baldwin Wallace colleges, and the master's degree from the latter institution. In addition, he was soon to receive another master's degree from Columbia University, and honorary doctorates from Ohio Northern and Miami universities. He had broad experience in the field of public education, as teacher in rural and village schools and as superintendent in several towns and cities of Ohio. He was well known and highly respected by the educators of the state and, at the time of his election, was president of the Ohio State Teachers Association. His selection was approved by all, except the disappointed candidates.

A Building Program

Even before selecting a President, the trustees had appointed the firm of Howard and Merriam of Columbus as architects to draw plans for buildings for the new school. The General Assembly in 1911 appropriated $150,000 for the 1911-13 biennium to be used for construction purposes. It was also understood that future appropriations for construction would be limited to an additional $100,000. It was thought at this time that a total of $250,000 would be ample to take care of the needs of the new institution for many years.

The original plans called for only two buildings, a college building and a dormitory. These were to be located where University Hall and Williams Hall now stand. However, the building program was delayed almost a year because of defects in the titles of some parcels of land included in the site. Titles had to be quieted in the courts before the state would permit construction to begin. The contract for the Administration Building (now University

Hall) was approved by the Attorney General on January 20, 1913, but weather conditions prevented start of work until late in the spring. The first preliminary surveys were made on April 22, 1913, and construction was soon under way.

These delays, although they postponed the opening of classes by a year, were really beneficial to the new school. James M. Cox, who became governor in 1913, was very much interested in the cause of education, and appointed a joint legislative committee to make a statewide school survey. This committee employed a staff of experts whose findings aroused greater interest in education, and exposed the lack of adequate preparation and training of the majority of public school teachers in Ohio. Gov. Cox espoused the cause of the two new normal schools and the new appropriations were greatly increased beyond the $100,000 originally planned. In fact, the appropriations for Bowling Green for the 1913-15 biennium totaled just a little less than one half million dollars.

The original plans for the Administration Building included 25 classrooms, science laboratories, library, small auditorium, heating plant, and offices for the President. Before construction was actually started, however, the new and increased appropriations were assured, and the plans for this building were changed to enlarge the auditorium, add a gymnasium under this auditorium, and increase the number of classrooms by eliminating the science laboratories and heating plant. These changes were made possible by an appropriation of $41,000 for the auditorium and gymnasium, and $218,000 for a science and agriculture building, a domitory for women, and a heating plant.

To help in formulating plans for the new normal school, the President made a survey of the teaching population of northwestern Ohio, and tried to foresee the future needs of this territory. On this basis, the President and trustees decided that the new plant should be designed to accommodate about 1,500 students. Although it was to be some years before the student body reached this size, there was one feature of the original plans that ultimately presented a serious problem in the expansion of the physical plant.

These plans called for all of the buildings (present and future) to be located around a small circle. The first three buildings (Administration Building, Science Building, and dormitory) left two open spots for a future elementary training school and a second dormitory. The heating plant was located outside the circle behind the Administration Building, and a large frame residence facing Wooster Street (south of the Library) was remodeled for the President's home. These seven buildings, when completed, were to constitute the entire plant for the new school.

The next building to be completed was the training school, but its construction was delayed for a number of years, and the elementary school was housed in temporary quarters. Facilities for observation and practice teaching were, of course, important for a teacher-training school. Many such institutions at that time maintained both elementary and high schools on the campus. President Williams and the trustees thought the school population of Bowling Green was not large enough for two high schools, and that any facilities on campus would soon be too small. They came to this conclusion after visiting several institutions, where the campus schools were already becoming inadequate to take care of the increasing numbers in teacher training.

After conferences with the public school authorities in Bowling Green, a cooperative plan was agreed upon. This involved two points. First, the College would maintain a small elementary training school on campus to be used, in the beginning, for both observation and practice. Later it was planned to use it only for observation. The pupils in this school were not to be selected from all over the city (the plan in many schools), but were to come from a regular school district. Building, teachers' salaries, and all other expenses were to be paid for by the College.

Second, all of the facilities of the Bowling Green school system, both secondary and elementary, were to be available for observation and practice teaching, and the salaries of a certain number of teachers, those to serve as critic teachers, were to be paid by the College.

This plan, with some modifications, continued for many years and proved quite satisfactory. One immediate result was that it gave the new school at Bowling Green much better facilities for observation and practice than existed in most similar institutions at that time.

The small, circular arrangement of the buildings was to prove a serious handicap to the future growth of the College, and to development of a convenient and an attractive campus. The location of the dormitory was particularly unfortunate, since it occupied a site that was later needed for an academic building. Furthermore, since the original buildings faced the circle, little or no attention was paid to the appearance of the backs of the buildings. As a result, when it was necessary to locate other buildings to the east of the original group, they were on a back street. Unfortunately, similar mistakes have been made many times in the history of the institution. These have usually been due to failure to foresee the future growth of the University. The present campus bears witness to the resulting difficulties and to the manner in which they have been met.

A Name for the University

The trustees and President found it necessary at the very beginning to make decisions on two questions of the utmost importance to the future of the new institution. These had to do with the scope and character of the work to be offered, and the related problem of selecting a name for the new school. The trustees attacked the second of these two questions first. The Act of 1910 referred to the two new institutions as normal schools, but did not specifically give a title to either. At the meeting held on February 16, 1912, the trustees chose the name Bowling Green State Normal College. Dr. Williams was probably consulted in the choice of this name, although this was the meeting at which he was elected President. In any case, the name met with his partial approval.

The author remembers hearing him comment on this on several occasions. He believed that normal school was not only a misnomer, as applied to the institution he envisioned, but that this title was out of step with the then current trends, and was fast disappearing from the American educational scene. He stated that his personal preference would have been Bowling Green State Teachers College, but that he was not unhappy with the title chosen. There was never any legal authorization for the name Bowling Green State Normal College. In fact, the institution so designated was not to have a legal name for a number of years and, when it did receive one, it was soon changed.

The Curriculum

The Act of 1910 contained the following provision:

> The board of trustees in connection with the presidents of the normal schools shall . . . provide a suitable course of study for the theoretical and practical training of students who desire to prepare themselves for the work of teaching.

There is no evidence that the General Assembly, in passing the Lowry Act of 1910, had any intention of creating anything beyond a two-year normal school for the training of teachers for the elementary schools. However, the name selected by the trustees indicates that, as early as February, 1912, they had already given some consideration to the scope of the new institution, and thought of it as something more than a two-year normal school. In February, 1912, the President-elect and the trustees visited the Teachers College at Albany, New York, and the State Normal School at Montclair, New Jersey. The first of these was selected, since it offered degree courses, and the second because it was supposed to be one of the best of the two year normal schools. In addition, President Williams visited a number of teacher-training institutions and arts colleges in the Middle West. After these visits, the President and trustees had to make decisions not only concerning the curriculum to be offered the first year, but also with respect to the future function of the institution.

As we have seen, the Lowry law referred to the two new institutions as normal schools, and the traditional normal school of the past had been a two-year institution for the training of teachers for the elementary schools. However, a new trend was developing throughout the country, and was resulting in the establishment of four-year, degree-granting institutions for the training of both elementary and secondary teachers. Should the new institution follow tradition and the legal designation of normal school, and plan only a two-year course of study for the training of elementary teachers, or should it also offer four-year curricula for secondary teachers and school administrators? If it offered a four-year course, should it confer a degree, and what degree?

President Williams felt strongly that the day of the old-time, two-year normal school was past, and that the need for professional training in the fields of administration and secondary teaching would soon become as urgent as in the elementary field. He argued that, although the Act of 1910 contained no specific authorization, it contained no prohibition. Therefore, the new school should start as a four-year, degree-granting college for the training of administrators and teachers in both the elementary and secondary schools. The trustees and our sister institution at Kent concurred with this point of view, and both colleges started on this basis.* These decisions were not to go unchallenged, but Bowling Green State Normal College, from the beginning, offered four-year curricula and conferred degrees. There was to be no specific legal authorization for either for many years. In fact, the Normal School Bulletin issued by the state Department of Education, in 1914, refers to Ohio State University with its College of Education, and then states: "The four other state schools for the training of teachers offer two-year courses." This, it will be recalled, had been the thinking in Ohio for many years: a centrally located institution for the training of high school teachers and administrators and outlying two-year schools for the preparation of elementary teachers. Again it should be noted that neither the law nor the above statement specifically limited the four other state schools to two-year courses.

We have seen that there is a great deal of evidence to show that the trustees, from the beginning, were determined to develop ultimately a four-year degree-granting institution for the training of both elementary and secondary teachers. Four-year courses, however, were included in future rather than present plans. On August 25, 1914, the trustees adopted the following outline of courses to be offered during the first year:

1. Diploma Courses
    (a) Two-year courses in academic and professional subjects for elementary and rural teachers.
    (b) Two-year course for special teachers of manual training, domestic science, drawing, music and agriculture.
    (c) Three-year courses in academic and professional subjects for elementary and rural teachers.
    (d) Three-year courses for special teachers of manual training, domestic science, drawing, music and agriculture.

2. Short Courses in Professional Subjects
    (a) One-year course in professional subjects for elementary teachers with a bachelor's degree.
    (b) One-year course in professional subjects for district superintendents.

*However, the institution at Kent used the title Kent State Normal School.

(c) One-year course in professional subjects for directors of county normal schools.

3. Short Course for Rural Teachers
One-year academic and professional course for rural teachers.

4. Advanced Courses
The diploma courses will be extended into four-year professional courses whenever sufficient demand arises.

A few words of comment and explanation need to be given in connection with the above. First, in order to meet the new requirements for professional training, it was necessary for many teachers already in service, and for other individuals preparing to teach, to take at least one year of professional training. The one-year courses were intended to meet the needs of these students.

Possibly the courses for rural teachers also need a word of explanation. In 1914, there were still many one-room rural schools in Ohio, and the curricula were intended to meet the requirements of teachers in these schools. It was felt that their needs and problems required special preparation. The one-year course was dropped at the end of the first year, but the diploma course was offered until 1922.

The courses in agriculture also deserve some comment. The Act of 1910 contained the following:

In planning said buildings, ample provisions shall be made for the establishment of a well equipped department for the preparation of teachers in the subject of agriculture.

Agriculture was the only subject of instruction specifically included in this Act. This special mention was undoubtedly due to the fact that northwestern Ohio was at that time predominantly agricultural in its occupations, interests, and outlook. In addition, the legislators responsible for writing and introducing the bill creating the new schools were mostly farmers, or men close to and interested in farming. This was true of Mr. Lowry who sponsored and gave his name to the bill. In spite of all this, however, there was little real need for teaching of agriculture at Bowling Green. In addition, the College of Agriculture at Ohio State University was opposed to agricultural instruction in the two new schools. It maintained, and rightly as later shown, that Ohio State could meet all needs in this field, and that proper instruction in agriculture was too expensive to warrant developing departments in the new schools. As a result, the General Assembly soon ceased making any appropriations for the University farm. The trustees, however, decided to hire a man to farm the fields, since they thought the farm could support itself. This continued for several years and items such as brood mares, horseshoeing, hay, and cattle appeared frequently among the bills allowed by the trustees. After several years, the University farm was changed to a dairy, which supplied milk to the dormitory and to many citizens of the town.

Bowling Green State Normal College was never able to develop a strong Department of Agriculture, and instruction in this field was finally discontinued in 1938. It is interesting to remember that the lettering over the front door of the original science building read Science and Agriculture. This called forth many questions from visitors, until it was finally changed to Moseley Hall, in honor of E. L. Moseley, science teacher on the first faculty.

Although no four-year courses were included in this first outline of curricula, they were planned for the future. The three-year courses were intended as a first step in this direction. These were expanded to four years after the first year.

President Williams and the members of the first Board of Trustees foresaw the trend in teacher training and the future needs of the schools of northwestern Ohio. Their courage in planning curricula, establishing entrance requirements, and adopting a title in conformity with these needs and trends have meant much to the institution they started and to the people of northwestern Ohio.

College Standards

At the time of the establishment of the new institution at Bowling Green, the normal schools of the country were not standardized, and many of them were little more than secondary schools. Many had low entrance requirements and admitted students who had finished only the eighth grade. Even this requirement was often waived. President Williams from the first was convinced that, if Bowling Green were to be a degree-granting college, it must establish its entrance requirements for all curricula on the same level as the strong colleges of liberal arts. This would mean graduation from an approved, four-year high school. Many residents of northwestern Ohio did not understand these requirements, and some were opposed to them. President Williams once showed the author a number of letters in his files from parents seeking the admission of a son or daughter with only eighth-grade preparation, or even less. A Bowling Green mother wrote that she had a boy in the fifth grade who wanted to enter the new school when it was opened, and inquired what studies he would have to take. Some parents became quite irate when told their child could not be admitted.

Appointment of a Faculty

In the selection and hiring of a faculty, President Williams was confronted with a problem similar to that faced by the trustees in their selection of a president. Since the new college was established by the General Assembly to serve the schools and people of northwestern Ohio, and was supported by state funds, many thought that the positions on the faculty should go to politicians, friends of politicians, teachers and administrators in the public schools,

The City Park was the site of Bowling Green State Normal College.

Bowling Green Armory — where classes met in 1914 - 1915.

The first Commencement was held July 29, 1915 in the Chidester Theatre.

The college was very young when these students posed for the 1918 *Bee Gee.*

The former Administration Building as it looked soon after its completion in 1915.

Early in the spring of 1916, the Science Building, above, was completed enough to permit partial use.

The Training School Building, above, was completed in November, 1921.

Williams Hall, dormitory for girls, opened in June, 1915.

The University Library contained some 15,000 volumes when this picture was taken for the 1918 *Bee Gee.*

"Eunice in her room in Williams Hall "—from the 1918 *Bee Gee.*

The Normal College orchestra in 1917-18.

Book and Motor members pose on the steps of the former Administration Building in 1918.

The entire student body of 1935 formed the B G U in honor of the achievement of university status in that year.

and other worthy citizens of northwestern Ohio. There were many active candidates, each with strong backing. These included ministers and other citizens, and many teachers and school officials. A few had some qualifications for the positions they desired; most had little or none.

President Williams, in spite of strong pressures, decided that the faculty should be selected on the basis of qualifications alone without regard to geography, political influence, need of a job, or other considerations.

On September 15, 1913, he asked the trustees for leave of absence to attend Columbia University. His purpose in this was three-fold: (1) to secure a master's degree, (2) to take courses planned for college administrators, and (3) to recruit a faculty. The author first met President Williams during his period at Columbia and agreed to come to Bowling Green as a member of the faculty of the new college. President Williams found several other faculty members while at Columbia.

By the time classes started in September, 1914, President Williams had assembled a faculty of 10 members (in addition to himself), plus four critic teachers for the elementary training school. The members of the first faculty were:

George Wilson Beattie, agriculture; Mary Turner Chapin, home economics; Ernest G. Hesser, music; Dallas D. Johnson education; Josephine Forsythe Leach, supervisor of practice teaching and director of Toledo Branch; Rea McCain, English; Edwin L. Moseley, biology; James Robert Overman, mathematics; Ernest G. Walker, extension; Leon Loyal Winslow, industrial arts; Lucy Helen Meacham, first grade critic; Grace M. Poorbaugh, second grade critic; Effie Alexander, third grade critic; Margaret Burney, fourth grade critic.

Without exception, the appointees were all well qualified by both training and experience for the positions they were to hold. All either had the master's degree or equivalent advanced training in their special fields. Several were to render long and successful service at Bowling Green. Others were to carve out careers in other fields of education or in other institutions of higher learning.

In addition to their professional qualifications, the original faculty had two other characteristics—the members were all comparatively young, and only two of the group had previously taught in northwestern Ohio. They also were selected solely on the basis of their ability and training, without political or other pressures. These characteristics of the first faculty were of the utmost importance to the future of the new institution. Their age enabled several of the group to serve many years and gave continuity to the early development of the school. The decision of President Williams to select the faculty on the basis of qualifications only was even more important. It was a decision that meant much for the future, and it was one that he was to adhere to (with few exceptions) throughout his long term of office.

The pressures to use faculty appointments as rewards for political and other services did not cease with the appointment of the first faculty. They were to recur at intervals throughout President Williams' administration. Often they were very strong, and two or three times they became too strong to be resisted. On these occasions appointments were made because of outside dictation, but even in these cases the appointees were reasonably well qualified for the positions to which they were appointed. Because of President Williams' determination to select faculty members on the basis of qualifications and to resist attempts at outside dictation, Bowling Green throughout the first fifty years of its history was remarkably free of the political domination that has hampered many state institutions of higher learning.

CHAPTER FOUR

The First Year of Classes
1914-1915

IN JULY, 1911, the trustees told a reporter from the Bowling Green *Sentinel-Tribune* that they hoped the normal school might be open to students in September, 1912. However, it soon became apparent that this would not be possible, and in August the trustees announced that classes would probably start in the fall of 1913. Numerous delays made this impossible, and Bowling Green State Normal College did not open its doors to students until September, 1914. Even then, it had a governing board, a President, a curriculum (at least for the first year), and a faculty, but was still without buildings. As a result of the delay in clearing the title of a portion of the site and other delays due to weather, change of plans, and other causes, none of the new buildings was completed. However, the trustees and the President felt that it would be unwise to postpone the start of classes any longer. On July 2, 1914, the trustees instructed President Williams to make all necessary arrangements to open school in temporary quarters at the beginning of the 1914 school year. This decision was undoubtedly influenced by the fact that the sister school at Kent (which encountered no difficulties) had started classes in 1912.

Temporary Quarters

Following these instructions, President Williams arranged to rent portions of the Armory building on East Wooster Street. Classes met in this building and the weekly chapel services were held in the Methodist Church, which at that time was just across the corner from the Armory. The College Library was located in the basement of the same church with the author in charge as librarian. There was no reading room, but the library was open from 4:00-5:00 p.m., so that students could take out and return books. These hours were sufficient, since the numbers of books and students were both limited. It has

32

been said that one measure of a library is the number of its books in circulation. Judged by this standard this library was perfect—the shelves were empty almost every night.

For many years the College maintained an elementary training school. At that time, this was considered to be a necessary part of any teacher-training institution. During the first year, it was housed in the old Ridge Street School. Only the first four grades were provided, since that was the number of rooms available in the building.

For several years, prior to 1914, Toledo had maintained a two-year training school for the preparation of teachers for the elementary schools of the city. This school was now discontinued, and Bowling Green State Normal College agreed to provide instruction for the students in their second year. Since facilities were not available to provide for these students in Bowling Green, faculty members taught first-year classes three days a week in Bowling Green and commuted to Toledo by interurban on three days to teach second-year classes. The Toledo classes were held in the old Toledo Central High School, then located on the site now occupied by the Toledo Public Library. Classes for the summer session (June, 1915) were held in the high school building on South Grove Street. This building later became the junior high school, and is now the administration building for the Bowling Green public schools.

The dormitory for women, the first of the new college buildings to be completed, was occupied for the first time during the summer session of 1915. It was at first called North Dormitory, since a second dormitory was planned to be located on the site of the old Library. However, the first dormitory was promptly christened Williams Hall by the students. President Williams did his best to discourage the use of this name. His opposition arose partly from modesty, but more from another reason. The author recalls hearing him say that the College might regret naming a building for a living person, as one can never foretell what a man might do before his death. He then cited several cases to support this statement. However, popular use of the name proved too strong and, on March 10, 1917, the Board of Trustees made the name Williams Hall official.

One trustee of this period deserves mention. He was J. E. Shatzel, of Bowling Green, who served on the Board from 1914 to 1924. His many contributions were recognized when the second college dormitory was named Shatzel Hall in his honor.

Faculty and Administration

The normal school opened in the fall of 1914, with a faculty of 10 members and four critic teachers. During the first year, the President was the only full-time administrative officer. Josephine F. Leach, in addition to teaching a few classes, was Director of the Toledo Branch and supervised practice teaching in that city. Dallas D. Johnson taught classes in psychology and education and was Director of the Training School. He also supervised the observation of teaching in Bowling Green. Ernest G. Walker taught history and was Director of Extension Services. The author, in addition to teaching full time, acted as college librarian, and assisted the President in the duties of a registrar and in writing and editing the first catalog.

First Faculty Meeting

The first meeting of the new faculty was held in a room of the Milliken Hotel on Saturday before the start of classes. The minutes of this meeting (if any were kept) can not be found, but the author remembers some of the topics discussed. President Williams first spoke of the name of the new institution and gave the reasons for the name. He emphasized that we were starting a college, not a school, and asked us to do all we could to inform everyone of this fact. However, in spite of all of our efforts and in spite of the title, it was to be many years before the citizens of Bowling Green and northwestern Ohio would refer to the new institution by any name except normal school or normal.

President Williams next informed the faculty that the new buildings were not ready for use and explained the six-day schedule, three days in Bowling Green and three in Toledo. The disappointment of the group was great, since all had expected to begin teaching in new buildings. The shock was not quite so severe to the author, since he had visited the campus the day before and found Williams Hall under roof but far from completion. The Administration Building (now University Hall) was little more than four walls without roof, and the only sign of the new science building (about which he had heard so much) was a one-mule scraper starting excavation of the site. The author resolved, then and there, to start looking for a new position. This was a resolve that most members of the faculty made again and again throughout the early years, only to decide (in most cases) to remain just another year. Those who remained were challenged by the fact that there always seemed to be some new problem to be solved or some new project to be started or carried out. Teaching in a new school presented many difficulties, but it also offered many rewards.

After distributing and explaining the teaching schedules, President Williams raised the question of how the faculty members should expect to be addressed. The consensus seemed to be that, although we were teaching in a college, it would be presumptuous to insist on the title of professor. At least, all agreed they would not be offended if they were called simply Mister or Miss. As it turned out, the time spent discussing this question was wasted. From the beginning, the faculty members were almost always called professor by both students and citizens. This did not inflate their egos unduly, since they soon learned that this title was also customarily applied to all school officials and teachers, including those in one-room rural schools.

The group was next informed that it was planned to hold weekly chapel periods, with attendance required of all students and requested of faculty members, whenever possible. In addition, no smoking would be permitted in college buildings by either faculty or students, and smoking in public by faculty members would be frowned upon. Both the compulsory chapel and the ban on smoking continued for many years.

Neither of these announcements aroused any vocal opposition from the infant faculty, since both were customary in many institutions at that time. However, the same was not true of the next announcement. This was to the effect that, as soon as possible, study halls would be set up, which students would have to attend during all free periods of the school day, and that faculty members would be assigned to supervise these study periods. This aroused instant and strong opposition. The faculty members argued that study halls were customary in most high schools, but, so far as they knew, were not to be found in any college. If we call ourselves a college, the argument ran, we should follow college procedures. President Williams, with evident reluctance, finally agreed to try operating without study halls for a time, and nothing further was ever heard on the subject. The author was greatly encouraged by this discussion. It made him feel, for the first time, that the new institution might develop into a real college, and the new staff into a college faculty.

Curricula and Courses

We have seen that the Board of Trustees had, on August 14, 1914, adopted an outline of the general curricula to be offered by the new school. Before the start of instruction in September, President Williams had also prepared the list of classes and the schedule for the first semester. In general, the offerings were confined to courses for the preparation of teachers in the elementary schools, and were based on the requirements that had been prescribed by the superintendent of public instruction. First-year classes were taught in Bowling Green, and the second-year in Toledo. The required observation of teaching for first-year students was provided in the Ridge Street School, and practice teaching for the second-year students was carried on in the Toledo schools.

At the time of the first faculty meeting, each faculty member was given, by the President, a brief outline of the courses he was to teach. The detailed content of each course was to be worked out by the instructor as he went along. Because of the heavy teaching schedules, and the time consumed in traveling, the instructor was often lucky if he could keep a day ahead of the class. Some planning was done on interurban cars between Bowling Green and Toledo.

During the first year (and for several years to follow), a few preparatory courses were offered. These were necessary because of the decision of the trustees and President to require graduation from a four-year approved high school for admission to Bowling Green State Normal College. These classes were offered to enable graduates of three-year high schools to complete a fourth year and qualify for admission to regular college courses. Since the three-year high schools soon disappeared from northwestern Ohio, the preparatory courses were later discontinued. They were never intended to be a permanent part of the curriclum, but only to meet a temporary need; and wherever a four-year school was available near the student's home, he was encouraged to complete his high school work in that school.

Fees and Expenses

One of the strongest motives for the establishment of a state normal school in northwestern Ohio was the desire of the people of that area for free educational facilities near home. In the beginning, Bowling Green did provide a free education, or nearly so. In the meeting of August 25, 1914, the trustees voted that tuition be free, but students be required to pay the cost of materials used in laboratory courses. This policy of free tuition continued several years, but with rather strong opposition from the General Assembly. Some members felt that the student's parents should bear part of the cost of his college education.

During this year, the majority of the students, whose parents did not live in Bowling Green, commuted daily from their nearby homes. Most commuters brought their lunches, so their only expenses were for books and transportation. Those who did not commute or reside in Bowling Green found the cost of rooms in private homes and meals in local restaurants quite inexpensive. Many brought food from home and did their own cooking.

Early Traditions

Early in the college year, the students started talking about the need for college colors and a college song. As a result, President Williams asked Leon L. Winslow, industrial arts; Mary Chapin, home economics; and one or more students to act as a committee to study the question of selecting college colors. After considering various suggestions, they recommended orange and brown, stating that these made a pleasing combination and (so far as they knew) were not in use by any other college.

The story was told, at the time, that Prof. Winslow suggested these colors after he saw them on a woman's hat during an interurban trip from Toledo to Bowling Green. However, Prof. Winslow would never either confirm or deny this story. The author recalls some discussion of these colors at an assembly period, but he can find no record of formal approval by students, faculty, or trustees. However, with or without formal action, orange and brown became the college colors.

The need for a college song was also satisfied during the first year, when Ernest G. Hesser, instructor in music, composed the school's first song. This was entitled *We Hail You, Dear Normal College,* and was dedicated to President Williams. This song was used for a number of years, but the title and words had to be changed in 1929, when the word Normal was dropped from the name of the college.

Every college needs a seal for use on official documents and publications. Early in the first year, President Williams asked Prof. Winslow to design one for the new school. Prof. Winslow welcomed this task as he was very much interested in any project involving design. After considerable thought and study, and a number of preliminary drawings, he submitted a design to the President and trustees. In presenting the seal to the trustees, Prof. Winslow wrote:

> Today most manufacturing concerns believe that it pays to have a trade-mark. Likewise, institutions of learning have their marks or emblems by which they are known . . . The great seal of a college or university is placed upon all diplomas issued by the institution. It is caused to be placed there by the President and Board of Trustees, and it is what makes them valid. Though the values placed upon seals is conventional, yet custom has come to demand them as marks of authority.
>
> The seal for Bowling Green State Normal College is an adaptation of the Seal of the State of Ohio, as will at once be evident. In the center of the seal is a shield containing the essential elements of the State Seal. These elements, however, have been rearranged and conventionalized, according to the rules of the heraldry by which seals and coats-of-arms are fashioned. The hills and water are seen in the left quarter of the seal, while the rising sun of the State Seal appears in conventional style in the right quarter. The field of the lower half of the shield is given over to two sheaves of wheat. The crest which appears directly above the shield consists of a motor and a book mounted on the customary scarf. The motor is intended to symbolize industry, progress, and the concrete application of knowledge or of ideas, while the open book appearing behind it stands for knowledge alone or pure science, literature and the like. . . . Agriculture . . . is suggested by the sheaves of wheat upon the shield. The sun being the source of light is emblematical of truth and power, while the hills suggest that there is something beyond towards which to strive. They point upwards to the heights of a liberal training and culture. The inscription around the seal reads: "Bowling Green State Normal College, 1910." At the left and right of the year in which the legislation founding the new institution was enacted appear three buckeyes to further connect school with state.

Prof. Winslow's design was approved by the trustees and it became the official seal of the College. It has continued in use until the present, with several changes. Aside from those changes in the inscription around the shield, which were necessitated by the changes in the name of the institution, the chief alteration has been the omission of the crest showing a book and motor mounted on the customary scarf. These were omitted because they became unrecognizable and, therefore, meaningless when the size of the seal was reduced for jewelry, stationery, and similar uses.

Prof. Winslow also designed a monogram to be used as the official college emblem, and awarded for participation in athletics and for other similar uses. In submitting this to the trustees, he wrote:

> A seal is of necessity a formal emblem and it is used only where dignity demands it. In order to have an informal mark of recognition, institutions have established letters, monograms, numerals, etc., for use in college activities and for letter paper and programs of entertainment, for banners, pennants and the like. Our monogram very well represents the Normal College, and is the official mark of recognition presented to members of the various athletic teams and worn by them as a mark of efficiency in various college activities.

The monogram (with necessary alterations as the name of the institution was changed) was used as Prof. Winslow described for several years, but has been largely dropped in recent times. Styles change and the seal is no longer confined to official documents. It is used not only on stationery and jewelry but even appears on sweaters.

Organizations and Activities

From the beginning, both the faculty and the President believed that a college should give a well-rounded education to its students, including many social as well as academic experiences. During the first year, the divided student body, the limited physical facilities, and the crowded programs of the faculty were all serious handicaps. However, it was possible to start a number of extracurricular organizations and activities for Bowling Green students.

The first organizations included two literary societies, Wilsonian and the Emerson. These were both cultural and social as described in the first catalog:

> The aim of these societies is to increase the power of oral expression, to acquire habits of logical thinking, to develop those social graces which make for real culture, and to uplift the profession of teaching.

The Wilsonian Society continued until 1934, and the Emerson until 1940. Both made fine contributions to the life of the College, socially and intellectually.

The first year was also marked by the founding of another organization, which for many years played an important part in the life of the institution. One morning, the author, on leaving a class in the Armory, was stopped by Prof. Winslow with a question, "Don't you think we need an honorary society?" We found seats and discussed the question at some length. We agreed that an honor society would be a fine thing, but also agreed that it would be impossible for a new school to secure a charter from any national group. Obviously, there was only one answer; we would have to start one of our own. Then, the "cat jumped out of the bag." The bag, in this case, was a large envelope from which Prof. Winslow now drew the drawing of a key for the new society. In his design for the college seal, he had included an open book behind a motor. After designing the seal, it occurred to him that Book and Motor would be a good name for a society. Its purpose would be to foster and honor high attainment in the pursuit of knowledge and in its application to living. With this idea in mind he drew a design for a key for such an organization, and it was this that he now handed the author for his inspection. The design was for a gold key consisting of the college monogram surmounted by the book and motor.

Since the author approved of Prof. Winslow's idea and design, the next steps were to solicit the interest of other members of the faculty and to write a constitution for the new organization. Interest among the faculty was almost unanimous, so the author and Miss Rea McCain (English) wrote a constitution which was quickly approved by the faculty members. Before the end of the year, four members of the sophomore class in the Toledo branch were elected to membership.

Possibly, the history of the founding of Book and Motor was unusual, if not unique. Ordinarily, the idea of the society comes first and is followed by the selection of a name and an emblem. With Book and Motor, this order was reversed. It was truly a case of a name and an emblem hunting an appropriate organization. However, Book and Motor from the first became a valuable part of college life, and continued to be so until 1965, when it was superseded by Phi Kappa Phi, a national honorary society.

One of the most active members of the original faculty was Ernest G. Hesser, the teacher of music. As a result of his enthusiasm and leadership, a number of musical organizations were started during the first year. One of the first of these was the girls' glee club, which adopted the name Treble Clef Club. This organization, according to the first catalog, was limited to twenty-four voices chosen according to singing ability. The author recalls that this group sang during at least one assembly period before the end of the year.

During the first summer term (1915), Prof. Hesser organized a summer school chorus known as the Philharmonic Club. This group was limited to 75 members, and studied a number of standard choral works for mixed voices. It gave a public concert toward the end of the summer term. This concert was a feature of the summer sessions until 1920, when the Philharmonic Club was discontinued with the withdrawal of Prof. Hesser from the faculty.

In the spring of 1915, Prof. Hesser started another musical group which played an important part in the cultural life of the college and community for a number of years. This was the May Festival Chorus, composed of about 200 members from the student body, Bowling Green, and Wood County. According to the first catalog, this chorus gave a program of great choral works and oratories at the time of the Spring Musical Festival.

No college can neglect the purely social side of the students' lives. This fact was not overlooked by the President and faculty although, during the first year, time and facilities were both quite limited. The author can remember at least one party (there were probably more) which was held in the drill hall of the Armory. Both students and faculty were permitted (even encouraged) to dance. This aroused a storm of criticism from the citizens of Bowling Green and northwestern Ohio, since many church groups were at that time strongly opposed to dancing. President Williams, however, in spite of the fact that he did not dance himself and was also a strong Methodist, believed that dancing under proper supervision was a useful part of the social training of young men and women. The criticism continued for a number of years, but the Bowling Green students continued to dance with official approval.

Extension Courses

Because of the new professional requirements, it was necessary for many teachers in northwestern Ohio to obtain additional training. Many of them wished to do this by means of extension classes and attendance at summer sessions. During the first year, Bowling Green State Normal College conducted Saturday classes in Bowling Green in addition to classes in 24 other centers. The total enrollment in these classes was almost 600 students.

One faculty member devoted most of his time to organizing and teaching extension classes. The agriculture teacher taught off-campus during the first semester. In addition, most of the other faculty members taught extension classes on one or more evenings or on Saturday afternoons. For example, the author recalls that he taught three mornings in Toledo, three days in Bowling Green, and one evening in Findlay. During the second semester, on Saturday mornings he taught a large class in psychology in the drill hall of the Armory. During the first year, because of the small size of the faculty, many instructors had to teach outside their fields of specialization. Quite recently, the author was reminded by a retired high school principal that he had been a member of that Saturday class.

Summer Sessions

Since many Ohio schools (particularly the one-room rural schools) closed late in April, Bowling Green State Normal College offered a special spring quarter of eight weeks, starting April 26, 1915, and paralleling the last weeks of the second semester. Classes were taught by the regular faculty members and were in addition to an already over-full schedule in Bowling Green and Toledo. Some relief was afforded by the fact that the extension courses for the second semester were scheduled to end by the last of April. This spring quarter was reduced to six weeks in length in 1916, and the name changed to first summer term. The first summer term continued for several years, until the demand fell off with the disappearance of the one-room school.

For the summer term of six weeks, following the end of the special summer quarter, the faculty was augmented by 13 additional members. Some were from the faculties of other colleges and universities, and the remainder were teachers or administrators in the public schools of Ohio. The practice of recruiting a summer school faculty from the public schools was customary at that time. In many cases the summer school was not a part of the regular college program. It was organized and run by a group of college and public school teachers who desired summer employment. The faculty shared the money received from fees. Credit for work taken in such a summer school was not always granted, even by the college on whose campus it was held. Because of this situation, President Williams, from the beginning, emphasized that the summer sessions at Bowling Green were part of the regular offerings of the College, carried college credit, and were staffed by regular college faculty, plus others of at least equal qualifications. For years this was the cause of considerable discontent on the part of the schoolmen of the territory, many of whom had expected (and thought they were entitled to) summer employment at the College.

During the summer term of 1915, 70 courses were offered in 10 departments. These offerings included a few high school subjects and most of the required courses in the two-year curriculum for elementary teachers. In addition, courses for the preparation of high school teachers were offered for the first time. These included both subject matter and methods courses. At the first opportunity, Bowling Green State Normal College served notice that it would cover the fields of both elementary and secondary education.

College Enrollment

If any evidence were required to prove the need for a state institution to train teachers for the schools of northwestern Ohio, it was furnished by the attendance during the first year as shown below:

Enrollment, 1914-1915

Academic year	304*
Extension	598
Summer School, 1915	615
	1,517

Only 58 men were enrolled during the academic year. The offerings were mostly in elementary education, and few men were preparing for that field.

Attendance at extension classes and summer school greatly exceeded that during the regular academic year. This was to be true for a number of years, or until the teachers already in service in the schools of northwestern Ohio caught up with the new professional requirements. The law passed in 1914 provided that applicants for any elementary certificates, on and after January 1, 1915, had to "possess an amount of professional training . . . not less than six weeks of classroom instruction, in a recognized institution for the training

*This includes the enrollment for the special spring quarter.

of teachers." The law increased the amount of professional training required by six weeks for each year until January 1, 1920, when it reached a full year.

The law of 1914 also provided for life certificates. These required, on and after January 1, 1915, not less than a one-year course or its equivalent in a recognized institution for the training of teachers. On and after January 1, 1920, this requirement was increased to two years.

These progressive increases in professional requirements were provided so that teachers then in service might be able to continue teaching and meet the requirements by taking extension courses and attending summer school. The plan resulted in heavy enrollments in both extension and summer classes for many years. The more ambitious teachers were not satisfied with meeting the minimum requirements but were anxious to secure a life certificate. Some of these, after meeting the minimum standard of one year, took a leave of absence from their teaching positions and entered college for a full year. Many, however, completed the second year entirely by extension and summer school work.

Further inducements for securing training beyond the minimum were offered teachers by the fact that many towns and cities required graduation from a two-year diploma course for all their elementary teachers, and gave teachers in service a number of years in which to come up to this standard. In addition, increases in salaries were often given for each additional six weeks of training.

First Graduates

The inheritance of a second-year class from the Toledo Teacher Training School enabled Bowling Green State Normal College to graduate its first class on July 29, 1915. At this time, the diploma in Elementary Education was presented to the 35 students who had completed their second-year at the Toledo branch and the summer session at Bowling Green. Since the event marked an important milestone in the history of the new institution, it was attended by all members of the Board of Trustees and by Frank W. Miller, State Superintendent of Public Instruction. The exercises were held in the Chidester Theater (since destroyed by fire). Music was provided by the Philharmonic Club and Prof. Hesser. The commencement address was delivered by Dr. Charles H. Judd of the University of Chicago.

CHAPTER FIVE

Early Years, World War I
1915-1918

WORLD WAR I HAD a comparatively small effect upon the fortunes of the new school. Enrollments remained about the same throughout the period, since there were very few men in college to be affected. There was some talk of the College getting an ROTC unit, but this proved to be impossible because of the small number of men. The principal effect of the war was to delay the building program.

Classes in Toledo were abandoned at the beginning of the second year, although there was considerable pressure for the establishment of a permanent Toledo branch. During this year, the superintendent of the Toledo schools was appointed to the Bowling Green Board of Trustees. He was very anxious to have the normal school offer classes in Toledo for the training of teachers for the city schools. However, the trustees and President decided against the Toledo branch. The pressure for such a branch continued for several years, until it was relieved by the development and growth of the University of Toledo.

First Buildings

By September, 1915, the new Administration Building was near enough to completion to be used for the first time. This building contained an auditorium, gymnasium (now the Joe E. Brown Theater), Library, general classrooms, and special quarters for home economics, industrial arts and music. Until the new Science Building was completed, the Administration Building also housed all classes, laboratories and shops, and the six grades of the elementary training school.

The heating plant, although not completed, was put into operation late in the fall of 1915, just in time to prevent suffering from cold classrooms and dormitory. Early in the spring of 1916, the new Science Building (now Moseley Hall) was nearing completion, and agriculture, science, industrial arts and the four upper grades of the training school were transferred to this building. The first and second grades remained in the Administration Building.

The contract for the Elementary School Building (now Hanna Hall) was let in July, 1916, and the third annual catalog contained the statement that the building would be ready for use at the opening of the next regular academic year in September, 1917. Events were to prove that this prediction was overly optimistic. Many delays occurred including shortage of materials due to the war and the bankruptcy of the contractor. The builiding stood half-finished for several years. A careful observer can still detect the line on the walls where

44

construction was finally resumed, since the new brick did not quite match the old. The building was not completed and ready for use until November, 1921. In the meantime, the six grades of the training school continued to be housed in the Administration and Science buildings.

The completion of the Elementary School completed the school plant as originally planned, with the exception of a second dormitory. It soon became evident, however, that the original plans were inadequate and that additional buildings would be needed in the not too distant future. As early as 1918, a plan was drafted for future development. This plan showed 11 new buildings in addition to the six (including the President's home) then completed or under construction. These included a high school, a gymnasium, a library, a classroom building, an auditorium, a museum, a woman's building, a dormitory for men, and three additional dormitories for women.

It had already become apparent that the original quarters for the Library, on the third floor of the Administration Building, were entirely inadequate, so the proposed plan showed a library building where the second domitory had been originally planned. Only three of the proposed buildings were actually constructed on the planned sites. They are the Library, Men's Gymnasium and Shatzel Hall. The plan also included an athletic field which was later constructed.

The Emerging Campus

During the years 1915-18, little money was available for improving the campus. However, during the summer of 1915, the grounds around Williams Hall and the Administration Building were graded and seeded, and temporary wooden walks were built. These were to be the only campus improvements for some time.

The buildings had been planned to face a circle, but as yet no circle existed. A north and south street, known as Wayne Street, was located just in front of the Administration Building, where it was met by the east end of Court Street. Both of these were public streets, and the citizens of Bowling Green for a number of years were very jealous of this fact, since they afforded the easiest access to the cemetery just north of the college. Funeral processions were a common campus sight during these years.

Finally, on October 1, 1917, the Bowling Green City Council passed an ordinance vacating Court Street, east of Thurstin, and Wayne Street, from Wooster to Ridge. This opened the way for the campus improvements which followed in 1918.

The College Catalogue

During the first year of classes, the President and faculty planned the detailed curricula and courses. These were described in the first annual catalogue, which was dated May, 1915, but not published until the fall of that year. No catalogue was published in the spring of 1916. However, when the third annual catalogue, dated May, 1917, was being printed, Dr. Williams decided, for the record, to change the calendar, Board of Trustees, and lists of students and graduates, add a new cover and title page, and print a few copies as the second annual catalogue, dated May, 1916. These two catalogues were identical except as noted above. They were both issued in the early fall of 1917.

During the early days of the College, the actual date of publication of the catalog was often later than that shown, although the delay was never again as long as a whole year. The chief cause was the fact that President Williams would never publish a new catalogue until the supply of the previous one was exhausted. Sometimes he would wait too long, and the college would be without catalogues to send to prospective students. Often not enough copies were left for the files, and some numbers became so scarce as to be collector's items. These delays are apt to be confusing to one who is unaware of the above circumstances. Thus, most of the early catalogues contained the lists of students attending the summer sessions, although the cover stated that they were published in May. The faculty list was not always for the current year. A new faculty member hired before the actual publication was usually included. All of this sometimes makes it difficult to determine exactly when certain additions and changes were made. In most cases, however, the author has been able to resolve such questions by consulting the minutes of the trustees' meetings and other sources (including his memory). In a few cases, it has been impossible to locate the exact time of an event.

Early Faculty

Six additional members were appointed for September, 1915. These were: C. J. Biery, rural education; F. G. Beyerman, physical education; Robert Cummins, extension; Harriet S. Hayward, Supervisor of Practice Teaching; W. P. Holt, geography; and J. W. Zeller, history.

A few courses in the above fields had been taught during the first year by members of other departments, but these new appointments made it possible to increase the offerings. J. W. Zeller, instructor in history, had been State Commissioner of Elementary Schools in 1910 and influential in securing the passage of the Lowry bill of that year. His appointment to the Bowling Green faculty was a fitting recognition of his contributions to the cause of education and teacher training in Ohio.

In the fall of 1915, the fifth and sixth grades were added to the training school, and two additional critic teachers were employed. These were: Estelle Rich, fifth grade, and Erma Ferguson, sixth grade. Arrangements were also made to use the entire Bowling Green school system and several rural schools for observation and practice teaching. These combined facilities were at least the equal of any in Ohio at that time.

Six additions were made to the faculty in the fall of 1916. These were in English, extension, foreign language, home economics, industrial arts, and music. No additions were made for the 1917-18 school year.

Administrative Appointments

In the summer of 1915, Marie E. Simpson was appointed librarian (relieving the author of these duties). The work of selecting and cataloging books for the new Library soon became too heavy for one person, and an assistant librarian was appointed in 1916. Two additional appointments to administrative positions were made during the first summer. These were Calvin J. Biery, who, in addition to his teaching duties, was to be Director of Practice Teaching in Rural Schools, and W. F. Shaw, who became high school inspector.

At this time, each of the five state teacher-training institutions was required to employ an individual to devote full time to the inspection of high schools. Before the opening of school in September, 1914, the trustees appointed a Mr. Boone to this position, but he resigned before school started, and no successor was employed at that time. Mr. Shaw, who had been superintendent of the Bowling Green schools, taught courses in education in the summer, and during the academic year devoted full time to the inspection of high schools in northwestern Ohio.

Bowling Green State Normal College secured its first dean in 1916, when Mr. Walker was appointed Dean of the Faculty. This position was created to relieve the President of some of the details of plannning and administering the academic program. Mr. Walker also continued as Director of Extension Teaching.

The last administrative appointment during this period came in 1918 when Maud F. Sharp became the first Dean of Women. Until this time the President had performed the duties of both dean of women and dean of men. Since the number of men in college was so small, the President continued to act in the latter capacity, and no dean of men was appointed until 1930.

Curricula Established

Teaching was not the only task for members of the faculty during the first year. They also had to work with the President on the curricula and course offerings for the future. Certain basic decisions had already been made, as we have seen, but much more remained to be done. The results of the year's work by the President and faculty are contained in the first annual catalogue, dated May, 1915. It contained the following statement of the Functions and Scope of the Normal College:

In order to furnish adequate training for all classes of teachers, the State Normal College will maintain the following courses:

(1) A one-year professional course for college graduates.

(2) Four-year courses leading to the B.S. degree in Education for supervisors, superintendents, principals, and teachers in secondary schools.

(3) A two-year diploma course for grade teachers in city and village schools, permitting emphasis on primary or grammar grade work in accordance with the needs of teachers.

(4) A two-year diploma course for rural teachers.

(5) A two-year diploma course for teachers of each of the following special subjects: agriculture, industrial arts, home economics, and music.

(6) A one-year course for rural teachers.

The catalogue outlined the above curricula in detail. They all had two characteristics in common. In the first place, each was planned to meet the requirements for a teaching certificate in a particular field. In the second place, they contained few or no electives. This was partly due to the requirements for teacher certification, but even more to the limited course offerings during the first few years.

The trustees had adopted an outline of courses to be offered for the first year on August 25, 1914. This included no four-year degree courses, but did end with the statement that the diploma courses will be extended into four-year degree courses whenever sufficient demand arises. When preparing the copy for the first catalogue, the President and faculty decided that there was already sufficient demand to warrant the offering of four-year degree courses for high school teachers and supervisors.

The four-year curricula for the training of secondary teachers were limited to four combinations, each in two subject-matter fields. These were the teaching combinations commonly found in the small high schools of the region. These first curricula were in agriculture and science, English and history, English and Latin, and mathematics and science. No other combinations of teaching fields were possible. This was the result of President Williams' feeling that it was useless and unfair to permit a student to prepare for a teaching combination in which he would probably be unable to secure a position.

The second, third and fourth annual catalogues outlined only two new curricula. These were four-year courses in home economics and industrial arts for the preparation of high school teachers in these subjects. These curricula were in addition to the two-year courses previously offered.

These catalogues also announced a significant change in the curricula for secondary teachers. Although they outlined courses in agriculture and science, English and Latin, and mathematics and science, they prefaced the outlines with the following statement:

The following outlines of courses exhibit several possible groupings of subjects. Other groupings may be made . . . For example, a student may make a combination of Latin and History, or of German and English, etc., but in doing so, care should be taken to group subjects that are frequently combined in the practice of assigning work to teachers in secondary schools.

When the first catalogue was published, several faculty members had argued that prospective high school teachers should be allowed perfect freedom in their choice of fields of primary and secondary specialization. President Williams was strongly opposed to this point of view. However, by the time the second and third catalogues were published, the faculty succeeded in gaining his somewhat reluctant approval of the compromise described above. The sole purpose of the new school was still to supply students with the training needed in and demanded by the schools of northwestern Ohio.

From the beginning, the trustees, President, and faculty all planned the new school is a degree-granting college. However, it was to be a teachers' college only. Liberal arts courses were offered, starting with the first summer, but for years they were only those which were needed for the preparation of teachers. However, high school graduates interested in fields other than teaching soon found that these liberal arts courses were numerous enough and of a high enough quality to permit them to study for one or two years at Bowling Green, and then transfer to a liberal arts or professional school. Even during the first year, there were a few students who enrolled with this in view and, in succeeding years, an increasing number of students took advantage of this opportunity.

Bowling Green State Normal College was indeed fortunate in the fact that its first President and the majority of its early faculty, while primarily interested in the training of teachers, felt very strongly that knowledge of subject matter was the first essential for good teaching. This led to the early development of strong departments in the traditional liberal arts fields, and paved the way for the ultimate transformation of the institution from a teachers' college to a university.

Departments and Courses

The first annual catalogue announced courses in 13 departments: agriculture, biological science, education, English, geography, history, home economics, industrial arts, library, mathematics, music, physical education, and the physical science.

The Library Department offered only one course. This was designed to enable the student to employ the resources of the library readily and effectively. This course was considered necessary, since most students entering the College at that time had had little or no experience in the use of a library. The course was taught by the librarian.

The chief expansion in offerings during this period was in the number of courses for high school teachers and school administrators. These were in both education and subject-matter fields. Such offerings were to show a slow but steady increase in the years to come. The President and faculty never wavered in their conviction that Bowling Green State Normal College had an obligation to train teachers and administrators for all levels of the public schools of northwestern Ohio.

In 1916-17 a Department of Foreign Language was added, and the catalogue for that year announced 12 courses in German and 12 in Latin. In addition, seven preparatory courses in Latin were prescribed for students with less than four years of that subject in high school. Increased offerings were also made in home economics and industrial arts, and in the courses for secondary teachers in other departments.

Fees and Expenses

Tuition continued to be free throughout these years. However, pressure grew for a change in this policy. At the meeting of the Board of Trustees, held on April 29, 1916, President Williams read a letter from W. L. Tobey suggesting that the presidents and representatives of the five state-supported institutions hold a conference concerning means of securing larger state appropriations. He quoted members of the state administration as stating that Ohio had reached the limit of support of educational institutions, and new ways would have to be provided for financing these institutions. The author remembers that several conferences were held at about this time to consider this question. Bowling Green, however, continued its free tuition policy for several years, although it became increasingly apparent that it was only a question of time until it would have to be abandoned.

Bowling Green State Normal College also made every effort to keep the necessary expenses of a student to a minimum. President Williams himself had to struggle to obtain an education. He wanted to make one available to all high school graduates of northwestern Ohio at the least possible expense. As a result, for a good many years, a college education cost less at Bowling Green State Normal College than at any other comparable institution in the country.

During these first years, rooms in the dormitory for girls were $1.25 a week and board was $3. The first annual catalogue estimated that total expenses for a year need not exceed $203. This figure included $30 for washing and incidentals and $20 for books and stationery. Theoretically, expenses were slightly higher for men, since there was no men's dormitory. In practice, however, most of the men lived more cheaply than the girls, since they brought food from home and did their own cooking. The cost of this food was relatively small, since most of the parents lived on farms. Both men and women also saved by sending their laundry home to mother, so many a student's yearly expense was actually less than $200.

Record Blizzard

On December 8, 1917, Bowling Green was hit by the worst blizzard on record. Even now, when a bad storm occurs, the newspapers and the weather bureau often describe it as the worst since 1917. During the storm, the author was on his way to a class in the Administration Building. He entered the campus at the corner of Ridge and Thurstin Streets. At that time, a foot path led through the grove of trees from that corner to the Administration Building. The falling and drifting snow was so thick that the author soon lost the path and his way. He wandered around through the trees until he finally emerged near the Elementary School Building, then under construction. This gave him his bearings, and he reached the Administration Building with badly frosted ears and nose, and too late for class. However, most of the students had also failed to arrive.

As a result of the storm, all railroad traffic came to a standstill, and coal shipments in transit failed to arrive. Since the supply on hand was almost exhausted, classes were dismissed until after the Christmas holidays. The County Fuel Committee was asked for enough coal to keep a small fire in the boilers. The request to this committee was necessary, since coal was rationed as a result of the war. Enough coal was obtained to keep a small fire in the boiler and furnish sufficient heat to prevent freezing. No damage resulted to buildings, plumbing, or contents. Sufficient coal finally arrived to permit the resumption of classes after the Christmas recess, but the supply was limited, and class and dormitory rooms were only partially heated.

The winter of 1917-18 continued to be unusually severe. The College received enough fuel to operate, but coal was rationed to the citizens of Bowling Green and Wood County. Residents could secure only a half a ton at a time, and the dealer was not permitted to deliver that until the previous supply was exhausted.

The Weekly Assembly

Weekly assembly exercises continued to be a feature of the College for many years, and both students and faculty were expected to attend. These assemblies usually opened with a brief devotional service, followed by announcements. After that almost anything could happen, ranging from a talk by the President, some faculty member, or an outside speaker, to a pep rally for an athletic or other student event. These exercises also furnished a forum for the discussion of student problems and affairs. The assembly periods served a useful purpose in the early years, and were usually well attended by both students and faculty.

Organizations and Activities

Only one new organization was started during these years. This was the Country Life Club, which was organized in 1915 by George W. Beattie, instructor in agriculture. The catalog of May, 1915, stated:

> This club is open to the entire student body. It is conducted on the plan proposed by the National Society. . . . The regular programs are given by club members who have investigated some interesting phases of country life. Specialists in rural life subjects appear before the club from time to time.

The popularity of this organization for a number of years reflects the fact that the majority of the students at that time came from rural homes. However, as time went on, its programs and activities ceased to be entirely rural in character, and it was discontinued in 1933. By that time, the student body was more urban and cosmopolitan. This club made many real contributions to student life during its existence and one that was permanent. In 1920 it started the college paper, the *BeeGee News,* and was responsible for its publication for several years.

The first purely social group for students was organized in either 1916 or 1917. A small group of men formed a secret fraternity and called it by the Greek name of Theta Delta Chi. The organization was not officially recognized by the College. Indeed, its very existence was unknown until later. The group soon suspended operations as a result of the shortage of men due to World War I.

During 1917-18, Calvin J. Biery, Director of Rural Education, organized the first college orchestra. It was small, but represented a beginning. In addition to Prof. Biery, who played first violin, the group consisted of three other violinists, a cornetist, a clarinetist, a trombonist, a drummer, and a pianist. The primary purpose of the organization was to furnish suitable music for many college functions, including basketball games. However, it was not a dance band, and a record player continued to furnish dance music.

The year 1917-18 also brought two additions to the growing list of activities at Bowling Green. The first was a course of lectures, entertainments, and musical events. Ever since the first year, Prof. Hesser and the author had talked about this need and, finally, a proposal was submitted to President Williams that such a course be started. He agreed to the need. However, he was afraid that it would not be possible to finance the course, since no state or other funds were available. Prof. Hesser, however, from his experience with the Spring Festival thought it would be possible to sell enough season tickets to the faculty and citizens of Bowling Green and Wood County to cover all expenses, at least for the first year. The course was introduced on a trial basis. President Williams appointed Prof. Hesser as chairman of a committee to arrange and manage the course. The author and one other faculty member (name forgotten) completed the committee.

The course for the first year (1917-18) included the Oratorio Artists (four singers and accompanists), the Zoelner String Quartet of Brussels, the Ben Greet Shakespearian Players, and a lecture by Dr. Edward A. Steiner. The course continued throughout President Williams' administration. Each year it brought well-known artists and lecturers to the campus. After Prof. Hesser left Bowling Green in 1920, the author became chairman of the committee.

The Spring Musical Festival, started in 1915, continued for several years. The first festival was produced entirely by local talent. Later, however, the chorus was assisted by artists and orchestras of national reputation. An amusing incident occurred at one of these concerts during a program by the New York Symphony Orchestra, with Walter Damrosch conducting. These concerts were held in the Methodist Church, and the temporary platform was rather small for the large orchestra. During one number, the author was appalled when he saw one of the double bass players disappear off the back of the platform, taking his instrument with him. He was relieved when, before the end of the selection, he saw the player climb back and resume playing. Mr. Damrosch paid no attention to the incident, and apparently did not even see it. Such was not the case, however, as he later, in an article in the *Saturday Evening Post,* mentioned the amusing incident that had occurred at Bowling Green, Ohio.

Other well-known orchestras also played at the Spring Festival in the years that followed. Among these the author recalls the Minneapolis and Detroit symphonies. The chorus was assisted by well-known soloists, who sang choral works such as Haydn's *Creation,* Greig's *Olaf Trygrason,* Gaul's *Holy City,* and Handel's *Messiah.* Unfortunately, the Spring Festival was discontinued in 1920, when Prof. Hesser left Bowling Green.

The year 1916-17 also saw the beginning of an athletic program. The fact that such a program had not been started sooner was due to two things. In the first place, President Williams, although he became an ardent fan in later years, did not feel that athletics were important in the development of the new college. In the second place, the number of men in school was small, and dropped almost to zero during the war. The first official interest in the development of athletics resulted from the appointment of F. G. Beyerman, in 1915, as instructor in physical education. Although he was hired, primarily, to teach courses in physical education and conduct gymnasium classes, he was interested in the development of an athletic program at the first opportunity.

Although some baseball and basketball had been played by college students before that time, the first organized college team to play a regular schedule appeared in 1916-17. In that year, a team in basketball, coached by Mr. Beyerman, played a schedule of eight games, and won two and lost six. The first successful season was in 1917-18, when Bowling Green played a schedule of 10 games, with six wins and four losses. Games were played with Bluffton College, Ypsilanti Normal, Adrian College, Findlay College, Defiance College, and The University of Toledo. It is interesting to note that Toledo is Bowling Green's oldest athletic rival, and that the first year of competition set the pattern that has been frequently repeated to the present. Bowling Green won in Bowling Green and Toledo won in Toledo. A baseball team representing the College played two games in the spring of 1918 and lost both.

Bowling Green State Normal College found it difficult to maintain athletic teams during the early years, since the number of men in college was small in the beginning and was reduced further during the war period. At one time the basketball schedule was maintained with only six men on the first team and, of these, only two had ever played before. Three of the remaining four had never seen a game of basketball before entering college.

The spring of 1918 was marked by the issuance of the first student publication at Bowling Green State Normal College. For several years, Prof. Winslow had been interested in starting a college annual. In the fall of 1917, he decided to undertake this task with the assistance of a board of students from the sophomore and senior graduating classes. The board was composed of Elsie C. Meyer, editor-in-chief; Stella Canright, business manager; Clair W. Wilkinson, art editor; and eight associate editors. The result of the combined efforts of this board was a book of 174 pages with numerous illustrations. The publication was financed by the sale of copies to faculty and students, with additional aid from a group of 27 sponsors and 16 pages of advertisements.

The title page of the *BeeGee* contained the statement, "Issued Annually by the Students of the State Normal College, Bowling Green, Ohio." Unfortunately, these plans for annual publication were not realized for a number of reasons. Not the least of these was the fact that Prof. Winslow left Bowling Green to become supervisor of art in the public schools of Baltimore, Maryland. A college annual was not published again until 1924. In the meantime, the college paper was started, and took the name of *BeeGee News*. When an annual was started for the second time, a new name had to be found.

Extension Courses

These years also saw a change in the character of the extension work offered. The first catalog contained the following:

> The extension work as conducted by this school is not entertainment; it is not a series of lectures; it is the usual classroom work brought to the community.

This statement was included in the catalog because the extension work offered by many colleges in the region had, before this time, been more like Chautauqua offerings than college courses.

However, the demand for the type of extension service to which the communities of northwestern Ohio had been accustomed in the past continued. The second and third catalogs announced, in addition to credit courses for teachers, offering of lectures and entertainments designed for communities, clubs, and school organizations. This change of policy was the first indication, and the only one for some time, that Bowling Green State Normal College was interested in anything but teacher training.

Summer Sessions

In 1916 the special spring quarter was renamed the first session, and was reduced from eight to six weeks. It again paralleled the last weeks of the second semester. The courses offered were all from the curricula for elementary teachers. No additional faculty members were hired for this session.

The second session, also of six weeks, offered 90 courses in 11 different departments. These included, in addition to a few preparatory courses, a wide selection for elementary and secondary teachers, and school administrators. The faculty for the second summer session numbered 36 individuals, 23 from the Bowling Green faculty, and 13 from other colleges and from the public schools of Ohio.

Two sessions were announced for the summer of 1917, but some questions were raised. The minutes of the trustees' meeting of May 5, 1917, show that President Williams was called to Columbus by the State Superintendent of Public Instruction to consider the advisability of cancelling the second summer term. It will be recalled that the United States entered World War I on April 6, 1917. The state superintendent feared that so many men would enter the military service, and so many women would work in war plants, that the enrollment would be too small to warrant the expense of maintaining the term. President Williams opposed the proposition as announcements were already out. He also believed there would be no great shrinkage in the enrollment. Both the first and second summer terms were offered, as planned, and proved President Williams was right. Indeed, the enrollment in the second term showed an increase of 67 over the corresponding term of 1916.

The third annual catalog, dated May, 1917, again announced two terms for 1918. However, a change of plans occurred during the year, and three terms were held. These included a five-week term, six days a week, in addition to the two previously offered. This third term reflected the increased demand from teachers in service who wished to complete the equivalent of 12 weeks, and whose schools did not dismiss in time for them to attend the first summer session.

No significant changes were made in the courses offered. These were still mainly for teachers in the elementary grades, plus a few courses for administrators and high school teachers.

Enrollments

The enrollments for the first four years of classes are summarized below:

	1914-15	1915-16	1916-17	1917-18
Academic Year	304*	403*	274	257
Extension	598	247	578	713
First Summer Term			205	332
Second Summer Term	615	638	739	806
Third Summer Term				409
Total	1,517	1,288	1,796	2,517

The above figures seem to show an increase of almost 100 students, or over 30 per cent in the attendance for the second academic year; and a decrease of over 100, or 32 percent, for the third year. However, these figures are misleading. This is due to the fact that, for the first two years, the enrollment for the first summer term was included in that of the academic year. No record is now available, but the author remembers that the enrollment in this

*These figures include the enrollment for the first summer term.

term, during the spring of 1915, was comparatively small, and that it was larger in 1916. This probably means that there was only a small increase in attendance during the second academic year, and this is in accordance with the author's recollection. In fact, the attendance during the academic year was quite stable for several years, and did not again exceed 300 until 1920-21.

Even World War I had little effect on attendance, because Bowling Green was predominantly a girls' school. There were only 58 men in school in 1914-15, 64 in 1915-16, 24 in 1916-17 and 28 in 1917-18. Even after the war, Bowling Green State Normal College did not attract many men until it increased the offerings in courses for high school teachers, and for those interested in fields other than teaching.

Enrollments in extension classes dropped from 598 in 1914-15 to 247 in 1915-16, a decrease of almost 59 per cent. This was largely due to diminishing enthusiasm, on the part of teachers in service, to meet the new professional requirements. However, renewed pressure by superintendents and school boards soon forced teachers back into extension classes, and the enrollment mounted to 578 in 1916-17 and to 713 in 1917-18.

Summer enrollments followed somewhat the same trends as those in extension, and for the same reasons. The summer of 1916 showed a slight increase, but this was followed by bigger increases in 1917 and again in 1918, when the combined attendance at the three sessions reached a total of 1,547. Teachers in service could no longer postpone taking the additional education required for renewal of their teaching certificates.

The number of two-year diplomas and four-year degrees conferred during the first four years are summarized below:

	1915	1916	1917	1918
Two-Year Diplomas in:				
Elementary Education	35	40	46	41
Home Economics		8	6	10
Industrial Arts		0	2	0
Music		3	8	3
B.S. in Education			1	8

The summer of 1917 was made notable by an important first in the history of Bowling Green State Normal College. The determination of the trustees, President, and faculty to develop a four-year, degree-granting college bore its first fruit, when, at the end of the second summer term, the degree of Bachelor of Science in Education was conferred on Miss Margaret L. Grant of Bellevue, Ohio. This first degree was followed by eight more in June, 1918. No outsider can possibly realize the great satisfaction the granting of these degrees gave to all who had helped make it possible. Bowling Green State Normal College had proved (at least to itself) that it was more than a two-year school. However, the opposition to the development of a four-year college did not cease for several years. In fact, the actual conferring of degrees served to increase this opposition.

CHAPTER SIX

From Normal School to College
1918-1929

THE YEARS FROM 1918 to 1929 were very important in the history of the Bowling Green institution. After the end of World War I, in November, 1918, the President and faculty redoubled their efforts to develop the school into a strong, fully recognized, degree-granting college. The success of their efforts is shown by the fact that in 1918-19, Bowling Green was a normal school with an on-campus enrollment of 208 students, mostly in the two-year diploma courses and with no legal authority to train high school teachers or school administrators or to grant degrees. In 1928-29 it was a legally constituted, four-year degree-granting institution, with Colleges of Education and Liberal Arts, and an enrollment of 957 students.

The Normal College Challenged

One of the most important events in the history of Bowling Green State Normal College occurred in the early part of this period. The private liberal arts colleges of Ohio had always wanted the Bowling Green and Kent institutions limited to the two-year curricula for the training of elementary teachers. These colleges had been educating high school instructors and school administrators for many years and were very jealous of their prerogatives in this field. Ohio State University was also opposed to the two new schools developing into degree-granting institutions.

The opposition to the degree programs was greatly increased after Bowling Green State Normal College actually conferred its first degrees, and it reached its peak in the early 1920's. Bland L. Stradley, then university examiner at Ohio State University, became the leader of the opposition. He argued that Bowling Green and Kent were created as normal schools for the training of elementary teachers, and that they did not have either the faculty or equipment needed to train teachers for the secondary schools or to warrant the granting of degrees. A committee of three Ohio State faculty members, with Dr. Stradley as chairman, was appointed to investigate Bowling Green and Kent, and secure evidence to support their contention. The committee spent several days in Bowling Green, visiting classes, interviewing faculty members, and examining the records in the registrar's office. A similar visit was planned to Kent, but the author does not know if it was made.

After returning to Columbus, the committee wrote a report and forwarded it to President Williams. They admitted that the instruction they had witnessed was excellent, that the teachers were enthusiastic and well trained, that admission and other standards were high and rigorously enforced. In fact, they found nothing to criticize. However, they still maintained that Bowling Green had no right to train secondary teachers, or to grant degrees.

President Williams decided that attack was the best defense. If Ohio State could investigate Bowling Green, Bowling Green could investigate Ohio State. Acting on this, he appointed a committee of three: C. C. Kohl, history, chairman; C. F. Reebs, education; and the author. The committee visited the Ohio State campus and made a thorough investigation of the College of Education. They found much poor teaching. One faculty member in particular was poorly equipped for the courses he was giving. He was a former school official who had admittedly been appointed to the faculty for services rendered.

The greatest weakness discovered, however, was in the field of practice teaching. This was being done in the Columbus high schools under teachers with no special preparation or qualifications for the work of supervising student teachers. The work was being carried out with little or no supervision.

The committee returned to Bowling Green and wrote its report, and President Williams sent it to Ohio State University. In a few days he received a letter asking that the Bowling Green committee come to Columbus for a conference. This was held around the luncheon table in the old University Union. The Ohio State committee admitted that all criticisms were true, stated that it was aware of the weaknesses in its program, and was working to correct them as soon as possible. The committee even admitted that, as of that date, Bowling Green was doing a better job of training high school teachers than was Ohio State.

The meeting adjourned in a spirit of mutual friendship and respect, and Bowling Green never again encountered any opposition from Ohio State to the granting of degrees and the training of high school teachers. Dr. Stradley became a warm friend of Bowling Green, and helped the institution in many ways for years to come.

Looking back, this incident has its amusing side, but at the time it was very serious. In fact, it marked the turning point in the attitude of the other colleges in Ohio. Now, for the first time, Bowling Green State Normal College was recognized as an institution of collegiate rank, and legal recognition of this fact was now only a matter of time. It would certainly have come, in any case, but it is equally certain that it would not have come, as early as it did, if it had not been opposed by Ohio State University.

Buildings and Campus

In the fall of 1918, the physical plant was still limited to the four original buildings and the President's home. By 1929 this number was increased to eight by the addition of the Training School Building (finally completed in 1921), a second girl's dormitory (Shatzel Hall) in 1924, the Library in 1927, and the Men's Physical Education Building in 1927.

When the bids for the Men's Physical Education Building were opened, they were all above the estimated cost and the money available. Rather than reduce the size of the building, President Williams decided to build only part of it (as much as funds would permit), and add the rest later. The portion of the building containing classrooms and offices was not built, and the front was closed in with a temporary wall. No attempt was made to make this front look finished, since President Williams wanted the finance committees of the General Assembly, when it next visited the campus, to be sure to see that the building was not finished, and that a new appropriation was needed for its completion. When influential citizens visited the campus, President Williams always made a point to show them the unfinished gymnasium. This strategy was successful, and (several years later) an appropriation was secured to finish the building according to the original plans.

The year 1918 saw a major improvement in the campus. The old board walks, muddy streets, and muddier paths finally disappeared. They were replaced by circular walks and a drive in front of the Administration Building, and a mall and drives from the circle to the east end of Court Street. Campus lights also were installed. More walks, drives, lights, and landscaping were added between 1918 and 1929 and, in the latter year, ornamental brick and stone gateways (there were never any gates) were built at the three main entrances to the campus, on Wooster, Thurstin and Ridge Streets. By the end of this period, the campus had assumed the appearance it was to present for many years. It is still remembered in this way by hundreds of former students and graduates.

One of the most outstanding trustees of the early years was Dr. H. J. Johnston, a prominent physician of Tontogany, Ohio, who served on the Board from 1920 to 1935, and again from 1939 until his death in 1943. Dr. Johnston and D. C. Brown were President Williams' chief advisers and supporters for many years. Each was a man of wide influence and power in northwestern Ohio. Although neither ever played politics, the fact that one was a leading Democrat and the other a leading Republican certainly was of considerable value to the College. Dr. Johnston's services to the University have been recognized by naming Johnston Hall (the first hospital and health center) in his honor.

Growing Faculty

By April, 1929, the faculty, which numbered 23 in 1918, had grown to 48 and also had started to rise in educational qualifications. Whereas, in 1918, only one member held the doctor's degree, by 1929 the number had increased to four, and several other faculty members were studying for and would soon receive this degree.

During the early years, the faculty was capable and well trained for the work it did, but it was typical of the faculties of most teacher-training institutions of the time. The usual qualifications of a faculty member in such a school was the master's degree, teaching ability, and some experience in public school work. Doctor's degrees were few in number and were not considered essential or even important. In fact, in some schools, they were looked upon with suspicion. This was never the case at Bowling Green but, in the early years, the school could neither afford nor attract many holders of advanced degrees.

In the normal school years, faculty members were classified under two titles of department heads and instructors. With the change of status, in 1929, conventional ranks were introduced. The catalog published in May of that years lists eleven professors, nine associate professors, six assistant professors, and ten instructors.

Several additions were made to the administrative staff during this period. The first of these occurred in 1923 when C. D. Perry was appointed registrar. This appointment relieved both the President and the author of some of their duties, since they had shared the work of this office. In 1920, with the resignation of Ernest G. Walker from the faculty, the office of Dean of the Faculty was discontinued. No new appointment was made until 1928, when Clyde Hissong was appointed dean of instruction.

The year 1928 saw the start of another new administrative service at Bowling Green, when Helen B. Todd was appointed associate professor of Hygiene and Physical Education. Miss Todd held the M.D. degree and, in addition to her teaching duties, started a health service for students. In 1938, she was given the title of Director of Health Service.

Faculty Meetings

Faculty meetings were held frequently during the first part of President Williams' administration, but less frequently during the later years. Even at its first meeting, the faculty showed signs of its desire to participate in making decisions and determining policies.

This continued to be the case throughout the early part of this period.

The President used the faculty meetings to keep the faculty informed of problems to be faced and tasks to be accomplished. Discussion was invited, and sometimes the final decisions were left to the faculty. More frequently, however, they were made by the President. The topics discussed covered a wide range—academic, financial, and social.

The author recalls one question that aroused vigorous differences of opinion among the faculty members. For a number of years, the graduation exercises of the new school were very informal, although some faculty members felt that greater formality and pageantry would be much more impressive. As a result, the faculty proposed that it should wear academic robes at all commencement exercises. The question was not settled at one meeting. If the author remembers correctly, it took three elections and the final vote in favor of robes was quite close. The opposition presented two main arguments: (1) robes were undemocratic and (2) expensive to buy or rent. However, after several commencements, the majority of the faculty agreed that the exercises were much more dignified and impressive, and that the robes were worth all that they cost.

Faculty Committees

As the college faculty increased in size, fewer general faculty meetings were held and more business was carried on through committees. The only faculty committee mentioned in the first catalog was the Appointment Committee. The names of the committee members are not given, but the author remembers that the chairman was John E. Talbot, Director of the Training School. The catalog states:

Careful attention will be given to securing positions for capable teachers and to supplying the wants of superintendents and supervisors. This service will be rendered free of charge.

There were several other committees in the early years although they are not mentioned in the catalog. One of the earliest was the Social Committee, which was appointed in 1915 or 1916, and had charge of all parties and social events sponsored by the College. Prof. Biery was the first chairman of this committee which was, at that time, composed of three faculty and four student members. When Dean Sharp was appointed in 1918 as Dean of Women, she became the chairman of this committee. This was the first standing committee to have both faculty and student members.

Another early committee was the Entertainment Course Committee, which had charge of the lectures and musical events that were brought to the College from time to time. Prof. Hesser, instructor in Music, was the first chairman of this committee, and the author was a member. After the establishment of an activities fee, this committee was given the added responsibility of apportioning the money realized from these fees among the participating activities.

With the start of an athletic program, in 1917-18, President Williams appointed an Athletic Committee to have charge of all intercollegiate contests. Prof. Beyerman, instructor in physical education, was the first chairman, and there were two additional faculty and four student members.

Student Government

The first student participation in the administration of the College took the form of student membership on administrative committees. The first of these were the Social Committee (1915 or 1916), and the Athletic Committee (1917), each with four student members.

In 1915-16 the girls residing in Williams Hall organized a dormitory government board of eight students, and the matron as an honorary member. The 1918 *BeeGee* states:

> The purpose of the Board is to maintain social harmony and insure respect for the rights of others. It meets at regular intervals to deliberate upon matters pertaining to the welfare of the students who live in the dormitory as one family.

A second women's organization with wider membership and broader functions was started some time prior to 1923. This was the Women's League, first mentioned in the catalog dated in May of that year. It contained the statement:

> The Women's League is a self-government association of the women students of the college. The object of the association is to regulate all matters pertaining to the student life of its members which do not fall under the immediate jurisdiction of the faculty. All women upon matriculation into college automatically become members of the League.

This definition of functions was quite general, but, in practice, the League usually confined its activities to discussing and making recommendations concerning dormitory regulations. Its recommendations were subject to the approval of the Dean of Women and the President of the College.

Curricula, Departments and Courses

The years from 1918 to 1929 saw few changes in the curricula offered at Bowling Green. Apparently the offerings as planned in 1914 were well suited and adequate to the needs of the normal school. The only exceptions were in the two-year diploma courses in the special subjects. The two-year curricula in commercial education, industrial arts, home economics, and music were extended to three years in 1927-28, and to four-year degree courses in 1928-29.

These years saw a number of changes in and additions to the departments and course offerings. One change was the result of the war. In 1918-19 German was dropped from the Foreign Language Department, and Spanish and French were added. German was returned in 1927-28. These changes reflected the fact that most high schools dropped German from their offerings during this period and substituted Spanish or French or both.

One other change was made to serve more effectively the needs of the schools of northwestern Ohio. In 1919-20 a Department of Commercial Education was added for the training of teachers of commercial subjects, since courses in this field were becoming more numerous in the high schools of the territory.

The only other change resulted from increases in both faculty and enrollments. In the beginning, the catalog listed science courses under two headings of Biological Science and Physical Science. However, the courses were administered in a single department and taught by the same instructor. It was not until 1923-24, when an instructor in chemistry and physics was appointed, that separate Departments of Biological Science and Physical Science were created.

Two courses in the field of speech were offered by the English Department as early as 1919-20. These were two-hour courses in public speaking and debating. Two courses in drama, two hours each, were added in 1921-22. Students in these courses produced several plays each year under the direction of Miss Rea McCain, chairman of the English Department.

Fees and Expenses

The catalog dated May, 1918, announced the first fee charged at Bowling Green. With the start of the Entertainment Course, and the athletic program, in 1917-18, the College was confronted with the problem of financing these activities. No state funds were available for either of these purposes, so it was decided to charge a student-activity fee of $2 a semester, which would entitle the student to admission to all programs of the Entertainment Course, and to all athletic events. This fee, the first of any kind to be imposed, was for extra-curricular activities.

No further fees were charged until the 1921-22 school year. The announcements for that year show a major change of policy, namely the imposition of a registration fee of $10 a semester. This fee was the result of a growing feeling on the part of the General Assembly that the state could no longer afford to pay the entire cost of a student's college education, but the parents should bear a part of this expense. This was the beginning of a policy which has continued to the present time, with the parents and student paying an ever-increasing share.

This same year, 1921-22, also saw the increase of the student activity fee from $2 to $2.50 a semester. This change was due to the fact that admission to all college debates and plays, and a paid-up subscription to the college paper, were added to the activities covered by this fee. The next catalog added social events to this list. In 1927 the registration fee was increased to $22.50

and the activity fee to $5 a semester. No other additions to, or increases in fees, were made during this period.

The necessary expenses of attending Bowling Green remained low throughout these years, although they increased somewhat. With the 1918-19 school year, board in Williams Hall was raised to $3.50 a week. This increase was largely the result of complaints concerning both the quantity and the quality of the dormitory food. The girls said they would rather pay more and receive better meals. In fact they said the cost would be less, since they would not have to buy so many sandwiches and other snacks. The author does not remember that there was any great reduction in complaints, or that they have ceased even to this day.

The only other increase in living expenses during this period came in 1924 when room rent in the dormitories was increased to $1.50 a week. Even with these increases in fees and dormitory charges for board and room, the total estimated expenses for a year were still below $300. Bowling Green continued to be an institution where a student could get a college education at a minimum cost.

Beginning Traditions

During this period, several traditions were started in connection with the athletic program, and most of them were due to the efforts of Ivan E. Lake. *Doc,* who was graduated in 1923, was a loyal booster as an undergraduate and has continued to be so as an alumnus. He received the Distinguished Alumnus Award in October, 1964. He has also been of great assistance to the author in supplying information concerning the early days.

The first of the new traditions came in the fall of 1922, when the first Homecoming was held at the time of a football game. These exercises, which were started through the efforts of Mr. Lake, have become an annual event.

In the early years the athletic teams were nicknamed the Normals, and the athletic award was the monogram designed by Prof. Winslow. Later the award was changed to a block N. By 1925, although the term Normal had not yet been dropped from the official title of the institution, everyone wanted to emphasize the fact that Bowling Green was something more than a normal school. The members of the men's physical education staff were particularly interested in a change, since they wanted to induce more men to enroll at Bowling Green and did not think they would have much success as long as the school was known only as a teacher-training institution. As a result, the athletic award was changed to a block BG, but the nickname Normals persisted for a number of years.

In 1927, *Doc* Lake, then a reporter and sports writer for the Bowling Green *Sentinel-Tribune,* suggested that the college athletic teams be nicknamed The Falcons. The name met with instant and general approval, and is still used today. Certainly, Falcon was a happy choice, since this bird is famous for its fierceness, speed, and courage. Bowling Green's good judgment was confirmed when, in 1955, the falcon was adopted as the mascot of the Air Force Academy at Colorado Springs.

Tornado Hits Campus

On March 27, 1920, the campus was struck by a tornado which badly damaged the Administration, Science, and Training School buildings (the latter still uncompleted), and did even greater damage to the power plant and smokestack. Classes were recessed until repairs could be made to the Administration and Science buildings, and until the weather was mild enough to make heat unnecessary. The power plant repairs and the building of the new smokestack took longer, and were completed just in time to prevent serious suffering from cold buildings after school started in the fall.

Not all of the damage was due to the wind. Although the attempt was made after the storm to drain all pipes, it was found that some of them had been incorrectly installed and did not drain completely. Cold spring weather resulted in frozen pipes and widespread damage to the plumbing in the Administration and Science buildings.

New Name, New College

The Act of 1910 established two additional state normal schools, one in northeastern Ohio and one in northwestern Ohio. The Act, however, gave no official title to either of these schools. The trustees and President Williams, in their determination to establish a four-year institution, did not like either the term normal or school, but compromised by adopting the name Bowling Green State Normal College. Although this name was in use for almost 20 years, it never had any legal sanction and was never liked by President or faculty.

For a number of years preceeding 1929, there was a growing feeling on the part of the public and the administrators and faculties of the two sister institutions that the scope of these schools should be widened to meet the growing needs of northern Ohio. In 1929 the citizens of Kent and the Kent Chamber of Commerce were instrumental in having Sen. V. D. Emmons of Summit County introduce a bill in the State Senate, which proposed to change the two institutions to universities with separate colleges of liberal arts and education and graduate divisions. At first, Bowling Green had no knowledge of and was not included in the proposed bill. However, when friends of the College in the General Assembly acquainted President Williams with what was going on, he requested that Bowling Green be included in the bill, and this was done. President Williams thought that the bill was premature and went too far, but felt that, if a change were made in one of the two sister institutions, it should be made in both.

The Emmons bill aroused considerable opposition as many citizens and legislators shared President Williams' feeling that its provisions went both too far and too fast. Ohio State University also opposed the establishment of two new, state-supported universities, and was even more strongly opposed to the proposed graduate programs.

When it became evident that the Emmons bill, in its original form, could not pass, President Williams proposed that representatives of the Bowling Green and Kent institutions meet to discuss the possibility of a new bill that would meet the objections to the old. Kent agreed, and the meeting was scheduled for Columbus to make it convenient to consult state officials and legislators, if the need arose. Bowling Green's representatives were President Williams, Dr. Clyde Hissong, and the author. When we arrived at the meeting place, we were met by a delegation from the Kent Chamber of Commerce. President Williams refused to talk with this group, since it contained no representative of the Kent State Normal School, and the three members of our group adjourned to a hotel room to talk matters over.

President Williams thought a new bill that would meet the criticisms of those opposed to the Emmons bill could be presented to the General Assembly with an excellent chance of approval. Through such a bill he hoped to accomplish two things that he had desired for a long time. First, he wanted legal sanction for the name college instead of school, and to eliminate the word normal, which he had never liked. Second, he was anxious to secure legal sanction for the granting of degrees. Although no one in recent years had seriously challenged Bowling Green's right in this respect, and over 500 degrees had already been granted, President Williams had always cherished the hope of getting legal authority at the earliest opportunity. His chance, he believed, had finally arrived. So, in the hotel room, and in consultation with the other two Bowling Green representatives, President Williams drew up the rough draft of a revised bill which he hoped would accomplish the two things he desired, and at the same time meet the objections to the original bill. No copy of this rough draft can now be found, but, as the author of this history remembers it, it was almost identical with the bill that was finally passed.

After being revised in the Education Committee of the Senate, the Emmons bill was sponsored in the House by Myrna Hanna of Bowling Green, the Wood County representative. After passing both houses and going to a conference committee, the title of the bill was changed to the Emmons-Hanna Bill. It was finally passed on April 2, 1929, and went into effect on July 2 of the same year.

President Williams was often criticized for being too conservative. However, this reputation was in many instances (as in this case) an asset in dealing with members of the General Assembly and state officials. Most of these had great confidence in his judgment and felt that any proposition he backed was sound and worthy of careful consideration. Both Bowling Green and Kent profited by this situation.

The Emmons-Hanna Act contained the following section:

Section 1. On and after the passage of this Act, the Bowling Green State Normal School, and the Kent State Normal School, . . . shall be known as the Bowling Green State College, and the Kent State College, respectively.

So, after almost 20 years, the institution at Bowling Green finally had an official name. It was not yet a university, but it was officially a college and no longer a mere normal school. Probably no one who was not connected with the institution in its early days can realize the handicap imposed by the title of normal. Probably this change of name did as much as any one thing to hasten the day when the people of Bowling Green, of the state of Ohio, and of the nation would recognize Bowling Green as an institution of collegiate rank.

The Emmons-Hanna Act also accomplished Dr. Williams' second great objective. Section 2 gave legal authority for the granting of the Bachelor of Science degree which the institution had be conferring for years.

Section 2. The boards of trustees of said normal school shall . . . (have) authority to provide courses for the training of elementary teachers . . . and also to provide standard courses leading to the degree of bachelor of science in education.

Bowling Green graduates could no longer jokingly refer to their degrees as illegal or bootleg.

The College of Liberal Arts

President Williams, from the very beginning, had been determined to establish the new institution on a four-year, degree-granting level. His interest, however, was primarily in the field of teacher training and his ambition was to develop a strong teachers' college, and no more. The faculty in the early years was selected with this object in view, and, as a result, most of them were not interested in the development of a college of liberal arts. In fact, many faculty members were strongly opposed to such a development, as they thought it would tend to weaken the teacher-training program. However, from the very first, there was a small but active group of faculty members, who were interested in liberal arts as well as teacher training, and who believed that the development of a strong arts college would strengthen rather than weaken the teacher-training program. President Williams, although not primarily interested in such a development, was not actively opposed. As a result when, in the Columbus hotel, he drew up his suggestions for a revised bill he was willing to include authorization for the offering of liberal arts courses and the granting of liberal arts degrees. He was afraid, however, to propose the establishment of colleges of liberal arts as he thought this would be opposed by those who were against expanding the two institutions into universities.

The Emmons-Hanna Act, in conformance with President Williams' suggestions, contained the following:

Section 3. The boards of trustees of Bowling Green State College and Kent State College, respectively, are hereby further authorized to establish courses leading to the degrees of bachelor of arts and bachelor of science. . . . On recommendation of the faculty, the board of trustees may confer such honorary degrees as are customarily conferred by colleges of liberal arts in the United States.

Since Section 3 did not specifically authorize the establishment of a college of liberal arts, some faculty members were strongly in favor of continuing as an undivided college offering courses in both education and liberal arts. However, history repeated itself, and the trustees again went further than the letter of the law. On the recommendation of President Williams, they at once took action dividing Bowling Green State College into a College of Education and a College of Liberal Arts.

Organizations and Activities

During these years the students were gradually developing more independent social activities, but these did not do away with the need for a program of events sponsored by the college and open to all students. Each year a number of parties and dances were held under the supervision of the Social Committee. Weekly assemblies continued and became somewhat more varied. Outside lecturers and musical programs by both college and professional groups were often included in the exercises. The Entertainment Course was also continued, and brought lecturers, plays, operas, and musical artists and groups for evening appearances. All of these activities were financed by the student activity fee, and students were admitted free.

Musical activities were an important part of college life at Bowling Green from the very beginning. This continued to be the case throughout these years. Although the May Festival and the Philharmonic Club were discontinued in 1920, they were soon succeeded by other organizations. The orchestra, started in 1917-18, was discontinued for a time, due to lack of enough players. It was revived in 1922, under the leadership of Merrill McEwen of the Music Department.

In the fall of 1923, the first college band was organized under the leadership of E. C. Powell, instructor in Industrial Arts. Everyone who could toot a horn was invited to join, and about 20 students and faculty members responded to the invitation. According to the 1924 *Key*, after much noise and effort this aggregation developed into a smoothly playing band. Perhaps "smoothly playing" was largely wishful thinking, but at least it was a band. It made its first public appearance early in the football season.

Activities in the field of speech and drama were started at an early date. In 1919-20 the English Department offered a course in public speaking and another in debating and, in 1921-22, a course in drama was added. The catalog dated May, 1921, contained the following statements:

Intercollegiate debates are arranged by the Debating Class and are held annually.

The Drama Class . . . gives plays twice each semester, care being taken to present only the best of classical and modern drama.

The first student publication came in 1918, with the *BeeGee,* but it died after one issue. The next publication was the *Bee Gee News,* a monthly newspaper with 10 issues a year. This was started in 1920-21 by the Country Life Club, and its faculty adviser, George W. Beattie. It was later changed to a weekly, and continued to be sponsored by Prof. Beattie and the club for a number of years. The paper was financed by the activity fee, and every student received a free copy.

The First *Key*

Since 1918 there had been considerable interest in reviving the publication of a college annual. However, President Williams had been reluctant to authorize it, since he did not think it could be successfully financed. In the spring of 1919, the sophomores published a 52-page class booklet, but this was the last effort for several years. Since an annual could not be published, Prof. Beattie and the editors decided to issue a commencement number of the *Bee Gee News.* This was published on June 15, 1923, and consisted of a 48-page, illustrated summary of the events of the college year.

Instead of satisfying the desire for an annual, the commencement number of the *Bee Gee News* seemed only to intensify it. In the fall of 1923-24, a group of students, headed by C. D. Fox, came to the author with the statement that the President had agreed to approve the publication of an annual, if I would assume the financial responsibility. I was, of course, reluctant to do this. However, after talking to Dr. Williams and a number of students, I became convinced that the interest was great enough to insure the success of the publication. Therefore, I consented, and operations were soon under way.

Since the annual was to be published by the sophomore and senior graduating classes, they elected an editorial board. This consisted of the author and Caroline Nielsen, instructor in Foreign Language, as faculty advisers; C.D. Fox, editor-in-chief; Esther Russell, assistant editor; and 12 additional staff members. Since the publication had to be financed through the sale of copies to students, alumni, and others, and the sale of advertising, three important members of the staff were, Lester Scherff, advertising manager; Donnal V. Smith, sales manager; and Ivan E. Lake, alumni editor.

In order to promote sales among the students, one whole assembly period was devoted to a discussion of the proposed project. The author presided, and a number of faculty members and students spoke of the need for and the value of a college yearbook. The students were then informed that the annual would be possible, if enough of them would pledge to buy a copy. Cards were distributed, and enough pledges were soon received to give a reasonable guarantee of financial success. With President Williams' approval, it was decided to go ahead with the project.

The assembly also solved another problem. Since the college newspaper had appropriated the name *Bee Gee,* which was the title of the 1918 annual, a new name had to be found. Among the speakers at the assembly was R. B. McCandless, instructor in physical education and coach of the football team. In the course of his talk, Mr. McCandless referred to his college annual as the key which unlocked memories of his college days. This gave the author an idea and, when Mr. McCandless sat down, he suggested that *The Key* would be an appropriate name for the new annual. The suggestion was enthusiastically received, and the name was approved by acclamation.

The preparation of copy and the assembling of pictures did not get under way until after the Christmas holidays. At times it seemed that it would not be possible to finish the copy in time for publication before the end of the school year, but finally everything was completed and in the hands of the printer. Finding a printer had presented a problem as contracts for annuals are usually made a year ahead. Finally, a firm in Kalamazoo, Michigan, agreed to take the contract. However, they fell behind their schedule and *The Key* was delayed. One day they telephoned the author that they were ready to start printing but that, if the book were to get to the binder on time, there would be no time to submit proofs. So the author went to Kalamazoo and approved each page as soon as it was set up. So far as is known only one serious mistake was made. The printer found two pictures of seniors and two names which had become detached. Which name belonged to which picture? The author did not know either of the individuals so he could only guess. His guess was wrong, but *The Key* was delivered just before commencement.

The combined campaigns for sales and advertising proved so successful that, when the books were balanced, there was a profit of several hundred dollars. This success assured the publication of *The Key* in 1925. Part of the balance from the 1924 *Key* was used to pay deficits in several succeeding issues and, finally, the remaining amount was used partly to defray the cost of a portrait of President Williams after his retirement.

Athletic Program

The years from 1918 to 1929 saw a great expansion in athletic activities. This expansion was strongly encouraged by one member of the Board of Trustees, D. C. Brown, of Napoleon, Ohio. Mr. Brown was not only a fan, very much interested in athletics, but was also a firm believer in the educational value of an athletic program. His influence led to the employment of coaches for the various sports, and to the building of the men's physical education facility in 1927.

Intercollegiate basketball, as we have seen, was started in the 1916-17 school year, and baseball in the spring of 1918. These were followed by football in the fall of 1919, when there were only 36 men in college. The first coach was Raymond E. Ladd, a former star at Denison University and, for many years, Probate Judge of Wood County. Only three games were played, and Bowling Green lost all three. However, in 1921, Bowling Green established a new intercollegiate football scoring record by beating Findlay College 151 to 0.

In 1919 Bowling Green State Normal College and three other schools formed the Northwestern Ohio Intercollegiate Athletic Association. The other members were Bluffton College, Defiance College, and Findlay College. Later, the University of Toledo joined the Association. The college catalog dated May, 1919 contained the statement:

Whenever possible, teams are formed in football, basketball, baseball, tennis and track athletics, and contests are held with the other colleges of this association.

However, baseball and football remained the only two sports until 1922-23, when it was possible to add track and tennis to the list. Cross-country, started in 1927-28, completed the athletic program for this period.

Fraternities and Sororities

The first social groups organized at Bowling Green State Normal College had dual objectives, combining social activities with a more serious purpose. They were usually organized by the faculty for the benefit of the students. The two literary societies and the Country Life Club were of this type. With increased enrollments and the formation of departmental clubs, the need for organizations of this kind lessened. They were superseded by others whose purposes were purely social and were organized by the students themselves.

There were no national fraternities or sororities at Bowling Green during President Williams' administration. This was popularly believed (by students and others) to be the result of President Williams' opposition, but this was not really the case. President Williams discussed this question with the author on a number of different occasions and always stated that he would not be against national fraternities when the time came. However, he was convinced that it was too early to invite such groups to come to the Bowling Green campus. He felt that the institution could not, at that time, attract the better organizations. His attitude was always, "Let's wait until we can get the best." President Williams also expressed this point of view to a number of student leaders. *Doc* Lake, of the class of 1923, states that President Williams once expressed the desire to proceed with caution, and the hope that some day Bowling Green might command the attention of the strong national groups.

In spite of President Williams' opposition, several attempts were made to form local chapters of national Greek organizations. These were organizations most of whose chapters were in teachers' colleges. President Williams felt that Bowling Green could soon do better, if it waited. At least one attempt almost succeeded. President Williams received a tip one Sunday afternoon that a local group was in the process of being inducted into a national organization. He arrived on the scene in the middle of the ceremonies, and ordered the organizers from the campus.

Everyone admitted, however, that purely social organizations for both men and women were needed. As a result, a number of local groups were formed. The first of these, Theta Delta Chi, was started secretly in 1916 or 1917, but discontinued as a result of the war. With the return of more men to the campus, in 1919, Theta Delta Chi resumed activities. Before long, President Williams learned of this organization and summoned the officers for a conference. He told them that he was not opposed to the organization, but objected to the use of the Greek name. As a result, the group changed its name to the See More Society, and received official approval. The name of this society was later changed to Seymore.

In 1922 a group of eight members of the Seymore's formed a new organization which they called Ye Olde Five Brothers fraternity. *Doc* Lake was one of the members of this group and one of the earliest and most vigorous advocates of bringing strong Greek fraternities to the campus as soon as possible. *Doc* gives the following account of the way in which the Five Brothers gained its name.

> They gained their eventual local name as the result of a baseball trip when a package of strong tobacco and some corncob pipes were purchased and tried on some pledges on the rear platform of the train. That tobacco was named Five Brothers and one had to stand the test of the Five Brothers to become a member.

The Seymore society was disbanded (since most of the members joined the Five Brothers), and for several years the latter organization had no competition. However, a few of the old Seymores returned to the campus for the 1926 Homecoming and, joining with two former members who were still in school, pledged some new men and reorganized the society. This group, although descended from the old Theta Delta Chi and Seymore society, adopted the new name of Delhis.

Early in 1927 a third group of men was organized and chose the name of Commoners. According to the account in the 1927 *Key* this was a group, "the ticket of entry to which is not birth, wealth, social rank, or any other superficial standard but simply the ability to do." Throughout its life, high scholarship and worthwhile contributions to college life continued to be characteristic of this group.

Although there were many more women than men enrolled during these years, social groups for women were started somewhat later. The first two came in 1923, with the organization of the Five Sisters and Skol. The former was designed to be affiliated with the Five Brothers; hence the name.

The Seven Sisters sorority was founded in 1924. It took its name from the fact that there were seven in the original group. All of these were graduated, and the organization ceased to exist until it was reorganized in 1926. The Three Kay society, founded in 1927, was the last organization to be founded during this period.

Rising Enrollments

During the period from September, 1918 to June, 1929, attendance during the regular academic year showed a substantial increase. The enrollment during the 1918-19 year was 208. It increased slowly but steadily until 1924-25 when it was 681. The next year, 1926-27, showed a further sharp increase to a total of 927. The enrollment remained at this level for the remainder of this period, and was 957 in 1928-29.

We have seen that, in the early years, Bowling Green was largely a girl's school, and that World War I resulted in a still further reduction in the number of men enrolled. In the fall of 1918, there were less than half a dozen (exact figures are not available) men in school, but after the end of the war, on November 11 of that year, this number was increased to 17 by the return of men from service. The number of men then rose from 31 in 1919-20, to 60 in 1920-21, 109 in 1921-22, and to 205 in 1928-29. This shows that even before the legal change to college status, Bowling Green was attracting more men. Many of these were enrolled in pre-professional courses and remained at Bowling Green for only one or two years.

While on-campus enrollments for the academic year were increasing during this period, the number of students attending extension classes was dwindling. This was because state appropriations failed to increase as rapidly as on-campus enrollments. This made it necessary to transfer extension instructors to the campus, and gradually to discontinue extension offerings. The college provided instruction to 570 students in extension centers in 1918-19, to only 166 in 1925-26, and to almost none for several years following that time.

During the period from 1919 to 1929, enrollments in the summer sessions first increased for a few years and then decreased. In the summer of 1919, the enrollment was 1,239; by 1921 it had increased to 1,603; but in 1929 it was only 1,248. The decrease, which was to continue for a number of years, was largely due to the fact that teachers in service were gradually catching up with the requirements for continued certification. This decrease in demand led to the dropping, in the spring of 1928, of the first summer term, paralleling the last six weeks of the second semester.

The number of graduates hit an all-time low in 1919. The combined number in June and August of that year was 31 in two-year diploma courses and three in degree courses. This total was even less than the 35 receiving diplomas at the end of the first year. Following 1919 the number of graduates increased slowly but steadily until, in 1929, there were 241 in diploma and 43 in degree courses.

CHAPTER SEVEN

From College To University
1929 — 1939

D<small>R.</small> WILLIAMS' LONG SERVICE to the Bowling Green institution, which began in 1912, did not finally reach an end until April, 1939. He retired in 1937, at the age of 70, and was succeeded by Roy E. Offenhauer who held the office of President until December 29, 1938, when he died as a result of an automobile accident. Dr. Williams became acting president on January 2, 1939, and served in that capacity until April of the same year, when he was succeeded by Frank J. Prout. Since no major changes were made during Dr. Offenhauer's short administration, it seems best to consider the period from September, 1929 to April, 1939, as a unit.

These years were very important ones in Bowling Green's history. In 1928-29 it was a normal school with an enrollment of 951, mostly in two-year diploma courses. In July, 1929, it became a college, and in May, 1935, it became a state university with Colleges of Liberal Arts, Education, and Business Administration, and a graduate program leading to the master's degree. The enrollment increased to almost 1,800 students, of whom 1,157 were in four-year degree courses and 55 in the master's program.

Another Challenge—College or Hospital

However, this development was not without serious obstacles. In 1933 a new danger arose and for a time threatened the very existence of Bowling Green State College. This threat was the direct result of the Depression. The state colleges and universities were supported by fees and by state appropriations from the general revenue fund. This fund, at that time, was derived largely from excise taxes on the earnings of corporations doing business in the state. The decline in these earnings, due to the Depression, greatly reduced the general revenue fund. It forced the General Assembly to cut appropriations and eliminate activities wherever possible.

At that time, as is true today, the welfare institutions of the state of Ohio were unable to meet legitimate needs. Since it was impossible to finance the building of new institutions, the welfare section of the Senate Finance Committee proposed that one of the state colleges be suspended and converted, at least temporarily, into a mental hospital. Since Bowling Green was the smallest of the state institutions of higher education, it was selected for the suspension.

The proposal at first met with substantial support. Its advocates argued that the physical plant at Bowling Green could be converted to the new use at little cost, and that the educational needs of the state could be met by the private colleges, the remaining state colleges, and the Ohio State University. Although the majority of the educators of the state were against the proposal, there was one group in favor. During the Depression, the private colleges of the state were having financial difficulties so serious as to threaten the very existence of some of them. Many of the friends of these institutions backed the proposed change, since they hoped it would bring the private colleges increased enrollments and larger incomes from fees.

However, the proposal met with strong opposition throughout northwestern Ohio. Some of this was spontaneous, and some was promoted by the friends of Bowling Green State College. Dr. Williams felt that the campaign against the proposed change would be more effective, if it were carried out by an agency outside the College. With his encouragement, citizens of Bowling Green and the surrounding territory organized the Northwestern Ohio Educational Protective Association. Dr. Williams also appointed a faculty committee, with the author as chairman, to advise and work with the Protective Association.

In the campaign that followed no attempt was made to deny, or minimize, the welfare needs of the state, but the emphasis was placed on the growing needs of higher education, and on the services that Bowling Green State College was rendering to the citizens of northwestern Ohio. Considerable stress was placed on the fact that a college education at Bowling Green was both nearer home and less expensive than elsewhere. Evidence was submitted to show that many students attending Bowling Green, and many future high school graduates in the territory, would be unable to go to other institutions, if Bowling Green State College closed its doors. This argument proved to be strongest of all those used.

Several pamphlets were published and distributed widely throughout northwestern Ohio. Almost every town and village in the territory was visited. Most visitors were members of the college faculty, but some were citizens of Bowling Green who volunteered their services. These visitors sometimes spoke before groups, but devoted most of their time to talking with prominent and influential local citizens, and soliciting their support. Almost without exception their support was enthusiastically given, and most of those visited promised to write their senators and representatives and urge other citizens to do the same.

This campaign aroused such public sentiment in favor of retaining the Bowling Green institution as a college, that the proposed suspension was defeated. The crucial vote came in the Finance Committee when the motion was made to delete the appropriations for Bowling Green State College from the general appropriations bill. This motion was defeated by a vote of 14 to 5. All fear of any further attempts to delete the Bowling Green State College appropriations was removed when in 1934, Martin L. Davey, a resident of Kent, was elected Governor of Ohio. The proposal to close

Bowling Green State College was forgotten. It was superseded by agitation to raise both of the northern Ohio state colleges to university status.

Although the final outcome was an overwhelming victory, the danger was very real for a time. Without the support of its many friends, Bowling Green State College might well have been suspended, and suspension would have probably resulted in permanent closing. Even if it were eventually revived, it would have had to assemble a new faculty. Some faculty members jokingly stated that they would join the staff of the mental hospital and be ready to assume their professional positions when the college was revived. Other members jokingly threatened to enter the hospital as patients.

The College of Liberal Arts

The growth of the new College of Liberal Arts was quite slow for a number of years. This was due to several causes. In the first place, the people of northwestern Ohio continued for a time to look upon Bowling Green as a teacher-training institution. They usually looked elsewhere when seeking a liberal arts education. Furthermore, the interest of most of the faculty (including the President) was in training teachers. Until this situation was changed, through the gradual appointment of new faculty members with different and wider interests, students who enrolled for a liberal arts course were often persuaded to transfer to the College of Education. The greatest handicap to the growth of the new liberal arts college, however, was lack of funds. During the Depression years it was impossible to secure sufficient appropriations to provide for the needed expansion of offerings in the field of liberal arts, and to employ the needed faculty.

Bowling Green's development was just the reverse of that of many older institutions. In most of these, a college of education was grafted onto an existing college of liberal arts, and often, for many years, would be regarded as greatly inferior. At Bowling Green, however, the new College of Liberal Arts was the underdog. This was true for a number of years, until it was possible to build a faculty interested in the liberal arts program and convince the public that Bowling Green was truly more than a normal school.

Buildings and Campus

In the fall of 1929, the physical plant consisted of eight buildings. By 1939 this number was increased to 12 by the addition of the Practical Arts Building (now Hayes Hall) in 1931, the Women's Physical Education Building in 1938, and the Natatorium, and a men's dormitory (Kohl Hall) in 1939. In 1938, during Dr. Offenhauer's administration, the University also purchased a brick house across Wooster Street from the Training School for a President's home. This was occupied by Dr. Offenhauer and family, while President Emeritus Williams and family remained in the frame house, in which they had lived since 1914.

In 1937 the stadium was completed, and the auditorium was enlarged to include a large, fully equipped stage for dramatic productions. At the same time a large pipe organ was installed in the auditorium. Before the stage was remodeled, it was so small that a player who left at one side and had to make his next entrance from the opposite side had to crawl under the grand piano (behind the rear curtain), or run down the stairs on one side to the floor below and up the stairs on the other side. In this case, he often arrived late or without enough breath to say his lines.

When the Practical Arts Building was constructed, Dr. Williams expected to buy a set of chimes, and the tower on the top of that building was planned to house them. However, the money he expected to use for the chimes had to be spent for another purpose, and the chimes were never purchased. The tower remains to this day, and is often referred to as the chicken coop or pigeon loft. At a later date, during Dr. Prout's administration, chimes of a different type, requiring no tower, were purchased.

In the late 1930's, all of the older buildings on the campus were repaired and repainted. These improvements and most of the new construction, during this period, were financed by money from the Public Works Administration (PWA) and the Works Progress Administration (WPA), supplemented by local- and state-appropriated funds. The programs of both the PWA and the WPA were planned by the federal government in an attempt to alleviate some of the economic effects of the Depression.

Williams and Shatzel Halls, the first two dormitories, were built from funds appropriated by the General Assembly. In 1939 a new method of financing dormitories and other revenue-producing buildings was employed. In that year, Bowling Green State University issued $100,000 in revenue bonds to help finance the construction of Kohl Hall. The following year, however, a Supreme Court decision declared a proposed issue by the Ohio Institutional Building Authority to be in violation of the Ohio Constitution, which limits state indebtedness. Following this decision, the office of the Attorney General felt that dormitory bonds might also be in violation of the Ohio Constitution. As a result, no more bonds were sold on the open market until 1954.

No major changes were made on the University grounds during this decade. Additional drives, walks, and lights were installed, but the campus retained the same general appearance it had presented since 1918. Even the construction of the new buildings made little change in the front part of the campus, since all of these, except the Practical Arts Building (Hayes Hall), were in the rear of the older buildings.

The Trustees

E. T. Rodgers, one of the most outstanding trustees to serve on the Board, was first appointed in 1923. He served until 1928 and again from 1943-61. Since most of his services were rendered during the latter term, they will be discussed in a later chapter.

Most of the trustees of Bowling Green State University have been men, but there were two exceptions during this period. The first woman to serve on the Board was Myrtle B. Edwards of Leipsic, who was a member from 1928 to 1935. She was followed by Bessie S. Dwyer of Montpelier, who served from 1936 to 1941. No other woman was appointed until 1961.

Frank J. Prout's long years as President of the University have caused many people to forget that his services began before he assumed that office. He was a member of the Board of Trustees from 1934 to 1939, and played a major role in saving the University from political domination. His steadfast refusal to play the political game led to the final defeat of a political candidate for the presidency, and to the election of Dr. Offenhauer.

Faculty and Administrative Offices

By April, 1939, the faculty, which numbered 48 in 1928-29, had increased to 73. This growth was due to the increase in enrollment, the addition of the College of Liberal Arts, and later the addition of the College of Business Administration, and the master's program.

With the change in status from normal school to college and to university, and with the accompanying addition of the new colleges and the master's program, the problem of upgrading the faculty became a major one, and was to continue so for many years. Considerable progress was made during this period, in spite of the handicap of limited funds. In 1929 only four faculty members held the doctor's degree; but by 1939 the number had increased to 31. In addition, other members were studying towards doctorates and several received this degree during the next few years.

After the passage of the Emmons-Hanna Bill, in 1929, the author was appointed the first Dean of the new College of Liberal Arts. At the same time the Office of the Dean of Instruction was discontinued, and Clyde Hissong (who had held that office) became Dean of the College of Education.

Early in 1930, Dr. Williams called the author into his office, and asked him to read an announcement which Dr. Williams was going to make during the assembly exercises later that morning. The announcement was to the effect that he was appointing the author Dean of Men, effective immediately. The author protested vigorously, and refused to serve. He believed he already had enough duties and furthermore had no interest in such a position. Dr. Williams, who had been performing the duties of Dean of Men, stated that he no longer had the time for this work, and he was not in a position to employ anyone at that time. He asked the author to help him out for the rest of the year. Stated this way, the author could not refuse. Dr. Williams inserted the word acting in the announcement, and agreed to serve for the rest of the year. Thus, he became Acting Dean of Men in addition to his other duties, and continued to serve in that capacity for six years. These were really busy years. The author taught 10 hours, edited the catalog, organized and administered the new College of Liberal Arts, and served as Acting Dean of Men.

The year 1936-37 was even worse. The College of Business Administration was established by the General Assembly in 1935 and opened its doors to students in the fall of 1936. During the first year, however, no dean was appointed for this college and to the author, in addition to all of his other duties, fell the task of organizing and administering the new college. However, in the fall of 1936, he was relieved of part of his duties when G. Glenn Swanson became Acting Dean of Men. Further relief came in 1937, when Ralph G. Harshman was appointed Dean of the College of Business Administration. In 1937, William C. Jordan became the first full time Dean of Men. Mr. Jordan was Business Manager from 1925 to 1937. These appointments were among the last administrative acts of Dr. Williams before his retirement in the spring of 1937.

Faculty Committees

During this period, as in the past, many routine administrative duties were performed by standing committees of the faculty. These were faculty committees only in the sense that they were composed of members of the faculty. They were appointed by the President and were responsible to him. These committees were not listed in the catalog until 1936. The issue published in May of that year lists 10: Activity Fees, Alumni Relations, Athletics, Entertainment and Assembly, Executive, Graduate Instruction, Library, Placement, Social, and Student Employment.

The Activity Fees Committee was the result of dividing the functions of the old Entertainment Course Committee. The latter, with John Schwarz as chairman, now had charge of the Entertainment Course and the weekly assembly exercises. The new Activity Fees Committee, with the author as chairman, continued the task of deciding upon the distribution of the money secured from activitiy fees among the various participating activities.

The Act of 1935 authorized Bowling Green State University to offer work leading to the master's degree. For several reasons, all concerned felt that for some time the graduate offerings would have to be small in number and limited in scope. The most important reasons for this feeling were the limited demand for graduate work, the lack of qualified faculty in several departments, and the insufficiency of the available funds. It was decided, therefore, not to establish a graduate school under a dean, but to administer the graduate work by means of a graduate committee. This committee was appointed in 1935 to plan and administer the new master's program. Clayton C. Kohl was the first chairman.

By 1939, the number of standing committees had increased to 15. The additions were: Gifts, Endowments and Memorials; Personnel; Policies Commission; Promotion of Research; and Public Relations. The Committee on Gifts, Endowments and Memorials was the University's first attempt to secure financial support from sources other than fees and state appropriations.

With the attainment of university status, the administration felt that it was necessary to increase the amount of research being done by the faculty. This feeling was shared by many (but not all) faculty members. The Research Committee was given the task of encouraging scholarly production on the part of as many faculty members as possible. It was composed entirely of members of the teaching faculty (no administrators) with F. C. Ogg as chairman. This committee did effective work, although for years faculty research was greatly hampered by lack of funds and by heavy teaching schedules. These latter were also due to inadequate appropriations.

University Organization

Before the College of Liberal Arts was established in 1929, Bowling Green State Normal College was a small, single-purpose institution, and its administration was quite simple. The establishment of the new college complicated matters. It not only necessitated the appointment of new administrative officers, but also raised questions concerning the respective duties of the various officers and the even more important question of how the faculty should be organized to serve best the dual-purpose college.

In 1929-30 President Williams appointed a committee to study these questions and to make recommendations. The members of the committee were the two newly appointed deans to represent the administration, and Dr. Clayton C. Kohl, chairman of the Social Science department, to represent the faculty. This committee with the author serving as chairman, drew up a list of duties of the deans and registrar which was approved by the President. In addition, the committe report provided for an Executive Committee, composed of the President, the two deans, and the registrar. This committee was to pass on all exceptional and peculiar cases arising from the administration of the academic requirements and regulations. Gradually, the functions of the Executive Committee were expanded. During the latter part of Dr. Williams' administration, and for all of Dr. Prout's, it was a policy-making body, discussed and usually decided on most academic and student personnel problems. When, in 1937, a dean of the College of Business Administration was appointed, he was added to the Executive Committee.

The question of faculty organization proved much more difficult and was destined to plague the college for many years. In fact, no satisfactory solution was found until 1951, by which time it was even further complicated by the change from a dual-purpose college to a triple-purpose university. Even before the 1929 committee was appointed, the faculty had considered this question and had been unable to reach an agreement. The majority of those members who had been in favor of the creation of the new college also wanted some kind of division of the faculty, but could not agree on any plan. On the other hand, those faculty members who had either opposed, or been indifferent to, the establishment of a liberal arts program (and they were in the majority) were strongly opposed to any division. They argued that, if a division were to be made on any logical basis, the result would be that the College of Liberal Arts would have most of the faculty and the College of Education a big majority of the students.

The committee members represented almost as many points of view as the faculty, and were unable to agree on any plan of division that would be acceptable to either the faculty or the President. They agreed, therefore, that no division would be made, and that all departments and faculty members should serve the College as a whole, rather than particular colleges. In spite of several attempts to change this plan of two (later three) colleges served by one faculty, it survived until 1951.

For purposes of routine administration, the two deans agreed that each would assume primary responsibility for the administration of certain departments, but that important decisions concerning any department would require the approval of both. The division agreed upon was, briefly, that departments and faculty members engaged primarily in the training of teachers should deal with the Dean of the College of Education, and all others with the Dean of the College of Liberal Arts. Obviously, this arrangement was not a permanent solution to the problem, but it worked fairly well for a time. The main reason for this was that the two deans occupied adjoining offices, were able to discuss questions that arose and to reach a reasonable and friendly decision.

The question of separate college faculties was renewed with new vigor, when, in 1935, Bowling Green became a university with a College of Business Administration and a master's program. The same opposition to a division was encountered, and the same arguments used. The division on a college basis would still have left the College of Education with a small faculty and a large enrollment, and the new College of Business Administration would have had only one department, that of Business Administration. It was finally decided that the formation of college faculties would have to wait until the Colleges of Liberal Arts and Business Administration had more students and the Colleges of Education and Business Administration developed more departments. The departments of instruction were, therefore, divided among the three deans for purposes of routine administration. The division was as follows:

Dean of College of Education	Dean of College of Liberal Arts	Dean of College of Business Administration
Biology	English	Business Administration
Education	Foreign Language	Business Education
History	Mathematics	Economics
Home Economics	Music	Geography and Geology
Industrial Arts	Physical Science	Physical Education
Psychology		Sociology

This type of organization, a single university faculty serving three different colleges, remained in operation until the end of Dr. Prout's administration in 1951. Although it had a number of weaknesses, it really operated quite smoothly. This was largely due to the fact that the three deans involved were able to discuss the problems that arose and reach an amicable and reasonable solution. These discussions were greatly facilitated by the fact that the deans occupied adjoining offices. The author, as Dean of the College of Liberal Arts, found that his greatest handicap was the lack of a faculty primarily interested in the field of liberal education and dedicated to the development of a strong program of liberal studies. The result was that he had to work through individual faculty members who shared his interest in building a strong College of Liberal Arts, and through committees chosen from these individuals. Fortunately, the number of such faculty members increased steadily throughout this period.

There was no delegation of authority during the first part of Dr. Williams' administration, but after 1929, the practice was for the Dean of the College to make recommendations to the Executive Committee regarding the academic program of his college. The deans also discussed all questions concerning more than one college before submitting recommendations. At first these discussions were informal, but, after the creation of the College of Business Administration, the three deans held more formal meetings. Although it never appeared in the catalog, this group of deans came to be known as the Council of Deans.

In practice, most decisions on academic questions were made in the Executive Committee. However, the President, as chairman, always had the right of veto. Occasionally questions were discussed in general faculty meetings, but seldom were decided by faculty vote.

Student Government

The first student participation in administration took the form of student representation on administrative committees. The committees were usually those that administered the various student activities that shared in the student activity fees. The first of these, as previously noted, were the Social Committee and the Athletic Committee.

Faculty committees were first published in the catalog in 1936. At this time, the Activity Fees Committee, which distributed the money from the fees among the various participating activities, was composed of three faculty and two student members. This committee had been in existence for several years, but in the beginning was made up of only faculty members. There is no record of the time when students were included. Following 1936, students were added to all of the other committees administering activities supported by activity fees. By the end of Dr. Prout's administration these included, in addition to the above, the committees in charge of the Artist Series, Music Activities, Publications (student), and Speech.

The May, 1931, catalog also contained for the first time, the following statements:

> The Inter-Sorority Council is made up of two representatives from each sorority on the campus. It has power to regulate the sororities in their relation to each other and to the college.

> The Inter-Fraternity Council is a similar organization composed of two representatives and a faculty advisor from each fraternity, with similar powers.

Sororities and fraternities were local social groups, since there were no national organizations on the campus at this time. The decisions and recommendations of these two councils were subject to approval by the Dean of Men, or the Dean of Women, and the President of the University.

The increase in the number of men enrolled in the University brought with it a movement for a student government body with broader powers than the Women's League, and including both men and women. This movement culminated in 1935. The *Bee Gee News* of March 20, of that year, contained a letter to the editor and an article on the subject. The letter summarized the work of student councils on other Ohio campuses and discussed a few of the fields in which a student council would become an indispensable tool in bringing about lasting, beneficial changes in our college life.

The idea continued to spread, and various campus orgnizations rallied to its support. Among these was the Emerson Literary Society, which at that time was one of the most influential student groups. At its meeting on April 3, 1935, this society passed a series of resolutions calling for the organization of a student council to supervise elections, coordinate campus organizations, provide a medium of contact between the student body and faculty, and perform several other functions.

The *Bee Gee News* article, mentioned above, started with the statement: "A much needed improvement for Bowling Green State College is a student council, if it would work." After considerable discussion and study, by students, faculty, and the administration, it was decided that it would work, and the catalog dated May, 1936, contained the following statement:

> All students registered in Bowling Green State University are members of the University Student's Association. The governing power of this association is vested in a Student Council, composed of twelve students and three faculty members. Its purpose is to coordinate campus activities and to act as the official student voice in affairs affecting the student's interest.

The actions and recommendations of the Student Council, as in the case of the Women's League which remained, were subject to the approval of the appropriate administrative officers, and of the President of the University.

The pattern and the machinery for student participation in the administration of the University was complete by the end of Dr. Williams' administration. It remained basically unaltered during that of his successor. The pattern was to afford students the opportunity for studying, discussing, and making recommendations concerning all matters directly connected with their non-academic life on campus. The machinery was the Student Council the Women's League, the Inter-Sorority and Inter-Fraternity Councils Students also served on the committee charged with distributing funds from activity fees, and on committees in charge of activities which received activity fee money.

Expanding Curricula

The decade from 1929 to 1939 saw many changes in and a great expansion of the curricula offered at Bowling Green. All of these, with two exceptions, were the result of the development from a normal school to a university. The first exception occurred in the College of Education as a result of increases in requirements of the state Department of Education for the certification of teachers. As a result of these new requirements, all two-year diploma courses were discontinued on September 1, 1938. The diploma curriculum in elementary education was increased to three years in 1938-39 and to a four-year degree course in 1939-40. The last two-year diplomas were granted in August, 1939. With this event, the final vestige of a normal school vanished, and Bowling Green became a four-year, degree-granting university.

The year 1938-39 also saw the dropping of the Department of Agriculture. This was not the result of the change to university status, but was due to the fact, as we have seen, that work in this field at Bowling Green had never been able to secure adequate support from the General Assembly. With the retirement of George W. Beattie, who had been the only member of the department, all offerings in this field were discontinued.

The Bowling Green institution, from the beginning, offered many courses in the field of the liberal arts. These had been sufficient to enable students to take the first two years of a general or pre-professional course at Bowling Green, and then transfer to other institutions. Following the Act of 1929 and the establishment of the College of Liberal Arts, four-year curricula were introduced leading to the degree of Bachelor of Arts or Bachelor of Science. The curricula for the Bachelor of Science degree differed from those for the Bachelor of Arts degree by requiring more mathematics and science.

For the first year, 1929-30, majors and minors were offered in six fields: English, chemistry, French, history, mathematics, and social science; and minors only in four additional fields: biology, Latin, physics, and Spanish.

By 1938-39 the major and minor fields included biological science, business administration, chemistry, economics, English, French, history and political science, Latin, mathematics, physical science, sociology, and speech. Minors only were also offered in geography and geology, home economics, music, physics, psychology and philosophy.

Prior to 1935, the offerings in the field of business were limited to curricula for the training of teachers in the commercial subjects. With the establishment of the College of Business Administration in that year, four-year curricula were offered for students wishing to prepare for a career in business. These led to the degree of Bachelor of Science in Business Administration. The May, 1935, catalog outlined a general course and opportunities for specialization in accounting, marketing, and secretarial science. The May, 1939, catalog offered majors and minors in accounting, business finance, and marketing, and a minor in secretarial science.

The Act of 1935, besides changing the name to University and establishing the College of Business Administration, authorized the granting of the degree of Master of Arts. Bowling Green State University immediately took advantage of this authorization and announced, in the May, 1935, catalog, master's programs in the Colleges of Education and Liberal Arts. In 1935-36 graduate work was offered only in the Departments of Education, English, History, Mathematics, and Social Science. The May, 1938, catalog added the Departments of Biological Science and Foreign Language to this list.

Departments and Courses

The change from normal school to college, in 1929, and to university, in 1935, resulted in the creation of several new departments, and an increase in the number of courses offered. The Department of Agriculture was dropped in 1938-39. Most of the other changes took the form of new department names, and the splitting of old departments into two or more new ones.

In 1920-21, the title of the History Department was changed to Social Science, since, by that time, it was offering courses in history, political science, economics, and sociology. In 1929-30, after the establishment of the College of Liberal Arts, this department was split into two, the Departments of History and Social Sciences. The latter included economics, political science, and sociology.

The year 1929-30 also saw the creation of a Department of Psychology and Philosophy. Courses in these fields had previously been offered in the Education Department. In 1932-33 the title of the Geography Department was changed to Geography and Geology, since it was offering courses in both subjects.

With the opening of the College of Business Administration in 1935 the title of the Department of Commercial Education was changed to Business Administration. In 1936-37 the Social Science Department was eliminated and separate Departments of Economics and Sociology were established. Political science was re-combined with the Department of History.

A few courses in speech were offered by the English Department as early as 1919-20. Gradually, the offerings in this field were increased until they became so numerous that, in 1938-39, a separate Department of Speech was created.

In 1939-40 the courses for the training of teachers in commercial subjects were removed from the Department of Business Administration, and a separate Department of Business Education was established. At the same time, the offerings in the Department of Business Administration were expanded and divided under the heading of general courses, accounting, business finance, business law, marketing, and statistics.

Fees and Expenses

The decade from 1929 to 1939 saw the addition of one new fee and one increase. In 1929 a health fee of $2.50 a semester for dormitory residents, and $1.50 a semester for others, was added. The student activity fee was raised to $6 a semester in 1936 and to $6.25 in 1937. With these increases, each student received a copy of the yearbook. The first *Key,* published in 1924, showed a profit, but several issues in succeeding years were unable to pay expenses, and were forced to use part of the profits from the first year. Since this could not continue indefinitely, it was necessary either to discontinue *The Key* or to find a better method of financing its publication. No issue was published in either 1933 or 1935, because of lack of funds. Faced with this situation, the student body suggested that the book be included in the activities fee, and that the fee be increased for this purpose.

These years also brought moderate increases in living expenses. In 1932, room rent was increased to $2 for a single room, but remained at $1.50 a week for each occupant of a double room.

Northwestern Ohio at this time was largely a rural area with very little industry. As a result, the effects of the Depression were not felt too seriously in this region for several years. By 1933, however, money was becoming scarce even in northwestern Ohio, and Dr. Williams wanted to reduce as much as possible the estimate of expenses, as published in the catalog. Board in the women's dormitories was reduced from $3.50 to $3 a week, and the item of $30 for washing and incidentals was omitted from the estimate. This reduced the total, for girls living in the dormitories, to $240 for a year. The elimination of washing from the necessary expenses was justifiable, since some of the girls did their own laundry in the dormitory, and most of the rest took or sent their laundry home.

At first glance, it would seem that the necessary expenses for men were greater than for women. There were no men's dormitories, and rooms in private homes and meals in restaurants cost more than in the women's dormitories. In fact, however, this was not true, since many of the boys brought food from home and did their own cooking. Most of them came from farms, and food sent from home cost little. Often milk was the only item of food the boys bought in Bowling Green and, in winter, even this was often brought from home.

After 1933 expenses increased once more, but only moderately. In 1934 board went back to $3.50 a week, but the total necessary expenses were still well below $300 for the year.

Kohl Hall, the first dormitory for men, was completed during Dr. Williams' last year as acting president, although it was not opened until the following September. This dormitory was named in honor of Dr. Clayton C. Kohl, former chairman of the Department of Sociology. This was the first time that a faculty member was so honored.

After the contracts for Kohl Hall were let, but before construction began, Dr. Williams became afraid that a dormitory for men would not fill. If this happened, the University would be unable to pay interest on the bonds which had been issued to pay for its construction, or to provide for the retirement of the bonds. On his recommendation, the Board of Trustees on March 6, 1939, instructed Dr. Williams to see the Attorney General and find out what could be done about cancelling the contracts. On March 15, Dr. Williams reported that the Attorney General had given the opinion that the University had obligated itself to the contractors, and that there was no legal way in which the contracts could be cancelled. This ruling later proved to be very fortunate for the University, since without this dormitory it would have been impossible to obtain service training programs during the war period.

Many of the men attending the University at that time had been cutting expenses by doing their own cooking. Dr. Williams was convinced that they would want to continue this practice. To meet this situation, and to make certain that the new dormitory would be filled to capacity, Dr. Williams changed the plans for Kohl Hall to provide for a Co-operative Boarding Club on the third floor. The May, 1939, catalog contained the following statement concerning this club:

> Meals will be prepared by a cook furnished by the university and served in the club dining room. Each week the cost will be prorated among the members, and credit allowed for any provisions brought from home. By this plan, it is hoped to furnish wholesome and well-balanced meals at a cost materially less than in the regular dining room. Club members will be charged $1.50 a week for room and 50c a week to apply toward upkeep of the club kitchen.

This club was probably suggested to Dr. Williams by several private co-operative boarding clubs which had been sponsored by the University for a number of years. These operated under similar plans and had proved both successful and popular.

From College to University

After the passage of the Act of 1929, many people in northern Ohio felt that provisions for higher education in their section of the state were still not equal to those in the southern half. The need for college training in business also was growing rapidly, and no state school in northern Ohio was authorized to offer courses in this field. Furthermore, the possession of a master's degree was becoming more important for high school teachers, and it was felt that additional facilities were needed for graduate work. These circumstances, coupled with the natural pride and ambitions of Bowling Green State College and Kent State College, and the influence of Governor Martin L. Davey, culminated in the passage of two companion bills, by the General Assembly, on May 15, 1935.

The first of these bills contained the following provision:

On and after the passage of this act, the Bowling Green State Normal School, and the Kent State Normal School shall be known as Bowling Green State University and Kent State University respectively.

This change of name was not made without argument. Several members of the General Assembly still felt that university was too pretentious, and that the name college was more fitting. However, one of the main objectives of the new legislation was to put the institutions at Bowling Green and Kent on the same basis as Ohio University and Miami University, and these latter had been known as universities for many years. Since they did not think it wise (or possible) to change the names of the two older institutions, the legislators decided to change Bowling Green and Kent from colleges to universities. Even at this time, no one in the legislature foresaw the future development of the state institutions in the four corners of Ohio. Today, the state is very fortunate to have five well-established and strong universities. Sometimes, a legislature acts more wisely than it knows.

The second act passed on May 15, 1935, contained the following provisions:

The boards of trustees of Bowling Green State . . . university and Kent State . . . university, respectively, are hereby further authorized to . . . create, establish, provide for and maintain a college of liberal arts and a college of business administration.

Since the Act of 1929 did not specifically create a College of Liberal Arts, some faculty members at Bowling Green maintained that the trustees had exceeded their authority when they established such a college. To remove this doubt (which existed only in the minds of a few diehard opponents of liberal arts at Bowling Green), Dr. Williams asked that the College of Liberal Arts be included in this act, although it had been in existence for six years.

The College of Business Administration began functioning with the school year of 1935-36. However, no dean was appointed, and the author was assigned the task of organizing and administering the new College. This was a difficult assignment, since he had no particular qualifications for planning a curriculum in business administration. His difficulties were increased further by the fact that there were, at that time, only two men on the faculty who were qualified to participate in the planning. One of these was interested only in the training of teachers of commercial education, and had been strongly opposed to the creation of a College of Business Administration. The other individual had expected to be appointed dean of the college and was badly disgruntled by his failure to secure this position. Furthermore, the two men were not only jealous of each other, but were also diametrically opposed in their points of view. As a result, they never agreed on any question. Finally, by ignoring these two men, and consulting catalogs and professors at other institutions, the author succeeded in preparing a curriculum for the opening of the new College. At the end of the second year, in the spring of 1937, Dr. Ralph G. Harshman was appointed Dean. This was the last administrative appointment of Dr. Williams before his retirement from the presidency.

The growth of the College of Business Administration was more rapid than that of the College of Liberal Arts in its early years. This was largely due to the fact that there was a growing demand for business training on the college level, and the private colleges offered little in this field. Furthermore, the worst of the Depression years were past, and it was easier to secure funds for the development of the new College.

The Master's Degree

The second Act of 1935 also authorized the Board of Trustees to include the usual technical or graduate instruction for the degree of Master of Arts. History repeated itself. Just as the Act of 1929 did not specifically create a College of Liberal Arts, the Act of 1935 did not specifically create a graduate school. It simply authorized graduate instruction leading to the degree of Master of Arts. The reason was the same as before. Ohio State University was still opposed to the development of graduate schools at the other four state institutions, and it was feared that its opposition would defeat the bill.

In spite of the lack of specific authorization, Dr. Williams and the trustees established a College of Liberal Arts. However, in the present case, because of the known opposition of Ohio State University, and in view of the small size of the graduate program, Dr. Williams felt that it would be unwise to establish a graduate school. As a result, the graduate program was administered for a number of years by a graduate committee composed of the deans of the Colleges of Education and Liberal Arts, and four faculty members. Dr. C. C. Kohl was the first chairman of this committee. Later, when the College of Business Administration offered graduate courses, the dean of that college was added to the committee. This type of organization and administration of graduate work was continued for a number of years.

Organizations and Activities

From the beginning, Bowling Green State Normal College believed in the value of extracurricular activities in furnishing a well-rounded education. This belief was well stated in the May, 1931, catalog:

> In order to provide adequately for the social as well as the mental development and training of its students, Bowling Green State College supplies a well-rounded program of student organizations and activities. It is believed that among these organizations and activities every student can find one or more suited to his needs and interests and in which he can develop those qualities of social ease and leadership necessary for a successful and happy life.

President Williams believed that all activities that were officially sponsored by the College should be available to all students at the least possible cost. This led to the establishing of the activity fee which, by 1939, entitled a student to free admission to all intercollegiate athletic events, debates, and certain lectures, entertainments, plays, and social events. It also included a paid-up subscription to the *Bee Gee News* and *The Key*.

In the beginning, the problem was to provide enough activities. However, by 1931 the picture had changed. The catalog published in May of that year (and several succeeding catalogs) contained the statement:

> Although students are encouraged to take part in student activities, care is taken to limit the amount of such participation so as to prevent interference with regular college work.

However, the limitations were not always effective and some students, then as now, majored in extracurricular activities.

For a number of years, Book and Motor was the only honorary society at Bowling Green. Several others were added by 1939. The first of these was Phi Sigma Mu, an honorary music fraternity, in 1926. This was followed by Pi Kappa Delta, forensics, in 1929; Beta Pi Theta, French, in 1936; Sigma Tau Delta, English, in 1936; Sigma Delta Psi, athletics, in 1936; Kappa Mu Epsilon, mathematics, in 1937; and Kappa Delta Pi, education, in 1939.

In addition to these national organizations, there were also a number of departmental clubs. Among these were the Home Economics Club, the Intermediate Teachers Club, the Kindergarten-Primary Association, the Industrial Arts Club, and Quill Type, an organization of students and faculty in business education.

As the years passed, the musical organizations and activities varied with the interests and talents of the students and faculty. However, there were always enough to constitute a valuable part of college life for both participants and listeners. The 1939 *Key* lists the Marching Band, Concert Band, Treble Clef (girl's glee club), Men's Glee Club, Concert Orchestra, A Cappella Choir, and Male Quartet.

The A Cappella Choir was a valuable part of the musical life of the campus during these years. In 1929 R. N. Tunnicliffe, chairman of the Music Department, organized a mixed chorus which gave a number of concerts each year. Later, the name was changed to A Cappella Choir. It frequently sang as a vested choir in the weekly assembly exercises and gave two public concerts each year, one of which was the traditional Christmas Concert.

The activities in both speech and drama were carried on under the supervision of the English Department until 1938, when a separate Department of Speech was created. Rea McCain, chairman of the English Department, supervised both speech and drama until 1919, when James W. Carmichael joined the English staff, and took over the work in public speaking and debate. Dr. McCain continued in charge of the drama activities until 1940, when Elden T. Smith was added to the staff of the new Department of Speech.

In 1930, Bowling Green State College was granted a chapter of Pi Kappa Delta, forensic society, and participation in events in this field was expanded. The May, 1931, catalog contains the statement:

Contestants in oratory, extempore speaking, and debate, for both men and women, are entered in the Provincial Convention, and the National Convention contests.

No new publications were started during these years. The *Bee Gee News* was published throughout this period, and *The Key* was published annually, except in 1933 and 1935. No *Key* was published in either of these two years, but the *Bee Gee News* published commencement numbers containing class pictures, and a brief record of the activities of the year.

Bowling Green's sports activities were not confined to intercollegiate competition. By 1939, according to the catalog published in May of that year, the University provided a varied program of intramural sports for both men and women. These included hockey, soccer, basketball, baseball, tennis, archery, volleyball, badminton, handball, table tennis, horseshoes, shuffleboard, and swimming.

Two changes occurred in the athletic program during these years. By 1932 Bowling Green had become too large and its teams too strong for the Northwest Ohio Athletic Association. It withdrew from that organization and, in the same year, joined the Ohio Athletic Conference. At that time, the Conference included 24 other Ohio colleges. Bowling Green competed in that organization until 1942, when it was again forced to seek stronger opposition.

In 1935 athletic relations were severed with the University of Toledo, Bowling Green's oldest rival. The rivalry between these two schools had become so great that few games ended without a riot. As a result, it was thought advisable to end relations, and to give the rivalry a chance to cool off. Athletic relations were not resumed until 1947.

No new men's social groups were organized during this decade, but there were two additions to the number of sororities. These were Las Amigas, founded in 1930 and PHRATRA, founded in 1933. This completed the list of local fraternities and sororities in Dr. William's administration.

The Silver Anniversary

In June, 1939, the University celebrated the completion of 25 years of instruction and the graduation of the twenty-fifth class. The fact that it was not the silver anniversary of the founding of the institution (this was four years earlier, in 1935) led to much confusion and misunderstanding. Ceremonies were held at the alumni dinner on June 3, and at a convocation on June 4. The programs included the introduction of the new President, Frank J. Prout, and of the five members of the faculty with 25 years of continuous service. These included, Dr. H. B. Williams, Dr. J. R. Overman, Dr. Rea McCain, Prof. G. W. Beattie, and Prof. E. L. Moseley. Brief talks were given by representatives of the first and twenty-fifth classes. Martha Harvey Parquette represented the Class of 1915, and Kermit Long spoke for the Class of 1939. Mrs. Marquette might have represented both classes as she received a two-year diploma in 1915 and the B.S. in Education in 1939. Dr. Williams spoke on the topic *Normal School to University*, and Gov. John W. Bricker gave an address.

Dr. Williams Retires

At the meeting of the trustees held on June 8, 1936, Dr. Williams informed the Board that he had reached retirement age on October 16, 1935, and could retire on August 31, 1936. However, if agreeable to the Board, he wished to continue service as President. The Board acceded to his wishes, and continued his services for the year beginning September 1, 1936. Nothing further concerning his retirement appears in the minutes of the trustees until July 1, 1937. At the meeting held on that date, the Board adopted a statement of policy as follows:

> Whereas, the State Teachers Retirement law provides that members shall retire when they reach the age of seventy years, with the consent of the employing board. Therefore, be it resolved by the Board of Trustees of Bowling Green State University that the teachers and employees of this University shall retire at the end of the school year when they reach the age of seventy years.

This policy was adopted by a vote of three to two. The trustees then, by unanimous vote, elected Dr. Williams, President Emeritus, with duties to be specified by the Board at a future date.

Dr. Williams was stunned by this action. He had intended to present the question of his retirement or retention for another year to the Board for its consideration, but he was surprised and deeply hurt by its summary action. He felt that his long service to the University deserved more considerate treatment.

At the meeting of August 25, 1937, Dr. Williams' duties as President Emeritus were defined. He was to:

1. Have charge of finishing all buildings then under construction.

2. Organize the alumni.

3. Carry out any other duties assigned by the Board.

These duties were satisfactory to Dr. Williams. He had long felt the need of more complete records of former students and graduates, and of an organization of the alumni to cooperate with the University administration, but neither time nor funds had been available. He welcomed the opportunity to devote his time to this project.

At this same meeting, the Board passed the following resolution:

Homer B. Williams, the first president of the University . . . be given a vote of thanks for his efficient leadership in the construction and development of the institution from a few unimproved lots and delapidated fields to its present attractive campus and recognized rank as a State University of approved standards.

This resolution did little to diminish the bitterness Dr. Williams felt at the treatment he had received.

The Election of a New President

The Board of Trustees made no public announcement of its plans for securing a new president. Between July 1, and August 25, 1937, of the same year, only one official Board meeting was held. The minutes of this meeting, August 3, 1937, made only one reference to the question of a new head for the University. They contained the following statement, without any elaboration or comment:

Carl Hawver and Archie King, graduate students, were present and addressed the Board on the matter of the selection of a man to succeed President H. B. Williams.

The uninvited presence of Mr. Hawver and Mr. King resulted from the fact that rumors were rife on the campus, in Bowling Green, and throughout northwestern Ohio, that the Board was holding secret meetings in Lima, Columbus, and other cities outside Bowling Green, and that they planned to appoint a man who had strong political backing, but limited qualifications, for the position of president of a university.

Frank J. Prout (later President of the University) was President of the Board of Trustees at that time. He strongly disapproved of the political plan and, as a result, was not notified of the secret gatherings. No minutes were kept of these rump meetings. Few official meetings of the Board were held, and these were not open to the public. The trustees refused to hear representatives of the faculty, students, alumni, or citizens. The sole exception was the case of the two graduate students mentioned above, and they crashed the meeting without invitation.

The faculty was greatly disturbed by the many rumors, and a group was organized to do all in its power to prevent a political appointment. This group decided that its best strategy was to back a candidate of its own and decided upon Clyde Hissong, Dean of the College of Education. The faculty group also started a thorough investigation of the qualifications and character of the leading (rumored) candidate. However, the Board still refused to hear any representative of the faculty.

Finally, late in August, the rumor reached the faculty group that the trustees were going to hold another secret meeting on the following day, and they now had three votes lined up for the political candidate. This was enough to insure his election, as the Board at that time had five members. A hastily called conference of some of the leaders of the faculty group was assembled to discuss possible means of stopping the election. After much discussion, the group decided (since the Board would not hear a faculty representative) that the only hope was to concentrate on one trustee, who was reported to have been the last to agree to back the politicians' choice. Two faculty members were selected to visit this trustee in his home, and to present all the information the group had been able to assemble concerning the candidate. C. S. Martin, chemistry, and D. J. Crowley, industrial arts, agreed to undertake the mission, and secured an appointment with the trustee for that evening.

After studying the information submitted by the faculty representatives, this trustee stated that he had been misinformed and misled, and that he could not, and would not, vote for the proposed candidate. As a result, at the trustees' meeting the next day, this candidate received only two votes, and the political plot was foiled.

With this defeat, the politicians apparently lost heart, and a compromise candidate was soon proposed. One member of the Board of Trustees at that time was from Lima, Ohio, so he suggested Roy E. Offenhauer, superintendent of the Lima schools. Dr. Offenhauer was well and favorably known to the other trustees, and was well qualified for the position. At an official meeting of the whole Board, held in the Argonne Hotel in Lima, on August 25, 1937, he was unanimously elected as the second President of Bowling Green State University, for a term of five years. That his election was evidently agreed upon before the official meeting was shown by the fact that both he and Dr. Williams were present at the meeting.

Dr. Offenhauer's Administration

Dr. Offenhauer assumed office in September, 1937. He was a man of great charm and impressive appearance, and soon won the hearts of student body, faculty, and citizens of Bowling Green. Everyone predicted a bright future for the University under his leadership. These high hopes were shattered, when Dr. Offenhauer was injured in an automobile accident. He died on

December 29, 1938, after only a year and four months in office. About all that can be said about his administration is that it showed great promise, but a year and four months were too short for many real accomplishments.

The plans for the new men's dormitory were started during Dr. Offenhauer's term in office, but construction had not started at the time of his death. On December 1, 1938, Dr. Offenhauer recommended to the trustees that this dormitory be named Clayton C. Kohl Hall, in honor of Dr. Kohl, Professor of Sociology, who had died on November 10. This was almost the last recommendation that Dr. Offenhauer made to his Board of Trustees. One other meeting was held on December 22, when Dr. Offenhauer reported progress being made on the buildings under construction. This was also Dr. Frank J. Prout's last meeting with the Board, as its President, since his term had expired.

Only two other events need to be mentioned, both in the realm of faculty affairs. The first of these was the culmination of several years of effort on the part of the faculty. On January 12, 1938, at the recommendation of President Offenhauer, the Board of Trustees adopted the 1925 statement of tenure principles of the American Association of University Professors as the policy of the University. This was the first official tenure policy for Bowling Green State University.

The Policies Commission

When Dr. Offenhauer became President, he believed that faculty should have a greater part in discussing and making recommendations concerning university affairs. To accomplish these purposes, he felt that a body smaller than the general faculty was needed. To meet this need, he appointed a Policies Commission, with the deans of the three colleges, the dean of men, the dean of women, and the registrar as ex officio members, and 10 members elected by the faculty. F. C. Ogg, of the Mathematics Department, was the first chairman of the commission.

This group was empowered to discuss academic and administrative problems and policies, and to conduct studies and investigations in these areas. It could report findings, and make recommendations to the faculty and President. However, it had no legislative powers. In the faculty meeting on January 20, 1938, Dr. Offenhauer stated that the commission was not to have power to put its findings into operation. Such power was still reserved for the President.

The Executive Committee, which was continued as before, was composed entirely of administrative officers. The new commission, while including administrative officers, had a faculty chairman and a majority of faculty members. It also had the power to initiate discussions and investigations. Although the Policies Commission proved unsuccessful, it was still an important first step in the direction of greater faculty participation in Univerity administration. Efforts in this direction were to continue for many years.

Dr. Williams as Acting President

After Dr. Offenhauer's death, the trustees asked Dr. Williams to return as Acting President. Although deeply hurt by his summary retirement, his continued interest in the welfare of the University moved him to accept. He served in this capacity until the election of Frank J. Prout, who assumed the presidency in April, 1939.

Enrollment Exceeds One Thousand

Attendance continued to increase slowly during this period. It exceeded a 1,000 for the first time in 1930-31, when the enrollment for the second semester was 1,002 students, and reached 1,310 in 1938-39. Dr. Williams was well satisfied with these figures. He told the author, on several occasions, that he thought 1,000 students was the ideal enrollment for a college, and that he hoped Bowling Green would never greatly exceed that figure.

Part of the increase in the early 1930's was the result of the Depression following the stock market crash of 1929. Job opportunities were scarce, or non-existent, and more young people entered college. Furthermore, Bowling Green probably received more than its share of these students, since, at that time, the cost of attending this institution was among the lowest of any accredited college in the country.

The number of women enrolled at Bowling Green from the beginning had greatly exceeded the number of men. After the establishment of the College of Liberal Arts in 1929, and the College of Business Administration in 1935, male enrollments grew more rapidly, and the proportions of the sexes started to change. In 1928-29 only 205 men were enrolled, but by 1938-39 this number had grown to 655. This growth in male enrollment was to continue until finally the number of men would exceed the number of women.

Post-Summer Sessions

The decline in summer enrollments, due to decreased demand from teachers in service, continued throughout the period from 1929 to 1939. This led, in 1934 to the dropping of the second summer term. Only one session was offered in that summer, but it was increased from six to eight weeks. The Summer Session Bulletin for 1934 contained the following statement:

> The Summer Session of the College has consisted heretofore of two terms of six weeks each because the state certification requirements were arranged in units of six weeks. Now the heaviest demand for summer work arises from students who wish to earn credit toward a diploma or degree.

> To meet the changing demand for summer work, the Summer Session of 1934 will consist of a single term of eight weeks, six days a week, and will be equivalent to a half-semester.

For a number of years a post-summer session of three weeks was held for students who wished to earn extra credit. Usually only one or two classes were offered. The student enrolled for one course and earned three hours' credit. In 1934 the enrollment was 602 in the regular session and 26 in the post-summer session and, in 1937, the correponding numbers were 712 and 95.

Summer enrollment increased sharply in 1938, with an attendance of 971 in the regular and 98 in the post-session. This was largely due to an increase in the requirements for elementary teachers, which was announced by the state Department of Education in 1938. The new requirements were to go into effect in the fall of 1939, but would not apply to teachers starting their training programs before September 1, 1939. The enrollment in 1939 was 937 for the regular term and 39 for the post-session.

During the early 1920's extension offerings were greatly curtailed due to increased on-campus enrollments. No substantial increase came until the late 1930's. The extension enrollment in 1936-37 was 46. This grew to 217 in 1937-38, and to 475 in 1938-39. These increases were due to the fact that the University faculty had finally grown large enough to provide more off-campus instruction.

Conferring of New Degrees

The years between 1929 and 1939 saw an increase in the number and a change in the nature of the degrees granted. The new College of Liberal Arts conferred the first Bachelor of Arts degree on Albert G. Jenkins of Toledo in August, 1931, and the first Bachelor of Science degree on Allen Scott of Bowling Green in July, 1933. Richard L. Beard of Findlay received the first Master of Arts in August, 1936, and the new College of Business Administration conferred the first Bachelor of Science in Business Administration on Dale Orwin South of Dunbridge, Ohio, in June, 1937.

In the spring and summer of 1939, there were 127 graduates from the two-year diploma courses. This group was the smallest for a number of years. It was also the last, since all two-year curricula had been discontinued. On the other hand, the number of graduates in four-year degree courses had increased to 244. Of these, 202 received the Bachelor of Science in Education degree; 24, the Bachelor of Arts; 5, the Bachelor of Science; and 13, the Bachelor of Science in Business Administration. In addition, 13 received the Master of Arts degree.

The Act of 1929 granted authority for the conferring of honorary degrees by the trustees, on the recommendations of the faculty. This was the first power granted to the faculty by statute. However, no honorary degrees were conferred until the retirement of President Williams. In June, 1938, he was awarded the degree of Doctor of Laws in recognition of his long and distinguished service in the public schools of Ohio, and in the building of Bowling Green State University. Dr. Williams had never been very favorable towards the policy of granting honorary degrees but, nevertheless, he was greatly pleased. All agreed that the honor was richly deserved, and that it was fitting that he should be the first to receive such a degree.

Election of Third President

In one respect the election of the third President of Bowling Green State University differed from that of the second—there was no attempt to exert political pressure. In other ways, however, the two elections were similar. In neither case did the trustees make any effort to find the best man for the position. Without preliminary discussion (at least in an official meeting) the trustees, on March 3, 1939, elected Frank J. Prout to the presidency. He assumed office on April 1, of the same year.

Fortunately, Dr. Prout was well qualified for the position. He had recently retired from the Board of Trustees and, as a result, was well acquainted with the history of the University and with the problems facing it in the future. At the time of his election, Dr. Prout was superintendent of the Sandusky, Ohio, schools. He was highly regarded by the public school men of the region. Before going to Sandusky, he had held administrative positions in several other Ohio school systems.

While the official title of the institution at Bowling Green had been changed, in 1935, from college to university, the public and the Board of Trustees still regarded it as a teachers' college, whose primary purpose was to train teachers for the schools of northwestern Ohio. As a result, the trustees, in seeking a president, thought only of public school men from northwestern Ohio. Even the governors of Ohio regarded Bowling Green State University as primarily a local, teacher-training institution. This is evidenced by the fact that, through all of its early history, the Board of Trustees (appointed by the Governor) was composed entirely of residents of northwestern Ohio, and usually included at least one public school administrator.

All of the first three presidents of the University had been connected with the Sandusky public schools. Both Dr. Wiliams and Dr. Prout were superintendents in that city at the time of their election to the presidency. Dr. Offenhauer, before going to Lima, had been principal of the Sandusky High School and superintendent of the Erie County Schools.

President Williams' Contributions

President Williams served for the longest term of any president. He was appointed in February, 1912, and held this office until September, 1937, when he had reached the retirement age of 70 years. On the death of his successor, he was appointed Acting President, and served in this capacity from January 2, 1939 to March 31, 1939. He thus guided the Normal College, College, and University for a total of 25 years and 9 months. Indeed, it would be more accurate, since Dr. Offenhauer's service was so short, to state that Dr. Williams' was the guiding hand for over 27 years.

Dr. Williams' administration was noteworthy for many reasons besides length. He planned the first curriculum and assembled a well-qualified faculty.

From the beginning, and throughout his term, he resisted all political and other pressures that might well have proved a serious handicap. He insisted on maintaining high standards in all the work offered, and always placed quality of offerings above quantity. He believed in growth and expansion, but only within the limits set by the resources of the college.

Possibly his greatest contribution arose from his never-flagging determination to build a college rather than a normal school. As a result, his administration saw the normal school develop into a state college, and then a state university. It aso saw the establishment of a graduate program on the master's level. In all these developments, he had the support and the cooperation of the Bowling Green Board of Trustees and faculty, and of the sister institution at Kent. However, Dr. Williams probably had more to do with these developments than any other one man. His well-earned reputation for conservatism and sound judgment gave him great influence with state officials and the state legislature. Without this, it is doubtful if either the change to a college or the later change to a university (including Colleges of Liberal Arts, Education, Business Administration, and a graduate program) would have been possible at the times they were accomplished. Growth in both physical plant and enrollment was slower than some people desired and expected. This in the early years was partly the result of World War I, when men almost vanished from the campus. The greatest handicap, however, was the lack of sufficient funds to make more rapid expansion possible. Bowling Green and Kent were established because of the lack of adequate facilities in northern Ohio for the training of elementary teachers. Local pride also played a major role. Since southern Ohio had two state-supported colleges (Miami and Ohio Universities), northern Ohio was entitled to equal treatment. This initial interest and pride soon waned, however, and when it came to supporting the new institutions, many people (including members of the state legislature) did not see the need of anything more than two-year normal schools. This attitude, as we have seen, was shared by many of the existing colleges in Ohio. They had been serving the state well for many years in training high school teachers and did not welcome, or see the need for, new institutions in this field. Ohio State, although it had ceased active opposition to the granting of degrees, was far from enthusiastic in its support of further developments. All of these institutions had loyal graduates in the legislature. Bowling Green and Kent had none. The result was that both Bowling Green and Kent had difficulty for many years in securing appropriations to support adequately existing programs, and to provide for desired expansions.

In the case of Bowling Green, this situation was aggravated by Dr. Williams' conservatism, which caused him to pare to the bone his request for appropriations by the legislature. He even took pride in keeping expenditures below appropriations, and returning to the state a substantial balance at the end of each biennium. A member of the Education Committee of the General Assembly once said to the author that returning state money after it was appropriated was not only unheard of, but that it was really a crime. Although we can not agree completely with this view, we must admit that in Dr. Williams' case economy was sometimes a virtue carried too far.

Dr. Williams' contributions far outweighed any hampering effects of too great conservatism. In fact, this conservatism was more often an asset than a handicap. Although, at the time, some people thought he built too slowly, we must admit that he built well. The subsequent history of the institution substantiates this verdict. He started with nothing—no official name, no buildings, no faculty, no curriculum, no students, and no specific authority for anything but a two-year normal school. He left a university including a College of Education, a College of Liberal Arts, a College of Business Administration, and a graduate program leading to the master's degree.

Dr. Williams was a hard man to know, and many people thought he was gruff and unsociable. However, underneath this rough exterior, he was really the kindest of men. He was feared by many students and faculty, but revered by all. The title of Prexy, by which he came to be universally known, showed both respect and affection.

Dr. Williams' conservatism caused him always to say no when first confronted with a new proposal. The author early formed the habit of never pushing an issue when first presented. He developed the system of first raising a question for discussion, but carefully avoiding any decision. Then he would return to the discussion informally, from time to time, and finally would obtain a favorable decision in most cases. Many times this came voluntarily from Dr. Williams, and was prefaced by the remark, "Overman, I believe I have a good idea." This was not a conscious stealing of the author's ideas, but it was proof of the effectiveness of his system of dealing with the President. Incidentally, the author later found the same system almost equally effective in his dealings with succeeding presidents.

To the author, Dr. Williams' two greatest characteristics were foresight and courage. It is true that he did not foresee the great expansion in enrollments that have come in recent years, but neither did anyone else. However, he had greater vision than either the public or the members of the General Assembly, with respect to the future needs of Ohio in the field of teacher training. He saw that the program for elementary teachers would ultimately be extended from two to four years, and that greatly expanded facilities would soon be needed for the training of high school teachers. From the beginning, as we have seen, he planned to meet these needs.

His courage was shown in many ways. He had the courage to resist political pressures in the appointment of faculty members and administrative officers. Above all, he had the courage to offer courses for secondary teachers and school administrators, and to grant degrees for many years before there was any legal authority for doing either. Furthermore, he had the courage to fight The Ohio State University, as an equal, when it challenged these acts. Indeed, Bowling Green State University owes much to its first President.

CHAPTER EIGHT

The War Years
1939-1945

O NE OF THE MAJOR problems confronting the new administration was the necessity for creating a new image for the Bowling Green institution. The legal title had been changed to university, but the majority of the public continued to regard it as a teachers' college. This attitude was shared by many of the faculty, most of whom had little interest in the development of a College of Liberal Arts, a College of Business Administration, or a graduate program (except in education). The majority of the faculty had been chosen because of their interest in the training of teachers, and many of these sincerely believed that the development of the other colleges would weaken the program in that field.

President Williams had built a strong teachers' college, but it remained for his successor to build a university. Fortunately, the new President was well-equipped for this task. Although he had spent many years in public school work, Frank J. Prout, third President of the University, was strongly convinced of the importance of a broad liberal education for teachers as well as for those preparing for other professions. From the beginning the new President was very much interested in building strong colleges in arts and in business. With the President's support and encouragement, Dean Ralph G. Harshman of the College of Business Administration and Deans Overman and Kenneth H. McFall, of the College of Liberal Arts, with the assistance of small but enthusiastic groups of faculty members, were able to bring about substantial progress in both of these colleges by the end of President Prout's administration.

President Prout was much more approachable than his precedessor and spent much time in informal visits and discussions with both students and faculty. These often took place in the corridors or on the campus. President Prout also had many more friendly contacts with the citizens of Bowling Green and the schoolmen of northwestern Ohio. President Williams had stayed aloof from both of these groups in order to discourage early efforts on the part of each to interfere with and dominate the affairs of the new College. These dangers were now largely past, and President Prout's friendly contacts were of great assistance in the development of a new image for the Bowling Green institution, and in meeting the many problems that arose during and following the war.

World War II

World War II slowed the development of the University during the first part of this period, but probably hastened it after hostilities ended. Although the war started in 1939, it had little effect on the University until after the entry of the United States into the conflict, in December, 1941. The difficulties confronting the University during the war years will be considered in this chapter and those of the post-war period in the next.

World War II brought several problems to Bowling Green State University. The first and most serious of these was the shrinkage in enrollments, due to the calling of young men into the armed forces. These decreased enrollments meant that the faculty was larger than needed and that the money available for salaries was insufficient as student fees decreased with enrollments. Since the shrinkage in attendance was largely in the number of men, Kohl Hall, the men's dormitory, presented a serious problem. Unless this hall was filled, the University would be unable to meet principal and interest payments on the bonds which had been issued for its construction. These payments had to be made from money received for room rent and food service.

The only solution to these problems was to secure war training programs. Even when these were secured they would not fully solve the faculty problem. Teachers would be required in fields in which they would not be needed when the war ended. Since most of the problems of this period were the result of changing enrollments, these must be considered next.

Fluctuating Enrollments

Attendance at the University during the first years of President Prout's administration was relatively stable. The on-campus enrollment for the first semester of 1939-40 was 1,462. It reached 1,600 in 1940-41, and then started to drop. It was 1,519 for 1941-42, and 1,383 for 1942-43. In 1943-44 the full effects of the war were felt, and attendance during the first semester fell to 842. This proved to be the low point, and the enrollment increased to 1,109 in 1944-45. Obviously, the decrease from 1,383 to 842, in a single year, presented serious problems to the University.

The decline in enrollments was largely due to the decreases in the number of men enrolled. During the first semester of 1940-41, there were 815 men in attendance. The number fell to 721 in 1941-42, to 643 in 1942-43, and to 69 in 1943-44. It then rose to 110 in 1944-45. The enrollment of women, however, changed little during the war years. There were 785 women in attendance during the first semester of 1940-41, 798 in 1941-42, 740 in 1942-43, and 773 in 1943-44. The number started to increase again in 1944-45, when it reached 999.

The enrollment figures given above include only civilian students. In addition to these, in 1943-44 there were approximately 400 Navy V-12 students on campus, and in 1944-45 there were about 240. The Navy V-12 program will be discussed in a later section.

The drop in the number of men was felt in all three colleges. In 1939-40 there were 949 students (of both sexes) in the College of Education, 306 in the College of Liberal Arts, and 194 in the College of Business Administration. In 1943-44 the corresponding figures were 538, 177, and 114. Attendance started to increase again in 1944-45, when the enrollment reached 603 in education, 341 in liberal arts, and 158 in business administration.

The decreased enrollments during the period from 1939 to 1945 were paralleled by corresponding decreases in the number of degrees conferred. In 1940 there were 230 graduates from the College of Education, 27 from the College of Liberal Arts, 25 from the College of Business Administration, and 13 from the master's program. In 1945 the corresponding figures were 130, 18, 13, and 4.

Government Programs

Dudley A. White of Norwalk, who was a member of the Board of Trustees from 1940 to 1945, made important contributions to the University, although his term in office was short. During World War II, he was a naval officer stationed in Washington, D. C., where he was of great service to the University in securing naval training programs for the University, and in dealing with the Pentagon during those critical years. His son, Dudley A. White, Jr., was appointed to the Board in 1963.

In the fall of 1939, Bowling Green State University was selected to participate in the Civilian Pilot Training Program, sponsored by the Civil Aeronautics Authority. This program was open to sophomores and upperclassmen and earned three semester hours of credit for those completing the entire course. A member of the University faculty was in charge, but the flight training was given at the Findlay airport.

In June of 1942, the Civilian Pilot Training Program was supplanted by a full-time program for Navy V-5 enlistees. Groups of cadets were given ground and flight instructions for periods of eight weeks. They were housed and fed on the campus and given class instruction by members of the University faculty. Flight instruction was given at the University airport (purchased in 1942), under a private contract with a flight instructor. The program was discontinued in 1945. Nearly 1,000 cadets participated, but they were not enrolled in the University, and were not counted in the enrollment figures.

In April, 1943, Bowling Green State University was chosen as one of the schools to offer the Navy College Training Program known as V-12. Class instruction under this program started in July, 1943. In the spring of that year, representatives of participating schools were called to New York, given outlines of the two-year curriculum, and briefed on its objectives. The Navy V-12 Bulletin, published November 1, 1943, contained the following statement:

> The courses of the fully prescribed programs have been molded so as to conform rather closely to those which are standard in the colleges and universities of the nation. The purpose . . . is to obtain adequately prepared men for Navy needs, within time limits required by the national emergency.

This Bulletin also stated:

> Each institution shall determine whether or not credit toward a degree at that institution will be given for the completion of courses in the various curricula. Inasmuch as the content of most courses is practically equivalent to that of standard college courses in the same subjects, it is hoped that credit will be given quite generally.

Bowling Green State University granted such credit, since instruction was given by members of the college faculty, and the standards maintained were at least equal to those of civilian courses.

The V-12 program divided the year into three terms of 16 weeks each. Since the University had already announced the calendar for 1943-44, no changes were made for the summer of 1943, or the year 1943-44. The regular program for civilian students was continued and separate classes were scheduled for the V-12 enrollees. Because of the inconvenience and added expense of this arrangement, the University calendar for 1944-45 was changed to conform with the V-12 program. Navy and civilian classes in the same subject were combined. With the termination of the V-12 program, at the end of the 1944 summer term, the University returned to its former calendar.

Although the service training programs helped solve the problem of too many faculty members, it created rather serious difficulties with respect to the housing of civilian students. The boys in the V-5 and V-12 programs were housed in Williams and Kohl Halls, and on the top floor of the Elementary School (Hanna Hall), which was altered to provide additional housing. The withdrawal of Kohl Hall (a men's dormitory) from civilian use caused little difficulty, since the number of men in college was greatly reduced. Conversion of Williams Hall (a women's dormitory) to military use created some difficulty, because the number of women in school did not decrease. To help solve the situation, the trustees, on April 15, 1943, authorized the housing of women in the Women's Physical Education Building. The on-campus housing shortage continued throughout the war period and became much more acute after the war was ended.

Wartime Shortages

The faculty in 1939-40 consisted of 73 members, 31 of whom had the doctor's degree. Increasing enrollments brought about an increase to 85 in 1940-41, 55 with the doctorate. Then, attendance started to decline, and the number on the faculty dropped to 77 in 1942-43. The quality, however, was maintained, since 33 of the number had the doctor's degree. Before the start of the 1942-43 school year, it became obvious that, due to the war, there would be a very large decrease in enrollments in all colleges, including Bowling Green State University. This created a very serious problem with regard to the faculty. On February 24, 1942, the trustees authorized President Prout to reduce the teaching staff in order to save approximately $29,000 for 1942-43. On March 20 they authorized the issuing of contracts to this reduced faculty. The contracts were to include the clause, "this contract is given subject to the exigencies of the present war."

The difficulty was partly solved by the fact that a number of faculty members asked for leaves of absence to enter the armed services, or other types of war work. Others decided to take advantage of the situation to pursue further graduate work, and several were granted leaves for this purpose. Even with all of these, however, the staff was still too large, and it was feared that further reductions would have to be made for 1943-44.

Luckily, this need was eliminated when Bowling Green State University was chosen as one of the schools to offer the Navy College Training Program, known as V-12. This created new problems for the University, since there would now be a shortage of faculty members instead of a surplus. This situation resulted in several individuals withdrawing their requests for leaves of absence, but this was not enough.

Since the Navy V-12 program was largely pre-engineering in character, the University would have to offer many more classes than ever before in certain subjects, particularly in mathematics, physics, and engineering drawing. The regular staffs in these departments, even if all were available, would be totally inadequate. The situation was rendered more difficult by the fact that colleges, all over the country offering the V-12 program, were faced with the same problem. Although there was a serious shortage in all three of these teaching fields required for the V-12 program, Bowling Green was able to secure a competent staff, before the program began in July. To augment the new instructors, the University hired a number of faculty wives. High school teachers in neighboring schools were employed for either full or part time. Several administrators also taught part time, and a number of faculty members from other departments helped. For example, the Dean of Students taught mathematics, and the University Architect taught engineering drawing.

Several of the individuals hired at this time were employed on a permanent basis, since they were well qualified and their services would be required after the war was over. It was necessary, however, to hire a number for the emergency only. In many cases, while well qualified to give the freshman and sophomore courses in the V-12 program, these individuals did not have the requisite training to join the permanent faculty. In addition, the University would not need so large a staff in mathematics, physics, or engineering drawing after the end of the war and the V-12 program.

Departments and Courses

Increases in enrollments and faculty, during the early years of this period, made it possible for most of the departments of the University to increase their course offerings, to some extent. Three new departments were created. The first of these came in 1939-40, when the Department of Business Administration was divided into Business Administration and Business Education. All courses for the training of teachers of business subjects in the public schools, and typing and stenography, were placed in the new Department of Business Education. The next change came a year later with the 1940-41 school year. Before this time, a few introductory courses in art, art appreciation and history, and elementary design had been offered in the Industrial Arts Department. The catalog, published in April, 1940, announced an increase in the offerings in this field, and the creation of a separate Department of Art. Twelve courses were offered by this department for the 1940-41 school year.

A few courses in journalism were offered in the English Department as early as 1939-40. The offerings in this field were greatly expanded in 1941-42, when a separate Department of Journalism was created. Eleven courses were announced by this department for the first year.

New Curricula

The addition of new departments, and increased offerings in the old ones, made possible a number of changes in the curricula offered. The College of Education added programs in distributive education in 1941-42 and dramatic arts in 1943-44. Minors were offered, for the first time, in art and speech in 1940-41, and in Spanish in 1942-43.

With the creation of the Journalism Department, in 1941-42, the College of Liberal Arts offered a four-year curriculum in this field. The same year saw the addition of a four year pre-professional social work curriculum. Since many of the students were preparing for transfer to professional schools after one or two years at Bowling Green, a number of pre-professional curricula, ranging from one to four years, were described in the catalogs of this period.

Increased offerings in old departments and the addition of new departments also enabled the College of Liberal Arts to offer new majors and minors. In 1940-41 a major was added in home economics and minors in art and German. Next year, 1941-42, increased offerings in the Departments of History and Political Science made it possible to discontinue the major in a combination of history and political science, and to offer a major in each of these fields. A minor in Spanish was added in the same year.

In 1939-40 the College of Business Administration discontinued the plan of majors and minors, and outlined four-year curricula in accounting, business finance, general business, marketing, and secretarial administration. A four-year curriculum in industrial management, and one- and two-year curricula in business training were added in 1942-43. No further additions were made during this period.

No significant changes were made in the graduate program during the war years. Enrollments decreased, and all of the University's resources (financial and otherwise) were needed for the undergraduate civilian and the government programs. Expansion of work in the graduate field had to be left until after the end of the war. The only change was the addition, in 1942-43, of a divisional major in the social studies. This was planned for high school teachers in this field, and included courses in economics, geography, history, political science, and sociology.

New Buildings

In 1941 the University started the policy of building small, cottage-type dormitories to house student social groups. Two of these were completed in 1941, and two more in 1942. These housed the Five Sisters, Skol, Seven Sisters and Three Kay local sororities. No new dormitories of this type were built during this period, but others were added after the war. The policy of furnishing University housing for social groups was a strong factor in bringing national sororities and fraternities to the campus.

For many years, the University had felt the need for a social center for students, and had considered the possibility of building a student union. President Williams, during his administration, had plans prepared for such a building. However, investigation indicated that the experience of several other colleges of the size of Bowling Green showed that student unions were not usually self-supporting. As a result, plans were dropped, and the building was not constructed.

Talk of a union was revived early in President Prout's administration and finally, on February 21, 1941, the trustees authorized the use of the balance of $10,000 in the Student Activity Fund for the construction of a student house on campus. This balance had been accumulated to meet any emergency that might arise in financing student activities. All agreed that this was the emergency. On March 18 of the same year, the trustees voted to enlarge the proposed building in order to provide rooms for from 10 to 12 men in the lofts. This action served two purposes. It helped meet the need for additional dormitory space for civilian male students, and it also made it possible, legally, to issue bonds for an additional $10,000 for dormitory purposes.

In order to reduce the cost to a minimum, the original plan was to have a log building built by students under the direction of a faculty member from the Industrial Arts Department. In addition, an attempt was made to use NYA (National Youth Administration) enrollees, transported by truck daily to and from Toledo. However, it soon became apparent that it would take too long to finish the building in this way, and a contract was let for its completion. It was ready for use in 1942, and was promptly named Falcon's Nest by the students. Although too small from the beginning, it still served a useful purpose for many years. When the new student union was started, the Falcon's Nest was sold to the Portage American Legion Post. It was moved to that village, and still serves as a legion hall and community center. When the new union building was constructed, the name Falcon's Nest was preserved by giving it to the cafeteria.

With the exception of the small, cottage-type dormitories, only one permanent building was constructed during the years from 1939 to 1945. This was the Johnston Health Service Building, completed in 1942. In addition to well-equipped hospital facilities and 36 beds, it housed the offices of the University Health Service. The availability of this building was another important factor in enabling the University to secure service training programs during the war. This facility was named for Dr. H. J. Johnston, a former trustee.

When, in 1942, the University was assigned a Navy V-5 program for the training of Navy pilots, it became necessary to buy land for a flying field. Negotiations were started for the purchase of a tract lying east of the cemetery and north of Ridge Street. Since this land was once owned by the grandparents of Mrs. John W. Bricker, wife of the Governor of Ohio, the new field was named Bricker Field. Gov. Bricker had cooperated with Sen. Fred Adams in securing air fields for each of the state universities. The trustees and the owners of this land failed to reach an agreement on the price, and the University finally purchased 120 acres north of the Poe Road. A portion of this was part of the H. J. Heinz farm, but the company purchased other land in order to make this tract available to the University. Runways, two hangars, a central control tower, and a large building to be used as a hangar and repair shops were constructed for the use of the V-5 unit.

In 1943 the trustees requested President Emeritus Williams to vacate the house he occupied. The house was converted into a dormitory to house the Las Amigas local sorority. This action was caused by the acute housing shortage for women. President Williams purchased a home on East Court Street, a block from the campus, and lived there until his death.

The Inter-University Council

Prior to 1939, each of the state-supported universities presented its own budget to the Director of Finance and the committees of the General Assembly. As a result, members of the Assembly would play one university against another, often to the detriment of all the institutions concerned. To meet this situation, the Inter-University Council was organized in 1939. This was a voluntary body composed of the presidents and business managers of the several institutions. From 1939 to 1963, the universities discussed their budget proposals in this Council and presented a single budget request to the General

Assembly. In general, this body functioned effectively, and its efforts resulted in more adequate and more equitable appropriations for the support of higher education in Ohio. Bowling Green State University may be proud of the fact that its business manager, E. J. Kreischer, played a prominent part in the organization and work of this body.

The impartial attitude which usually (if not always) characterized the actions of the Inter-University Council is well illustrated by an incident in its early history. For a number of reasons, Bowling Green State University had, from its beginning as a normal school, always been the underdog, with respect to state appropriations. To correct this situation, at the meeting of the Council held on February 14, 1941, Ohio State University requested that the Director of Finance transfer $30,000 from its requested budget to that of Bowling Green State University. This request was carried out and placed the Bowling Green appropriations more nearly on a par with those of the other state universities. This increased the Bowling Green appropriations not only for that year but for each ensuing year, since appropriations were always affected by the amount for the previous biennium. Thus, through the generosity and fair-mindedness of Ohio State University, Bowling Green was at last able to overcome the handicap under which it had labored for so long.

Organizational Problems

During President Offenhauer's short administration, the Policies Commission studied the perennial problem of University organization, and lines of authority and communication. The statement of 1929 had become inadequate because of the growth of the institution and the establishment of the College of Business Administration. In 1938 a committee which Dean Harshman chaired reported a plan to the Policies Commission. This report was discussed but it was never adopted, because of the death of President Offenhauer.

President Prout, on assuming office, was soon confronted with the same problem, and a working agreement was reached in a conference with the academic deans. This plan was announced in a letter to the faculty, dated April 28, 1939. The letter contained the statement:

> This plan is not necessarily permanent, but will be in force until further notice. It can be changed at any time, if change seems advisable.

The letter confirmed the division of the departments among the three deans, as previously made in 1935, and added the Art Department to Dean Hissong's (Education) list and Speech Department to Dean Overman's (Liberal Arts). It also defined lines of authority between faculty, department, deans, and the President, as follows:

> All matters concerning any department, or the members of the department, should first be taken up with the dean to whom the department is assigned. Said dean has full authority to act in all routine matters.

Final decision on all matters of importance, concerning the interests of more than one department, or of the university as a whole, will rest with the Council of Academic Deans, subject to the approval of the president.

It is understood that the line of communication is from faculty member to department head to dean to Council of Academic Deans and President. A faculty member should not go over his department head to the dean, or president; and a department head should not go over the dean to the president.

These definitions simply confirmed procedures that had usually been followed since the change from college to university.

There were a few changes in administrative officers during this period. For a number of years, the offices of Dean of Women and Dean of Men had been independent of each other, but with the 1939-40 school year the work in this area was unified under A. B. Conklin, first Dean of Students. Prof. Conklin also served as Dean of Men.

After his retirement in 1939, President Williams became President Emeritus and Director of Alumni Relations. For a number of years, he had felt the need for maintaining closer relations with the growing body of alumni and for more complete alumni records. On his retirement, he requested the Board of Trustees to make this work his chief assignment. He established an office on campus, and started the University's first file of alumni records.

Under President Williams, except during emergencies such as the threat to convert the University into a mental hospital, little attempt was made to inform the public on University affairs, or to promote its interests through publicity. The little news that was issued was usually given out by the President. In 1941, however, President Prout felt that the University suffered from the fact that the people of northwestern Ohio were often poorly informed concerning the services it rendered and the problems it faced. As a result, in 1941, the position of Director of News Bureau was created, and Paul W. Jones was appointed to the position.

As we have seen, the decreasing enrollments due to the war threatened the University with a surplus of faculty members. In an effort to relieve this surplus, a number of teachers were assigned to administrative duties. The University librarian resigned in the spring of 1942, and Dr. Frank C. Ogg of the Mathematics Department was appointed acting librarian. Although he had no training in this field, Dr. Ogg rendered fine service, particularly in improving the collection of books for the College of Liberal Arts and the graduate program. With the coming of the Navy V-12 program to the campus, Dr. Ogg's services were again needed in the Mathematics Department.

Dr. Ogg was succeeded by Dr. Paul F. Leedy, who was appointed University Librarian in 1944. Dr. Leedy was at that time Associate Professor of

English, but had developed a strong interest in library work. Although he already had a doctor's degree in English, he now studied for and received the Bachelor of Arts degree in Library Science from the University of Michigan. In spite of the handicap of inadequate finances for a number of years, Dr. Leedy made an outstanding contribution to the University by greatly increasing and improving its library facilities.

Prior to 1939, the dean of each college was the chief counselor on academic matters for all students enrolled in his college. By 1943 this task had grown to the extent that the office of Dean of Freshmen was created, and Kenneth H. McFall was appointed to the position. His duties, in addition to counseling with freshmen after their arrival on campus, included visiting high schools in northwestern Ohio, and advising seniors concerning their college plans.

Faculty Committees

A number of additions were made during this period to the list of standing committees. For several years prior to 1940-41, the University had been conducting an orientation program for new students. By 1940-41 this had grown, and a faculty committee, known as the Orientation Committee, was set up to plan and administer the program. In the same year, 1940-41, a Publications Committee was appointed. Its chief duty was to select editors and staffs for the *Bee Gee News* and *The Key*. With the completion of the Falcon's Nest in 1942, a committee was appointed to supervise its use. This committee, called the Student Union Committee, was composed of two faculty and three student members.

For a number of years prior to 1942-43, many faculty members had been complaining about students' deficiencies in written English. These complaints were not confined to the English Department, but came from all departments of the University. By 1942-43 this situation had become so serious that a faculty committee was appointed to plan and carry out a remedial program. This was called the Committee on Deficiencies in Written English.

With the June, 1940, commencement, the University instituted a system of graduation with honors. Three types of honor were conferred, namely, *cum laude, magna cum laude,* and *summa cum laude*. In 1942-43 a faculty committee known as the Honors Committee was appointed to administer the program.

For many years, the University had charged an activity fee, which was administered by the Activity Fees Committee. This committee apportioned the money received among several areas, including the Entertainment Course, and the athletic, music, social and speech activities. The money appropriated for the Entertainment Course, athletics, and social activities had, for some time, been administered by separate committees in charge of each of these activities. In 1943-44, similar committees were set up for music activities and speech activities.

The Policies Commission Fails

The Policies Commission never became an effective agent for faculty participation in administration. This was partly due to the untimely death of President Offenhauer before the functions and powers of the commission were fully established. The greatest difficulties arose from the conflict of duties and authority among the faculty as a whole, its standing committees, the Executive Committee, and the Policies Commission. This confusion is illustrated by the opening paragraph of a report the secretary of the commission made to the faculty in March, 1940. It read:

All who have had a part in the work of the Policies Commission have been confronted with its indefiniteness of purpose, confusion in procedure and ineffectiveness in outcomes.

Possibly there was another reason for the failure. Although a small group of the faculty was sincerely interested in participating in and contributing to the formation of University policies, it is doubtful if the majority were either interested or willing. In any case, as a result of all of these factors, the commission was finally discontinued in 1942.

Formation of the University Senate

On May 28, 1941, President Prout, on the recommendation of the Policies Commission, appointed a committee to consider the reorganization of, or a substitute for, this body. The early discussions of this committee convinced its members that a new body was needed to take the place of the Policies Commission, but that it would be futile unless the University adopted some general organization for the administration of academic affairs. They felt that President Prout's letter of 1939 was only a temporary solution to the latter problem. It also was inadequate, since it had not included either the Policies Commission or the Executive Committee. As a result, the committee asked for, and was granted, authority to consider the larger problem.

The committee consisted of the deans of the three colleges, plus three faculty members, with the author as chairman. After considerable study, this committee recommended a plan to the President, who submitted it to the faculty for study and discussion. As a result of these discussions, several amendments were made, and the plan, as amended, was adopted and approved by the President, on May 26, 1942. It was put into effect with the opening of the University in September, 1942.

One important feature of the new plan was the definition of lines of authority and communications between faculty members, department chairmen, deans, and President. These definitions, in the main, simply formalized procedures that had been usually followed in the past. However, some faculty members had been in the practice of ignoring their department chairman and trying to deal directly with their dean or with the President. Some department chairmen had, if they thought the dean was unsympathetic, taken their problems and suggestions directly to the President. Since these practices had led to confusion and ill feeling, the new plan attempted to prevent them.

The first report of the committee had recommended the formation of college faculties, but this suggestion was not approved by the faculty. The majority of the faculty were not yet ready for such a reorganization. The division of the departments among the three deans remained unchanged, except for the assignment of the new Department of Journalism to the dean of the College of Liberal Arts.

The most important part of the new plan was the creation of the University Senate. The committee members were unanimous in their firm conviction that, in order to build a strong university, the faculty should assume a larger role in discussing, and in making recommendations concerning academic problems. They also believed that the faculty, as a whole, had become too large to afford an efficient instrument for the accomplishment of this purpose, and that the existing Policies Commission was too small. It was for these reasons that they recommended the new body. The plan provided that:

> The University Senate shall be composed of chairmen of departments, professors, associate professors and assistant professors who have passed the probationary period.

The plan, as originally drafted by the committee, included only professors and associate professors. The assistant professors were added after discussion of the proposed plan by the faculty.

The powers and duties of the Senate were specified as follows:

> The Senate shall meet at the call of the President of the University who shall be its presiding officer. It shall have the power to study problems of interest to the University as a whole and to make recommendations to the Executive Committee and President.

The plan also provided that:

> The President of the University shall, in consultation with the dean, appoint one faculty member to represent each of the colleges of the University to constitute a Faculty Advisory Committee. The Committee shall meet at the call of the President of the University, who shall be the presiding officer, to discuss problems of interest to the University as a whole. The Advisory Committee shall also meet with the Executive Committee on request.

The Advisory Committee was included in the new administrative organization at the request of President Prout. The plan stated:

> The purpose of this committee is to enable the President to secure faculty opinions when, for lack of time, or other reasons, he does not wish to consult the Senate.

Finally, the new plan included the Executive Committee which had been in existence and operation since the establishment of the College of Liberal Arts in 1929. This committee, at this time, was composed of the President of the University (chairman), the registrar (secretary), and the deans of the colleges. Its powers and duties were specified in the plan as follows:

The Executive Committee shall meet at the call of the President. Subject to the approval of the President and Board of Trustees, it shall have final decision in all academic questions. Any member may request the President to call a meeting.

The plan of 1942 defined the official organization under which the University operated until 1951. It proved satisfactory in all respects but one. The deans of the respective colleges still had no faculty they could call their own. This weakness was most serious in the College of Liberal Arts. The College of Education had the Education Department, and the College of Business Administration had the Department of Business Administration. However, the Dean of the College of Liberal Arts had no group with which to discuss and plan the program of his college. He was forced to operate with a few departments and individual faculty members who were sincerely interested in the development of the liberal arts program. Among the latter, special mention should be made of Clayton C. Kohl, Charles H. Otis, Frank C. Ogg, Gay W. Allen, W. Heinlen Hall, Alfred M. Hayes, and Dr. Leedy. Two other men should also be mentioned. These were Dr. Harshman, Dean of the College of Business Administration, and Lloyd A. Helms, Professor of Economics. Although their primary interest was in the field of business, both believed strongly in the value of a broad, liberal education, and were always ready to contribute to the development of a strong program in the College of Liberal Arts.

A New Tenure Policy

A number of studies were undertaken during this period by committees of the University Senate. Probably the two most important were the Committee on Tenure and the Post-War Planning Committee.

The first action of the Board of Trustees came on January 12, 1938. At this time the Board adopted the 1925 statement of principles of American Association of University Professors as the official tenure policy of the University. While this was welcomed by the faculty, they felt that this general statement needed revision and amplification to meet the specific conditions at Bowling Green. This feeling resulted in the appointment of a Senate committee to study the whole problem of appointments, promotions leading to tenure, tenure, and leaves of absence. The committee consisted of G. W. Allen, F. C. Ogg, and Dr. Leedy, chairman. After careful study and investigation of tenure policies at other institutions, this committee presented a detailed statement to the University Senate. The plan (with some minor revisions) was approved by the Senate on March 18, 1944, and adopted by the Board of Trustees on May 5 of the same year. It was the official tenure policy of the University until it was revised in 1953.

This 1944 tenure policy provided permanent tenure for all full professors and probationary periods of two years for associate professors, five years for assistant professors, and six years for instructors. Permanent tenure could be secured in two ways, by promotion to higher rank or by being re-employed after the end of the probationary period.

Post-War Planning Committee

Near the close of the war, the North Central Association of Colleges and Secondary Schools, and other similar bodies, urged their member colleges to make careful plans for meeting the problems that they would have to face in the post-war period. Most colleges and universities undertook such studies, and the U.S. Office of Education acted as a clearing house to collect information and to make it available to all who were interested.

Even before the national movement was organized, the University Senate set up two central committees, and a number of sub-committees to study this problem and make recommendations. The Central Committee on Curricula was composed of representatives of each of the three colleges, with the author as chairman. W. H. Hall represented the College of Liberal Arts; H. C. Witherington, the College of Education; and B. L. Pierce, the College of Business Administration. The second central committee was the Committee on Buildings. Its members were W. H. Hall, E. J. Kreischer, and the author as chairman.

The representative of each college on the Central Curricula Committee also acted as chairman of a sub-committee of his college. Each of these sub-committees, in addition to the chairman, had two other Senate members, plus the dean of the college, ex officio. In addition, each department of the University set up a committee to make studies and formulate plans for post-war development. In many cases, these committees consisted of the entire staff of the department. The reports of the sub-committees were carefully studied by the Central Curricula Committee, which in turn submitted its report and recommendations to the University Senate on December 4, 1944. The Central Committee on Buildings reported at the same time.

In addition to curricula problems, the Central Committee studied the University and the probable conditions and problems of the post-war period. Several of its findings and recommendations are of sufficient interest to warrant some comment here. The first of these was the question of enrollments. The largest attendance before the United States entered World War II had been 1,600 students in 1940-41, but everyone realized that all institutions would face greatly increased enrollments when the war ended. Estimates ranged from 25 per cent to 100 per cent. Since Bowling Green had been growing more rapidly than most colleges before the war, the committee considered a 50 per cent increase to be a conservative estimate and recommended that plans be made on the basis of 2,500 students immediately after the close of the war. Although many considered this estimate too large, it proved to be much too conservative. The enrollment jumped to over 3,800 in the fall of 1946 and to almost 4,500 in 1947.

Another problem considered by both the central and sub-committees was the constantly recurring one of faculty organization. As we have seen, the University at this time was still operating with a general University faculty serving all three colleges. Many faculty members were dissatisfied with this arrangement, and a number of recommendations for change were made to the Central Committee. One sub-committee prefaced its report with the following quotation from Pope:

> For forms of government let fools contest
> That which is least administered, is best.

Nevertheless, this committee and most of the other sub-committees recommended changes in the existing plan. The three principal plans of organization proposed were (1) the existing university type with possibly some changes, (2) a divisional type, and (3) a college type. The Central Committee made no recommendation, but submitted all plans proposed to the Senate when it made its final report on December 4, 1944. Discussion in that body soon showed that the faculty was still sharply divided and that agreement was impossible. As a result, no change was made in the existing organization at this time.

The foreword of the Central Committee's report to the Faculty Senate contained the following statement:

> The committee regards its report as marking the beginning rather than the end of post-war planning. Such planning must be continuous for the duration of the war and several years following. . . . If this report serves to stimulate thought and discussion concerning the objectives of the University, conditions after the war, and ways of meeting these conditions, it will have served its purpose.

These hopes of the committee were more than realized. The fact that the studies and recommendations of the various committees proved helpful in guiding the course of the University after the war was possibly the least important outcome. The greatest gain came from the fact that so many of the faculty participated in the study. Never since the early beginnings of the institution had such a large proportion of the faculty become familiar with and interested in the functions and problems of the University as a whole. Even more important, they had enjoyed the opportunity of studying these problems, and participating in the planning of University policies.

Fees and Expenses

A few changes in fees occurred during this period. Beginning with the 1939-40 school year, the registration fee was raised from $22.50 to $30 a semester. In 1940-41 a physical activity fee of $1.50 and a library fee of $1 a semester were added. The first of these entitled the student to use of the physical education plant and equipment, towel and swim suit service. The library fee entitled the student to use the library facilities, and the money derived supplemented the inadequate state appropriations for the purchase of library books. With the opening of the Falcon's Nest, a student union fee of $1 a semester was added in 1942-43. Finally, the library fee was increased to $2 in 1945-46.

The cost of board and room also increased slightly. In 1939-40 room rent was $1.50 a week in rooms for two and $2.00 in single rooms. Board was $3.50 a week in the women's dormitories and $4 in the men's dormitories. Men who desired could reduce the cost of board by joining the Co-operative Boarding Club, which occupied the third floor of Kohl Hall. This club did not prove very popular, and it was discontinued in 1941-42. However, private co-operative boarding clubs for both men and women continued under University sponsorship as late as 1946.

By 1944-45 room rent had increased to $2.25 a week with a few rooms renting for $2.50. Board also increased to $4 a week for women and $4.50 for men.

These increases in fees and living expenses raised the total necessary cost of a year at Bowling Green from approximately $293.50 in 1939-40 to $308 in 1944-45. The cost of attendance at Bowling Green State University continued to be the lowest of any college in Ohio, according to a survey made by the Ohio College Association and published in 1947.

Summer Sessions and Extension

The summer of 1940 still showed the effects of the increase in training requirements for elementary teachers. There were 900 enrolled in the regular term, and 90 in the post-session. After 1940 the post-session was discontinued. Consequently, summer attendance dropped to 715 in 1941, and to 588 in 1942. Two terms of five weeks each were offered in the summer of 1943, with enrollments of 381 and 320. In addition, in July, 1943, the Navy V-12 program started with an enrollment of approximately 400.

Since the Navy V-12 program divided the school year into three terms of 16 weeks each, the summer terms in 1944 and 1945 were 16 weeks in length. However, to accommodate students desiring a shorter term (mainly teachers in service), a summer session of eight weeks was also scheduled. The attendance, in 1944, was 410 civilian students and 378 Navy V-12. In 1945 the corresponding figures were 379 and 140.

Off-campus offerings in extension classes rose, starting with the year 1937-38. To administer these increased offerings a director of extension was appointed in 1939. Attendance at off-campus centers was 429 in 1939-40, and reached 495 in 1940-41. This proved to be the peak. Off-campus attendance dropped to 406 in 1941-42, and to 189 in 1942-43. The Director of Extension was granted a leave of absence, in 1943, to enter the Red Cross service, and classes in off-campus centers were discontinued for the remainder of the war period.

CHAPTER NINE

The Post-War Years
1945-1951

M OST OF THE PROBLEMS of the first part of President Prout's administration arose from rapid changes in enrollments. This continued to be the case in the post-war years, but with a difference. Almost overnight, enrollments sky-rocketed, too few students changed to too many, and both faculty and physical facilities became inadequate.

The war with Germany ended in May, 1945, and with Japan in August of the same year. The effect on attendance was felt almost immediately. On-campus enrollment for 1944-45 was 1,349, of whom 240 were in the V-12 program. The V-12 program ended with the summer of 1945, but the enrollment for the first semester of 1945-46 reached a total of 1,651 and, for the second semester, 2,054. After that, enrollments rose to 3,856 in 1946-47, 4,472 in 1947-48, 4,525 in 1948-49, 4,682 in 1949-50, and 4,235 in 1950-51.

At first, most of the increase was due to the release of men from the armed services and the provisions made by the government for their college education. Enrollment of veterans started in the second semester of 1945-46 with 574. This increased to 1,813 in 1946-47, and to 1,875 in 1947-48. After that it started to decrease to 1,656 in 1948-49, 1,270 in 1949-50, and 624 in 1950-51.

Figures for the enrollment of non-veterans during this period were 2,043 in 1946, 2,597 in 1947-48, 2,869 in 1948-49, 3,414 in 1949-50, and 3,611 in 1950-51. These figures show that the growth of Bowling Green State University, which had started before the war, resumed as soon as the war ended, even without the somewhat temporary influx of veterans.

Enrollment of women continued to increase, but the big change was in the number of men. Of the 1,349 students in attendance during the first semester of 1944-45, 999 were women, 110 civilian men and 240 men in the V-12 program. In 1945-46 the figures were 1,312 women and 339 men. The big boom came in 1946-47, when there were 1,537 women and 2,319 men in school. In 1947-48 the corresponding figures were 1,644 and 2,828. The next two years showed little change, either in total enrollments or in the ratio of men to women. The attendance for 1948-49 was 1,698 women and 2,827 men. For 1949-50, it was 1,796 women and 2,888 men. The number of veterans enrolled (mostly men) dropped from 1,270 in 1949-50 to only 624 men in 1950-51. This loss was partly balanced by an increase in the number of civilian males enrolled. The figures for 1950-51 were 1,756 women and 2,479 men.

For many years, the Bowling Green institution was known as a women's college, since women greatly outnumbered men. This situation gradually changed until, in 1938-39, the number of the two sexes became equal for the first time. Except for the interruption of the war, the number of men continued to grow more rapidly than the number of women until, by 1950-51, there were 41 per cent more men than women. This change in the proportion of the two sexes was a result of the development from normal school to university. In the early days, the majority of students were in the two-year courses for the training of teachers for elementary schools, and almost all of these were women. The increase in the number of students in the College of Education who were preparing for high school teaching, establishment of the College of Liberal Arts and the College of Business Administration, and the beginning graduate program appealed to men as well as women. This soon resulted in changing the ratio of men to women.

This change in the representation of the sexes was largely the result of the development from normal school to university. It was also a strong contributing factor to this development. As long as Bowling Green continued to be a women's college, the public continued to think of it as a normal school. More men attracted more men (and more women also) and aided greatly in the development of the liberal arts, business administration, and graduate programs. For the first semester of 1945-46, there were 807 students enrolled in the College of Education, 561 in the College of Liberal Arts, 270 in the College of Business Administration, and nine in the graduate program. In 1946-47 there were 1,297 in Education, 1,497 in Liberal Arts, 1,060 in Business Administration, and 28 in the graduate program. These increases were, of course, partly the result of the influx of veterans. They were larger in liberal arts and business administration, since more veterans enrolled in these colleges than in the College of Education.

Although liberal arts did not maintain its lead after the number of veterans decreased, enrollments in both liberal arts and business administration continued, from this time on, to compare favorably with that in the College of Education. In 1949-50 there were 1,966 students in the College of Education,

1,298 in Liberal Arts, 1,220 in Business Administration, and 165 in the graduate program. In 1950-51 the corresponding figures were 1,773 in the College of Education, 1,146 in Liberal Arts, 1,061 in Business Administration, and 198 in the graduate program. Bowling Green was no longer primarily a teachers' college, but truly merited the name of university.

The number of degrees conferred by Bowling Green State University increased much more rapidly than the enrollments. This fact showed that the holding power of the University was increasing. Fewer students dropped out, or transferred, after one or two years; more remained to graduate. The total number of degrees granted was only 165 in 1945, while in 1951 it was 919. Of these 401 were in the College Education, 221 in Liberal Arts, 229 in Business Administration, and 68 in the graduate program.

Summer Session and Extension

Throughout this period, the University offered an eight-week session each summer. At first attendance increased, since most of the veterans wished to complete their college education as rapidly as possible. In the summer of 1946, the enrollment was 1,107, including 596 veterans. Attendance rose to 1,404 in 1947, to 1,446 in 1948, and to 1,688 in 1949. After that the number of veterans decreased, and summer attendance started to drop to 1,356 in 1950, and to 1,074 in 1951. Throughout this period (since most of the veterans were men), the number of men enrolled in the summer session exceeded the number of women. In 1947 there were 955 men and 449 women. In 1951 the figures were 631 men and 443 women.

In the early years of this period, the University occasionally scheduled special conferences for teachers and, starting with 1948, conferences, workshops, and other special programs became a regular part of the summer offerings. Two conferences were held in the summer of 1948, and three in 1949. By the summer of 1951, the number of special offerings had increased to five. These included workshops in art and health education, a symposium in speech therapy, a geology trip, and the Huron Playhouse. The Playhouse, or summer theater, was started at Huron, Ohio, in the summer of 1949, under the direction of Elden T. Smith, chairman of the Speech Department. A number of plays were given each summer. They became very popular with the residents of the area. The primary purpose, however, was to give students experience and instruction in the practical phases of theater arts.

Extension classes were discontinued in 1943, as an economy measure. When off-campus instruction started again, in the 1946-47 school year, it took a new form. A University branch, offering most of the required courses of the freshman year, was started in Sandusky, Ohio. During the first semester, 96 students were enrolled in the branch. This number dropped to 56 for the first semester and 46 for the second semester of 1947-48. After that the branch was temporarily discontinued. Off-campus classes at several other centers were again

An aerial view of the campus in the early thirties.

President Homer B. Williams guided the school in its first quarter century.

Dr. R. E. Offenhauer was president from September, 1937, until his death on December 29, 1938.

Dr. Frank J. Prout was president from 1939 to 1951.

Dr. Ralph W. McDonald was president from 1951 to 1961.

Dr. Ralph G. Harshman was president from 1961 to 1963.

John Begg

D. C. Brown

J. E. Collins

J. D. McDonel

Dr. Williams as he appeared toward the end of his long service to the University.

Dr. Prout as he appeared toward the end of his administration in 1951.

THE FIRST FACULTY

G. W. Beattie
Agriculture

Rea McCain
English

J. R. Overman
Mathematics

Mary T. Chapin
Home Economics

E. G. Walker
Dean

E. G. Hesser
Music

Not pictured:

D. D. Johnson
Director of the Training School

Joseph Leach
Supervisor of Practice Teaching

L. L. Winslow
Industrial Arts

Executive Council of Deans (1944) confers with President Prout. Left to right are Ralph G. Harshman (Business Administration), Clyde W. Hissong (Education), James Robert Overman (Liberal Arts), and A. B. Conklin (Dean of Students).

E. Tappan Rodgers, trustee for 23 years and President of the Board of Trustees from 1946 to 1961, helped lead the University into the modern era.

The former Administration Building gets a new facade and the University gains an Inner Campus when the traffic circle and through street is removed in 1958.

Overman Hall addition is completed during Dr. McDonald's administration.

The University Union, completed in 1958, adds a new dimension to student life and government.

Founders Quadrangle (1957) ushers in the era of a large university with facilities for 1,000 students.

offered, starting in 1947-48 with an enrollment of 37. Enrollments grew to 185 in the first semester of 1948-49, 210 in 1949-50, and 306 in 1950-51.

Rising Enrollments

Although almost all colleges and universities in the United States were faced with greatly increased enrollments after the war, the rate of increase at Bowling Green State University was much greater than that in most other institutions. Three factors probably accounted for this. In the first place, Bowling Green had started its growth before the beginning of the war. It undoubtedly would have continued at an accelerated rate, if the growth had not been temporarily stemmed by the war. The Navy V-12 program probably contributed to the post-war growth, since it brought men from different parts of the country to the campus. Since most of them were favorably impressed by the instruction and the treatment they received, the University became much more widely (and more favorably) known. Many of the men in the V-12 program returned after the war to finish their college education at Bowling Green State University, and often brought friends with them. A third factor, and possibly the greatest, was the fact that the costs for a year at Bowling Green were still among the lowest in the country.

The growth of Bowling Green State University becomes plainer (and more startling) when it is expressed in terms of percentages. The largest enrollment, before the war, was 1,600 students in the first semester of 1940-41. Thus, the enrollment of 3,956 for the corresponding semester of 1946-47 represented an increase of 147 per cent. Even more significant is the fact that enrollment within three years, from September, 1944, to September, 1947, jumped from 1,349 to 4,472, an increase of over 231 per cent. Obviously, such an increase in such a short time created serious problems for the University. Finding a faculty (although not easy), was not the most difficult. It was even harder to find enough space in which to teach and house such students.

Expanding Faculty

The fact that the enrollment of 4,472 for the first semester of 1947-48 was more than three times the 1,349 enrollment for the same term in 1944-45, meant that the faculty had to be tripled during a period when the number of qualified people was even fewer than usual, since enrollments in graduate schools had greatly decreased during the war. The problem was made even more difficult by the fact that most of the other institutions of higher learning in the country were also seeking new faculty members, and Bowling Green was not in a favorable position to compete. Faculty salaries had always been comparatively low and even less money than usual was available, since revenues from student fees and state appropriations did not increase as rapidly as the enrollments. The result was that the University was forced to resort to temporary measures. A number of permanent additions were made to the faculty during this period, but a large number of the new appointments had to be temporary, at the lowest rank, and at the lowest possible salary. This resulted in a serious drop in the quality of the faculty, as measured by their educational qualifications. In 1940-41 there were 85 members on the teaching faculty and 55, or almost 65 per cent, had doctor's degrees. By 1950-51 the number of full-time faculty members had increased to 233, but the number holding doctorates had decreased to 50, or less than 22 per cent.

Although the faculty was entirely adequate, and well qualified for the situation as it existed during these years, it was entirely too light at the top for a university faculty of the quality everyone desired for Bowling Green. In 1944-45 the teaching staff numbered 84 individuals, 18 of whom were on temporary or part-time appointments. By 1950-51 the total number had increased to 233 full-time and 15 part-time faculty. In addition, there were 39 graduate assistants, some of whom were doing some teaching. During these years, 174 new appointments were made, and 74 were at the rank of instructor. Many of these were made with the understanding that they could be terminated at the end of any school year.

It can be truly said that the quality of instruction did not suffer during these years. The largest increases in enrollments were in the freshman and sophomore classes, and all of the appointees were well qualified to teach courses on these levels. Many of them were outstanding high school teachers who wanted a taste of college teaching. They were willing to take temporary appointments, since they knew they would have no difficulty in returning to high school positions, equal to or better than they previously held. This proved to be the case. Other individuals used the temporary appointments as a means of earning money to continue their graduate work.

Faculty Salaries

Obviously, as soon as possible, serious steps would have to be taken to upgrade the faculty, if Bowling Green was to become a strong university. President Prout was well aware of this situation, but little could be done to remedy it during his administration because of the low salary schedule. It is true that salaries had increased somewhat after the war, but they were still inadequate. In 1950-51 the top salary for nine months was only $5,500 for a full professor, and only a few received this amount. The highest salary for an associate professor was $4,500; for an assistant professor, $3,700; and for an instructor, $3,100.

Although President Prout was forced to leave the solution of this problem to his successor, he did prepare the way for him as much as possible. On November 21, 1950, he presented data to the trustees to show that (1) faculty salaries at Bowling Green were seriously below those at sister institutions (average salaries at Kent, Miami, and Ohio Universities were $615.00 above Bowling Green), (2) too large a percentage of the faculty was in the lower ranks, (3)

Bowling Green was undermanned in administrative positions, and (4) Bowling Green had experienced the greatest percentage of increase in enrollment of any of the state universities. He further pointed out that neither the administrative nor instructional staffs had been geared to the increase, and that the instructional staffs had been built at the bottom, and not at the top.

The trustees expressed surprise at these facts and agreed unanimously that salaries at Bowling Green should be on a level with those at sister institutions. They voted that the budget requests for the next biennium should be sufficient to permit the necessary increases.

A Serious Housing Shortage

Building a faculty large enough to provide instruction for the rapidly expanding student body was not the only task confronting the University during these years. Even more serious was the problem of providing additional classrooms and living quarters for the students. This task was made more difficult by the fact that, during most of this period, there was not enough time, money, material or labor available for the erection of permanent buildings. On August 1, 1945, the trustees expressed concern over the rapid increase in enrollment and instructed President Prout to recommend additional dormitory buildings. However, on February 20, 1946, the President reported to the trustees that the State Board of Control (which controlled the release of state-appropriated funds) had definitely taken a stand against any state building until labor and material conditions had greatly improved. Although planning for permanent buildings continued, it was evident that the only possible way to meet the immediate housing needs was to secure temporary buildings, wherever they could be found, and to buy existing buildings located near the campus.

Expanding Campus

On July 11, 1945, the trustees authorized the purchase of the Leedom property, and the conversion of the house into a dormitory to house 20 girls. This property was north of Ridge Street and east of the cemetery. The house was enlarged, and afforded accommodations for 20 girls.

The next purchase came in November of the following year. On the twenty-fifth of that month, the trustees authorized the purchase of an empty brick building located on the northwest corner of Wooster Ave. and Thurstin St. At first, it was used for central receiving and storage, but later it was converted into a dormitory. This building was originally an underwear factory, but had been occupied by a chicken hatchery. After its conversion into a temporary dormitory, it was still known to townspeople as The Hatchery, but was named Ivy Hall by the students. Students sometimes said that a hatchery, by any other name, still smelled like a hatchery.

Several additional purchases were made during this period. In 1948 the

Graf Manufacturing Company, located across East Poe Road, south of Bricker Field, went out of business, and its plant was bought by the University. It was occupied by the Graphic Arts Department and the ROTC. Part of the building was also used for storage and by the maintenance department.

On November 11, 1949, the trustees voted to purchase the Urschel property, located south of the campus. This consisted of five acres of land, an abandoned quarry, the Urschel home, and a brick apartment building. The residence was used to accommodate University guests. The apartment building was converted into a dormitory for girls and named Urschel Hall. The quarry was used as a swimming pool for several years.

Temporary Student Housing

Although these buildings helped relieve the shortage of dormitories, they were not nearly enough by themselves. Temporary housing had to be secured, especially for men and married students. On November 23, 1945, the trustees instructed the President to buy from the government 40 trailers to house married veterans. On December 31, of the same year, they authorized the purchase of 15 pre-fabricated steel buildings to house 20 men each. On February 13, 1946, the President reported that the 40 trailers were in place and ready for occupancy, but that the steel buildings would not be completed in time for the second semester. At the same meeting, the President informed the trustees that Gov. Lausche had offered rooms in the Armory and in the state highway garage to house veterans.

On February 13, the President reported that the Federal Housing Authority had assigned Bowling Green State University two wooden barracks, each to house 50 men, and 10 additional trailers. At the same meeting, the Board authorized the purchase of land for the location of these barracks. On May 24, 1946, the President informed the trustees that the Federal Housing Authority had made available additional buildings and furnishings to house 900 men, and the Board authorized the purchase of several parcels of land for their location.

Other Temporary Buildings

Additional domitory accommodations was not the only need of the University during this period. The shortage of classroom space was just as serious. Early in 1946 Gov. Lausche suggested the possibility of relieving the crowded campus conditions by the establishment of a branch at Camp Perry, which was being released by the government. President Prout appointed a committee of faculty representatives and administrative officers to visit the camp and report on the feasibility of such a branch. He also instructed the committee, as an alternate plan, to consider the possibility of moving some of the buildings to the Bowling Green campus. The committee made the visit, but found that most of the buildings were locked and that the electricity had been turned off.

However, they succeeded in breaking in (through a window), and inspected the buildings with the aid of flashlights.

The committee, upon its return to Bowling Green, reported that it did not consider the establishment of a branch as either advisable or feasible, but thought that several of the buildings at Camp Perry could be moved to the campus and put to good use. The trustees, on March 1, 1946, instructed the President to study the cost of establishing a branch at Camp Perry and the cost of transporting the buildings to Bowling Green. However, the Board members were quite definite in their preference for the latter plan, which was finally adopted.

After some delay, the federal government released several Camp Perry buildings for transfer to Bowling Green, one of which was the mess hall. The University was especially eager to get this building, since it was equipped with modern facilities for cooking and serving meals, and such equipment could not be purchased at the time. However, at the last minute, the government ruled that the release covered only the buildings, and equipment was not included. After recovering from the shock of this ruling, the University decided that the building was better than nothing. Equipment was finally secured, partly from Kohl Hall and partly from other government sources. President Prout was able to announce to the trustees that the mess hall (rechristened Commons) would be ready for use in September, 1947.

Four other temporary wooden buildings were ready at the same time. These had been remodeled to house English, fine arts, speech, and a freshmen chemistry laboratory. The speech building was later enlarged and named the Gate Theater.

F. Eugene Beatty, later to become Director of Buildings and Facilities, was assigned the task of securing buildings, and equipment of all kinds from the federal government. Much valuable scientific and other types of equipment was released to educational institutions, but the competition was very strong. Mr. Beatty was both indefatigable and highly successful in his efforts to secure both buildings and equipment. The latter was just as important as the former, since much of it could not be purchased at the time, even if money had been available.

Buildings Constructed

Although it was not possible to build any large, permanent buildings during the early part of the post-war period, one existing structure was remodeled, and several smaller buildings were constructed. The remodeling came early in 1945, when rooms were built under the concrete stadium stands to house 80 men. The capacity was increased to 150 in 1947. The construction during this period was financed from a number of sources. These included state appropriations, local funds, and money received from various federal programs.

For a number of years, the city of Bowling Green had been faced with a possible water shortage and, as a result, the trustees considered making several water wells on the campus available for emergency use. These wells had been drilled during President Williams' administration, but had never been used as the water was not suitable for drinking.

President Williams, who had a keen sense of humor and enjoyed a joke even when it was on him, liked to tell an amusing story about these wells. At the time, there were a number of old gas wells on the campus which provided sufficient gas to heat the library building and the President's home. The President and trustees considered the possibility of drilling more wells in the hope of getting enough gas to heat more buildings. Since the city water supply at that time came from wells, they also discussed saving money by drilling for water. The question was, which should they drill first, water wells or gas wells? Finally, it dawned on President Williams that it was not necessary to decide this question. They would simply drill a well and take whichever they got, gas or water. It turned out to be water.

On September 19, 1945, the trustees authorized the construction of a pump house to draw water from one of these old wells. President Prout never missed an opportunity to secure more housing for men, so the plans for this building included living quarters for 12 men. The water from this well was, at first, used only for irrigation purposes. Later, during a serious water shortage, a chlorinator was installed and, with the approval of the Ohio Department of Health, the water was used for potable purposes.

Some additional relief for the critical shortage in student housing was afforded by the construction of several more cottage-type dormitories, which were occupied by sororities and fraternities. By the end of this period, there were 22 such cottages. These cottages were built for two reasons (1) to ease the housing situation (since it was impossible to secure money or material for a large dormitory), and (2) to encourage national fraternities and sororities to come to the Bowling Green campus. They succeeded in both of these objectives.

During the last few years of President Prout's administration, it became possible to build five more new buildings and additions to three old ones. These were completed by the summer of 1951. The additions were to the Library, Gate Theater, and Johnston Hall. The new buildings were a chemistry laboratory and a fine arts building (to replace the temporary frame structures), a new heating plant, an industrial arts building, and a chapel.

The new chemistry building was designed as the first unit of a larger science building. It was built north of Ridge Street and west of the cemetery. The old science building was now occupied by the Department of Biology and, at the suggestion of the faculty of that department, it was named Moseley Hall in honor of Edwin L. Moseley, a member of the original faculty and first instructor in biology.

The new heating plant was built to meet an emergency, since the old plant was too small to heat the existing buildings, and the boilers were worn out and beyond repair. Fortunately, the new plant was completed before the old one gave out completely, although this had seemed doubtful for a time. The boilers were removed from the old heating plant, the smokestack (long a Bowling Green landmark) was razed, and the building was converted to house maintenance offices and shops. The Industrial Arts Building was constructed at the airfield to be used as a hangar during the war, and by the Industrial Arts Department after the war. It was financed with money received from the federal government in connection with the V-5 program.

The chapel was built from a state appropriation for a music practice hall, supplemented by a gift from Sidney Frohman of Sandusky, Ohio. Still standing, it is a white frame, colonial building in the style of the early churches, built in the Firelands, east of Bowling Green. The first intention was to name the chapel for Mr. Frohman, but he declined the honor. It was named the Frank J. Prout Chapel in honor of President Prout, who had been instrumental in securing the gift to the University. Mr. Frohman's gifts did not stop with the chapel. He continued to show an interest in the University. Over a period of years, he made gifts totaling over $86,000. Part of the gifts were to the College of Business Administration, but most of the money was for the Sidney Frohman Scholarship Fund.

Few changes were made in the appearance of the campus during these years. Some additional walks were constructed, and trees and shrubs were planted. The trees were intended to replace the large oaks and other trees which had been deteriorating because of age. New campus lights also were installed. Probably the greatest improvement in the appearance of the main campus resulted from the attractive chapel and its landscaping.

One of the most important changes in the University grounds during this period did not affect the appearance of the campus at the time. This was land purchases. Although these were criticized at the time as being unnecessary, the President and trustees had the vision to see that additional land would soon be needed to accommodate the growth of the University. As a result, they bought various parcels of land near the campus whenever they were available and money was available. This foresight undoubtedly saved the University and the state many thousands of dollars. Campus acreage more than doubled during President Prout's administration, increasing from 105 to 274 acres, including the airport.

Housing Conditions in 1951

Measures taken during this period to relieve the serious shortages in both dormitory and academic space were (of necessity) mostly temporary. At the end of President Prout's administration, besides the small cottage-type dormitories, women were housed in Williams Hall, Shatzel Hall, Urschel Hall, and

Kohl Hall. All were badly overcrowded. For part of this period, girls were also housed in the Women's Physical Education Building.

The situation was even worse with respect to the men, most of whom (again with the exception of the few in the cottage-type dormitories) were housed in temporary frame, barracks-type structures. These were relocated on the campus from army bases, by the Federal Housing Administration, at no cost to the University except providing utilities and making the necessary site improvements. These buildings, known as North, East and West Halls, were overcrowded and represented a serious fire hazard. Men were also housed under the stadium stands and in Ivy Hall, the converted hatchery. These quarters were temporary and only slightly better than those in the barracks.

The situation was equally serious with respect to the University's academic facilities. English and psychology were still housed in temporary frame structures, and most of the other buildings were overcrowded. Part of the frame Commons was converted into classroom use. At first, the hatchery was to be used for classrooms or faculty offices, since there was a serious shortage of these facilities. However, the pressing need for student rooms forced the trustees to change their plans and convert this building into a dormitory.

Although forced to resort to temporary buildings, the trustees were determined they really should be temporary, and that they should be replaced by permanent structures at the earliest possible time. All were familiar with the situation on many college campuses where temporary buildings from World War I were still in use. This policy was carried out, although it probably took longer than the trustees had hoped. The last of these temporary structures did not disappear from the campus until 1962.

Why did the University not avoid serious shortages by limiting enrollment? Indeed, this question was asked at the time, but several things prevented the trustees from taking this course of action. In the first place the law in Ohio requires the state colleges and universities to accept all graduates of Ohio high schools who apply for admission. Furthermore, the Governor of Ohio felt that the state owed a particular obligation to the men returning from service, and stated that no veteran would be denied the opportunity for a college education. If the facilities of existing schools could not be expanded sufficiently, new schools would be started. The trustees, President, and a majority of the faculty agreed with the Governor's position. They also felt that some temporary buildings and faculty at an existing institution were infinitely better than entirely temporary buildings and faculty at new institutions. The other state universities shared these views and, as a result, not a single student was turned away because of a lack of necessary facilities. Bowling Green State University and all the other state universities of Ohio can be justly proud of this record.

The post-war years brought few changes in the general character of administrative procedures. Fewer general faculty meetings were held and the newly formed Faculty Senate was not as successful as had been hoped. However, it was more effective than its predecessor, the Policies Commission.

The Faculty Senate and Council

A committee in 1948 reported to the Senate that there had been no constructive accomplishments, and reported loss of interest, poor attendance, and lack of good general discussions at Senate meetings. Although this report was undoubtedly too pessimistic, the fact remained that, during this period, the Senate failed to become an effective organ for faculty participation in University affairs. Again, this was at least partly due to lack of any real interest on the part of the majority of the members of the faculty. This is shown by the fact that, during this period, most of the questions discussed by the Senate were submitted to it by the President or deans. Although the administrative plan did not specifically state that the Senate could initiate discussions, it did not prohibit such a procedure. The opportunity was there for much greater faculty participation, but it was not seized.

Probably the greatest weakness of the Senate, as a means of promoting faculty initiative and participation in University administration, was the fact that it met only at the call of the President of the University and that he was the presiding officer. Certainly, this situation did not contribute to faculty initiative and free discussion. However, these obstacles could have been surmounted, if the faculty had really wished to do so.

In 1948, and again in 1949, the Senate revised the provisions governing its operations, in order to make the organization more effective. These amendments provided for regular meetings and stated, specifically, that the Senate should be free to initiate an investigation on matters concerning the welfare of the University and to make recommendations. Another important change was the creation of a Senate Council which was to have complete charge of planning the programs and activities of the Senate. This council was composed of seven members, three appointed by the President of the University, three elected by the Senate, and a seventh elected by these six. The Council elected its own chairman.

Two other statements came under the heading of *Powers and Duties*:

(1) It is not the purpose of the Senate to usurp the powers and duties of the administration and, (2) the functioning of the Senate is based upon freedom of discussion and the acceptance of honest and sincere criticism of all persons concerned. Comment of a personal nature should be eliminated from such discussion.

Possibly, the fact that the Senate thought it necessary to include these statements is the best evidence that neither the administration nor faculty was, as yet, entirely ready for greater faculty participation.

The Senate discussed many important questions and made helpful recommendations. These included aims of the University grading system, reports of the Curriculum Committee, establishment of a program of honors study, cheating, evaluation and improvement of teaching, use of automobiles by students, audio-visual aids, library facilities, final examinations, and student counseling. Many of these recommendations were approved by the administration and were put into operation.

Advisory and Executive Committees

The Advisory Committee proved more effective than the Senate. This was largely the result of two factors: (1) President Prout worked better with a small group than with a large one, and (2) the faculty members appointed to this committee usually had a sincere interest in contributing to the academic development and administration of the University. Other faculty members interested in doing so could make suggestions to a member of this committee, or to his academic dean. In practice, this was seldom done. However, throughout President Prout's administration, the Executive Committee continued to be the guiding and advisory body for the University. Almost all problems were discussed and many decisions were made in this group. These decisions were usually final, although they were always subject to the approval of the President and the Board of Trustees. This was a convenient (and in many ways an efficient) method. However, it was certainly not democratic, or even representative, since the Executive Committee was composed entirely of administrative officers, who held membership by virtue of their administrative positions.

Other Faculty Committees

During this period, a number of additions were made to the standing committees of the faculty. The first (and one of the most important) was the Curriculum Committee in 1946-47. At first, this consisted of three faculty members, one from each of the three colleges. Later its membership was increased to six, and these were elected by the University Senate. This committee was especially significant, since it provided the first official representation of the faculty as a whole in the discussion, planning, and even initiating curriculum offerings. Before this time, these matters had been carried out by the deans of the colleges in consultation with each other and with the chairman of the departments under their supervision. The final decisions, however, were still made by the Executive Committee and the President of the University.

The year 1949-50 brought two new committees of importance. These were the Graduate Council, which succeeded the old Graduate Committee, and the Committee on the Honors Program. The latter committee was appointed to plan and administer a program of honors study as recommended by the University Senate. The next year (1950-51) saw the addition of the Automobile Committee, to supervise and enforce the new regulations concerning student use of automobiles.

Administrative Officers

In August, 1945, the trustees granted leave of absence to Dr. Hissong to enable him to assume the office of State Director of Education. Dr. Herschel

Litherland was appointed his successor as dean, and Dr. Walter A. Zaugg took his place as chairman of the Graduate Committee.

In the spring of 1948, the author asked to be relieved of the duties of Dean of the College of Liberal Arts in order to return to teaching and, on March 12, the trustees appointed Dr. Kenneth H. McFall as his successor. Dr. McFall had been assistant dean for some time. The author was given the title of Dean Emeritus, and continued to serve as a member of the Executive Committee.

Another change was included in the 1948-49 catalog. Until this time, the deans of the colleges had also acted as chairman of their respective departments. The increased loads that came with larger enrollments now required a division of these duties, and Dr. B. L. Pierce became chairman of the Department of Business Administration; Dr. W. A. Zaugg, chairman of the Department of Education; and Dr. F. C. Ogg, chairman of the Department of Mathematics. For a number of years, Dr. Ogg had been doing much of the work of the departmental chairman, but now was given the title for the first time.

The Graduate School

The year 1947-48 also saw a change in the organization of the graduate program. Prior to that time, graduate work had been offered in a Division of Graduate Instruction administered by the Graduate Committee. In this year, a Graduate School was organized under a director, Dr. Emerson Shuck, who had succeeded Dr. Zaugg as chairman of the Graduate Committee. He became the first director and, in 1951, his title was changed to Dean of the Graduate School.

Committee on Administrative Organization

After the report of the Post-War Planning Committee failed to result in a solution to the troublesome question of faculty organization, the Senate recommended to the President that he set up a new committee to make a further study of this problem. On May 7, 1945, President Prout appointed the three academic deans and two faculty members (F. C. Ogg and L. A. Helms) to this committee. However, for various reasons, nothing was accomplished. Probably the chief reason was that the committee members did not feel that the faculty was as yet ready to agree on any new plan.

Early in the fall of 1948, the Senate recommended to the President of the University the appointment of a new committee to study the whole problem of the organization of the administrative structure of the University. On October 15 of that year, the President appointed the Committee on the Administrative Organization of the University. The members were John E. Gee, W. H. Hall, L. A. Helms, F. C. Ogg, and the author as chairman. This committee had two characteristics. In the first place its members, with the exception of Dr. Gee, were all veterans of one or more previous committees that had studied the same problem. In the second place, it included no members of the administrative staff, since the author had given up his administrative duties the previous spring. This fact enabled him to devote more time to the work of this committee.

The committee studied the problem for almost two years. In addition to holding regular meetings its members investigated the administrative organizations in a large number of other universities, both public and private. Finally, on March 27, 1950, the committee submitted its final report to the University Senate. The complete report consisted of 42 typewritten pages, plus an organizational chart and appendix of 25 pages.

Part I of the report included sections on a historical summary of the administrative organization of the University, aims and functions of the University, functions of an administrative organization, areas of administrative service, a functional analysis of the existing organization, criteria for reorganization, types of academic organization, conclusions and recommendations, a proposed administrative organization for Bowling Green State University, and an organizational chart. Part II defined the powers and duties of the various administrative officers and the agencies of the University, as recommended in Part I of the report.

The report recommended that the administration of the University (under the trustees and President) be divided into four areas: academic, personnel, public relations, and fiscal. Each of these areas was to be headed by an administrative officer reporting directly to the President.

The part of the report that was to have the greatest effect upon the future administration of the University was the section dealing with the troublesome problem of faculty organization. This committee was the first (in a long line of predecessors) to reach an agreement on this question. As a first step, it divided the departments of instruction among the three undergraduate colleges. All departments primarily concerned with providing a broad, liberal education were assigned to the College of Liberal Arts; those primarily concerned with the training of teachers, to the College of Education; and those primarily concerned with education for a business career, to the College of Business Administration. The resulting division was as follows:

College of Liberal Arts: biology, chemistry, engineering drawing, geography and geology, mathematics, physics, history, political science, psychology, sociology, English, foreign language, art, music, and speech.

College of Education: education, graphic arts, health and physical education, home economics, industrial arts, and library science.

College of Business Administration: business administration, economics, journalism, military science and tactics, secretarial science, and business education.

The committee anticipated that, with the growth of the University, new departments would be created, especially in the Colleges of Education and Business Administration.

The committee recommended that the existing University faculty be divided into three college faculties, each under the jurisdiction of the dean of the college. It provided that a faculty member should belong to the faculty of the college to which his department was assigned. In addition, any instructor offering one or more courses in a different college would also be a member of the faculty of that college, as long as he taught such a course.

For several years, a number of faculty members were in favor of dividing the faculty on a divisional basis. The committee believed that such a plan had considerable merit, particularly for the College of Liberal Arts. They, therefore, recommended that the departments and faculty of this college be divided into three divisions, each with a chairman, as follows:

Division of Natural Sciences: biology, chemistry, engineering drawing, geology, mathematics, and physics.

Division of Social Studies: geography, history, political science, psychology, and sociology.

Division of Humanities: art, English, foreign language, music, philosophy, and speech.

One reason for the opposition of a number of faculty members to the formation of college faculties had always been the fear that this division would lead to rivalries, jealousies, and lack of cooperation between colleges. To prevent this possibility, the committee recommended that a vice-president and dean of faculties be appointed. As vice-president, he would be the executive head of areas of academic, personnel, and public relations administration, and, as dean of faculties, he would be directly responsible for the area of academic administration. The committee felt that eventually this office should be split into two, but that for a time one would be sufficient. As an additional means for unifying the academic program, the committee recommended the formation of a Coordinating Committee on Academic Instruction to be composed of the dean of faculties, the three deans of colleges, the director of the Graduate School and the registrar. The function of this committee, according to the report, should be to assure proper balance and coordination between the various colleges and schools of the University.

For a number of years, the administrative staff of the University did not expand with growing enrollments, and had become seriously undermanned. The new office of Vice-President and Dean of Faculties was recommended to help alleviate this situation as well as to coordinate the academic program.

The greatest administrative shortage, however, was in the offices of the deans of the three colleges. On occasion, the Dean of the College of Liberal Arts had the services of a part-time assistant to relieve him of the duty of advising students. The committee recommended the appointment of a full-time junior dean in the College of Liberal Arts and part-time junior deans in each of the other colleges. All realized that the counseling load was much greater in the College of Liberal Arts, because of the number and diversity of its programs.

The committee also tried to improve the effectiveness of the Faculty Senate in several ways. It recommended that the Vice-President and Dean of Faculties be the presiding officer, since he was to be in charge of the faculty and academic program. Its most radical recommendation was that certain well-defined legislative powers be immediately delegated to the Senate, subject only to the approval of the Executive Committee. It suggested several routine, academic questions, and recommended that, from time to time, other legislative powers, temporary or permanent, be delegated to it by the Executive Committee.

Finally, the committee recommended that the Senate be given power to study and discuss problems concerning the academic, personnel and public relations administration on its own initiatives, and to make recommendations to the Executive Committee. It further recommended, "that the Senate shall be kept informed . . . on all important questions concerning the university."

Following its presentation on March 27, 1950, the report was discussed by the Senate at several meetings, and was finally approved by this body. This approval included endorsement of the division of the single University faculty into three college faculties as recommended by the committee. Surprisingly enough, in view of the long and often bitter opposition of many faculty members, this section was approved with only one dissenting vote. This almost unanimous approval was the result of several factors. The safeguards against rivalries and jealousies between college faculties (such as existed on many campuses) influenced a large number of the faculty, and the divisional organization within the College of Liberal Arts attracted others. The main reasons, however, were probably (1) the fact that the shortcomings of the old organization had (with the growing size and complexity of the institution) become more evident to more of the faculty, and (2) through the appointment of new members, the character of the faculty had undergone a slow but sure change. The vote proved that there was only one member left who sincerely believed that Bowling Green State University should have remained a one-purpose institution for the training of teachers. This individual was firmly (and honestly) convinced that the teacher-training program in general, and in his own department in particular, had been seriously damaged by the addition of the new colleges.

Committee Recommendations

In a letter to the faculty, dated June 6, 1951, President Prout announced that as a first step in putting into operation the new administrative organization recommended by the faculty committee and given general approval by the Faculty Senate, the Executive Committee had on the above date approved the recommended division of departments among the three undergraduate colleges. This division had been previously approved by the academic deans and the department chairmen. The division into college faculties, as recommended by the committee, was also approved to become effective on September 1, 1951.

Another recommendation of the committee (somewhat modified) was carried out before the end of the 1950-51 year, to become effective at the same time. This was the creation of two new offices, dean of administration and dean of faculties. The President and trustees felt that the administrative organization, at the top level, was so seriously undermanned as to demand two new offices instead of the one recommended by the committee. The University was still too small to warrant the appointment of a vice-president, so the title was changed to Dean of Administration. This officer was to aid the President in non-academic administration of the University and head the personnel area. The Dean of Faculties was to be responsible for the administration of the academic program and the coordination of the three undergraduate colleges and Graduate School. The two officers were to be of coordinate rank and responsible directly to the President of the University.

Dr. Ralph G. Harshman was appointed Dean of Administration and Dr. B. L. Pierce was appointed to take his place as Dean of the College of Business Administration. The author reluctantly accepted the appointment as Dean of Faculties, with the understanding that he would serve for only a few years.

The above changes and appointments were made during President Prout's administration, although his successor had been elected on June 2, 1951. However, they were made after consulting the new President and with his approval.

Student Government

The University Students Association and the Student Council were organized during President Williams' administration to act as the official student voice in affairs affecting students' interests. A number of changes were made in the organization of the Student Council during President Prout's administration, and its name was changed to Student Senate. This body was composed of representative students and five faculty members.

Part of the time, the Student Senate and its predecessor, the Student Council, functioned successfully, but during some periods it was relatively inactive. In general, the students felt that neither body was an adequate means for representing student sentiment. The chief objection was that they were subject to too much faculty domination.

Fees and Expenses

After the war, both fees and living expenses started to increase. By 1950-51 the registration fee had been raised from $30 to $45 a semester, the health fee from $2.50 to $4, and the student union fee from $1 to $5. Total fees, exclusive of laboratory, music, and other special fees, increased from $47 to $67.50. Further increases were announced for 1951-52, when the total fees reached $74.50 a semester, as compared with $47 in 1945-46.

Board and room in University dormitories also increased. In 1945-46 rooms were $40.50 a semester; board was $81.00 for women and $90 for men. By 1950-51 these had increased to $45 for room and $126 for board. Board went up again in 1951-52 to $144 a semester.

Total expenses for a semester increased with fees and living costs. The 1945-46 catalog estimated total necessary expenses for a semester at $169.50 for women and $177.50 for men. The estimate in 1950-51 was $266.50. In 1951-52 it was $291.50. Although costs at Bowling Green were still lower than at many other comparable institutions, the difference was gradually and steadily diminishing.

In 1946-47 the University charged a nonresident fee for the first time. This was $25 a semester, but was increased to $37.50 a semester with the 1947-48 school year. Before 1946 the University wished to encourage out-of-state residents to enroll at Bowling Green, since it wanted to develop a more cosmopolitan student body. The increased enrollments following the war caused many people, including members of the General Assembly, to feel that the facilities of the state universities should be used primarily for the education of Ohio students, and that the state should not pay part of the cost of educating non-residents.

New Departments

Several new departments were created after the war. These usually came from splitting existing departments and were the result of increased offerings due to increasing enrollments. The Departments of Chemistry and Physics, History and Political Science, and Psychology and Philosophy each were developed into two departments.

Two new Departments, Engineering Drawing and Graphic Arts, also were formed by taking the offerings in these fields from Industrial Arts.

In the 1948-49 college year, a Reserve Officers' Training Corps (ROTC) was established in the University. Membership was voluntary, but was quite attractive. It carried with it deferment from the draft (within quota limitations) until completion of the student's education. Upon graduation from the University, the student also received a reserve commission as second lieutenant. With the start of ROTC, the Department of Military Science and Tactics was added to the catalog. During the last year of President Prout's administration, arrangements were completed for the establishment of a unit of Air Force Reserve Officers' Training Corps (AFROTC), starting with the 1951-52 college year. This resulted in the addition of a Department of Air Science and Tactics.

Courses and Curricula

Course offerings were increased in almost all departments, but the increases were greater in those that were divided. Foreign language also increased its offerings in French, German, Latin, and Spanish, and added Portuguese. These increases gave students in the Colleges of Education and Liberal Arts a wider choice of majors and minors. Several new curricula were added in each college to meet the needs of the rapidly expanding enrollment. Three of these were in the College of Education: public school art, public school music, (instrumental), and speech and hearing therapy. The College of Liberal Arts described several new preprofessional curricula including foreign and international service, public administration, and two in home economics. The greatest expansion came in the College of Business Administration. By the end of President Prout's administration, this college had added curricula in advertising, business statistics, insurance, personnel administration, and retailing to its offerings.

Increased enrollments after the end of the war resulted in an expansion of the graduate program. In 1945 the only graduate degree offered was Master of Arts, and the student was limited to eight departments of specialization. These were biology, education, English, foreign language, history, mathematics, social studies and sociology. By 1951 the number of fields of specialization had increased to 19 with the addition of business administration, business education, economics, geography, guidance and counseling, health and physical education, industrial arts, political science, psychology, speech and dramatic arts, and speech and hearing therapy. Four different masters' degrees also were offered. These were Master of Arts, Master of Science in Education, Master of Science in Business Administration, and Master of Education. All of these, except the last, included a thesis as one requirement for the degree.

The University Library

The University Library started in 1914, with a small collection of books housed in the basement of the old Methodist Church. The first professional librarian was appointed in 1915, and the book collection increased slowly but steadily. At the beginning of President Prout's administration in 1939, there were 45,000 bound volumes in the Library, but it was still inadequate for a growing University.

In the beginning, the library books were selected to meet the needs of a small undergraduate teachers college. When President Prout assumed office, it was imperative that the collection be increased and its character changed to serve the Colleges of Liberal Arts and Business Administration, and a graduate program. A beginning had already been made under Edmon Low, who was librarian from 1938 to 1940. More progress came while Dr. F. C. Ogg was acting librarian, but the big development was due to the efforts of Dr. Paul F. Leedy, librarian from 1944 to 1961. In spite of the library fees (started during this period), the funds available for the purchase of books were still too small. Nevertheless, the book collection grew by 1951 to more than 113,000 bound volumes, plus some 75,000 unbound United States Government documents. The improvement in the character of the books was just as great, particularly in areas serving liberal arts, business administration and the graduate program.

The increase in the number of books necessitated an addition to the library building. Even this was inadequate to house the growing collection, and plans for a larger addition or a new library building, were being discussed at the end of President Prout's administration.

Assembly Exercises

During President Williams' term in office, the compulsory weekly assembly periods were a valuable part of the college program and usually were well attended. However, as the college grew in size, interest waned, and the problem of enforcing attendance became difficult. Finally, the increased enrollments after the war made compulsory attendance impossible, since the auditorium was too small to hold all of the students. Several plans were tried to meet this situation, but by the end of President Prout's administration weekly exercises were abandoned. Assemblies, or convocations, were held at intervals as occasion demanded, and the catalog statement that attendance was expected was changed to read "attendance at these exercises is urged upon all students." Since no compulsion was applied, the auditorium was seldom crowded.

Organizations and Activities

In most respects, the University's policy with respect to student organizations and activities remained unchanged during President Prout's administration. The catalog still contained the following statement:

In order to provide for the social as well as the mental development and training of its students, Bowling Green State University supplies a well-rounded program of organizations and activities.

The principal change was in the number, which increased greatly with the larger enrollments that came after the war.

The social activities continued to be under the general supervision and direction of the Social Committee, composed of both student and faculty members and including both the dean of women and the dean of students. The number of activities increased to such an extent in the latter part of this period that it became a serious problem. Each fraternity and sorority sponsored at least one event, and the number increased with the rise in the number of these social groups. Several attempts were made to limit the number of activities, but with little success. Both faculty and students thought there were too many, but could not agree on the ones to be eliminated.

In 1946 a group of six students met with President Prout in his home and organized a society which is unique to the Bowling Green campus and which, throughout the years that have followed, has made important contributions to University life. This society is really secret. The meaning of its name and its members are unknown, its meetings are secret, and its activities are nocturnal.

At 3 a.m. on the morning following its organization, the residents of the campus and its surroundings were awakened by an announcement over the public address system by which the new society introduced itself and stated its purpose. Subsequent announcements, which ordinarily preceded athletic events or other important student activities, were usually by means of posters which were put up by night in prominent places on the campus. These were headed SICSIC sez, followed by a pep message recommending some course of action by the student body.

Although the secrecy surrounding the society has never been invaded, certain things are known. Its purpose, from the beginning, has been to develop campus spirit and support worthwhile activities. Its membership is confined to six, two each from the sophomore, junior, and senior classes, elected sometime during their freshman or sophomore years. The membership also is secret (and has never been divulged or discovered), until the names of the two senior members are revealed at the end of the year.

Activities connected with the academic program were expanded somewhat during this period, but showed no major changes. The Speech Department added radio broadcasting. Horseback riding was added to the activities in physical education and later dropped. Finally, three new student publications were started: a literary magazine (published twice a year), a freshman handbook containing information about University organizations and student activities, and a student directory. The first of these was sponsored by the English Department, and the last two by the Journalism Department. Each was published by a student staff.

The number of departmental and honorary societies increased greatly during President Prout's administration. In 1939 there were five departmental clubs and six honor societies. Of the latter Book and Motor was a local and the other five were national. At the end of this period, in 1950-51, there were 43 local organizations and 32 national. Most of these were departmental societies, but two were more general. These were Kappa Delta Pi, an honorary society in education, and Omicron Delta Kappa, a senior men's leadership honorary society.

For a number of years, the University staged a May Day celebration. In 1940 the Student Council suggested that these ceremonies be expanded to include the recognition of scholastic, athletic, forensic, and musical accomplishments of individual students and student groups. They proposed a special assembly program with an academic procession of seniors and faculty in caps and gowns. This program was to be followed by a recessional and a tree planting ceremony by the senior class.

The suggestions of the Student Council were carried out, and the first such exercises were held on Friday, May 10, 1940. These ceremonies were called Insignia Day, but the following year the name was changed to Honors Day. It has become an annual event.

Under President Prout's administration, the University continued to support a varied program of intercollegiate and intramural sports. In 1942 it withdrew from the Ohio Athletic Conference. During the remainder of this period, it scheduled games independently, wherever it could find suitable opponents. Withdrawal from the Ohio Conference was due to the fact that, with its growth in enrollment, University teams had become so strong that the other members of the conference were reluctant to schedule games with Bowling Green. In 1947, athletic relations, which had been severed in 1935, were resumed with the University of Toledo.

National Fraternities and Sororities

There were no national social sororities or fraternities on the campus during President Williams' administration. There were, however, by 1939, six local social groups for women and three for men. President Williams opposed national groups until the University could attract strong organizations.

President Prout, who was a fraternity member and an enthusiastic believer in the value of national social groups, thought that the time had arrived. Developments proved that he was right.

As an inducement to national sororities and fraternities to establish chapters at Bowling Green, President Prout started the policy of building small, cottage-type dormitories to house social groups. The first of these was completed in 1941, and was occupied by the Five Sisters local sorority. Three more similar dormitories were completed the next year, and housed the Skol, Seven Sisters and Three Kay sororities. By 1950-51 there were 22 such dormitories.

In addition to President Prout, a number of members of the administration and faculty (themselves fraternity members) worked to bring the *Greeks* to Bowling Green. Among them were Dr. Ralph Harshman, Dean of the College of Business Administration; Dr. Kenneth McFall, Dean of the College of Liberal Arts; John Bunn, Registrar; and Elden Smith, Chairman of the Speech Department. Several alumni also were active in this movement. The first of these, in both time and efforts, was *Doc* Lake, an alumnus of the Five Brothers local fraternity. *Doc* was probably the first and most active advocate of national social organizations, and was undoubtedly the first to open negotiations with such a group. His choice for the Five Brothers was Sigma Alpha Epsilon, which he hoped would become the first national on the Bowling Green campus.

Doc Lake's hopes for a first were not to be realized. Since Ralph Harshman, Kenneth McFall, and John Bunn were all members of Alpha Tau Omega, it looked for a time as if that organization would win the race. However, the Commoners (a local men's organization) moved with surprising speed, and became the first to gain a national charter. They were installed in the summer of 1942 as a chapter of Pi Kappa Alpha. After that, the progress was rapid. In

1943, the Delhi received a charter in Alpha Tau Omega. In 1945 *Doc* Lake's hopes were realized, and the Five Brothers became Sigma Alpha Epsilon. These were followed by Sigma Nu in 1946; Sigma Chi, Kappa Sigma and Theta Chi in 1947; Zeta Beta Tau and Delta Tau Delta in 1948; and Delta Upsilon in 1949. Five more chapters were installed in 1950, and one in 1951, bringing to 15 the number of national fraternities on the campus.

The campaign for the nationalization of the local social groups for women started in the fall of 1942. During 1943 four groups were chartered: Five Sisters became Alpha Xi Delta, Seven Sisters became Alpha Phi, Three Kay became Gamma Phi Beta, and Skol became Delta Gamma. Las Amigas received a charter from Alpha Chi Omega in 1944. Nationalization continued until, by 1950-51, there were 11 national sororities on the Bowling Green campus.

Although opinions may differ with respect to the value of national sororities and fraternities, and the contribution they may make to the total education of their members, no one can deny that the bringing of the Greeks to Bowling Green State University was one of the major developments during President Prout's administration. Certainly their coming resulted in many changes in the pattern of social life on the campus. Bringing these strong national organizations to the University was the accomplishment of which President Prout was most proud. The policy of housing these groups in state-owned dormitories on the campus, although it has much in its favor, also created problems that have not yet been solved at the time of this writing.

President Prout never lost his interest in the fraternities and sororities, and paid frequent visits to the houses. If he thought any small item was wanting for their comfort, he would see that it was obtained immediately. He often made purchases personally, paying for the items with his own money. When campus trees were trimmed or cut down, he would have them cut into firewood and often deliver the wood, personally, to fraternity and sorority houses.

Automobile Regulations

Student use of automobiles did not become a serious problem until near the end of the war. The catalog published in March, 1944, contained the first automobile rule:

> The use of automobiles by students attending Bowling Green State University is forbidden. Exceptions to this regulation must be secured from the Dean of Students.

Exceptions were granted only in the case of students who commuted, or who could prove that an automobile was necessary to the pursuit of their college work.

This prohibition was partly the result of lack of sufficient parking space on (or near) the campus, but this was not the principal reason. For some time, the citizens of Bowling Green and surrounding communities had complained about petters parking in cars, both on city streets and country lanes. Cars also were used for joy riding, and a number of serious accidents resulted. The President and trustees decided that the only way to meet these hazards was to prohibit the use of automobiles.

The first change in automobile rules came with the catalog dated March, 1947. This contained the statement: "A student who uses an automobile must register it with the Dean of Students." The next catalog contained more detailed regulations. It prohibited use of cars by freshmen, and continued the requirement for registration of cars by upperclassmen. It also stated:

> The University assumes no responsibility for providing parking space on campus for cars owned by students (or) for accidents on campus resulting from cars owned or driven by students.

At its meeting held on April 26, 1949, the trustees passed the following resolution:

> Whereas, the student use of automobiles has presented serious problems of safety, good conduct and proper use of time,

> Therefore, be it resolved that after September 1, 1946, a condition of enrollment shall be that a student shall not bring to this city or campus an automobile unless said student shall establish a just need for same.

On June 9, of the same year, President Prout presented to the trustees detailed regulations concerning the use of automobiles by students. These regulations included the following statement:

> Unmarried women students in the University are not permitted to make use of an automobile in any manner except upon special permission of the Dean of Women.

Copies of the above regulations were mailed to all students enrolled for the following year, since the catalog had already been published. The regulations appeared in the 1950-51 catalog for the first time.

The regulation that unmarried women students were not permitted to make use of an automobile in any manner was interpreted to mean just that. The author recalls that, on one cold winter day, he offered a ride to a woman student who was walking toward the campus and carrying a heavy load of books. She refused because it was against the rules. This strict interpretation was found to be unreasonable, so the 1951-52 catalog changed "in any manner" to "for social purposes."

Drinking Regulations

From the beginning of Bowling Green State Normal College, the serving of alcoholic beverages, in the dormitories, at college-sponsored social and athletic events, and on the campus was prohibited. However, for many years, the problem was not serious, and the penalties imposed upon offenders were not severe. No serious attempt was made to control drinking off campus, but there was very little of this. When disturbances did occur on campus, Steve, the college cop, would escort the culprits to their rooms. When minor disturbances occurred off campus, the Bowling Green police would do the same. At rare intervals, a few college men (the women did not drink in those days) would be jailed overnight, and released in the morning when sober.

After the war the problem of drinking became much more serious. There were more men in college, social customs and standards were changed, and the college men (many of them veterans) were older. Finally, a number of rather serious disturbances in Bowling Green and in taverns outside the city led the trustees (on May 17, 1947) to adopt the following regulation:

> Gambling, being drunk or disorderly, or bringing alcoholic beverages on campus is prohibited. Penalty for violation of above regulation is a minimum fine of $25.00; maximum penalty, suspension from university.

Gambling was included in the regulation, because of the recent exposure of a gambling ring in one of the men's dormitories. Several students had been found adding to their incomes by fleecing freshmen. Investigation disclosed the fact that the ringleader of the ring had been dropped by another university because of similar activities.

The catalog dated February, 1950, and subsequent catalogs for a number of years, contained the following statement:

> Any student convicted of an action, including drunkeness, which is derogatory to the good name and reputation of Bowling Green State University is eligible for dismissal. Enrollment in the University implies that the student accept the responsibility to be a good citizen of the community.

A number of dismissals resulted from the rather rigid interpretation and enforcement of this regulation.

Student Demonstrations

In October of 1949, the first of a series of student strikes and demonstrations occurred. These were to recur at intervals for a number of years. Several reasons were given for these disturbances. Among them was too much faculty domination of the Student Senate, lack of freedom of expression in the *B-G News*, and restrictions on the social use of cars. Although most students denied, in public, that the rules concerning the use of alcoholic beverages were a factor, many admitted in private that they were a major cause. At least these rules received the most publicity in the newspapers.

The fundamental, basic cause underlying all others was the growing feeling on the part of the students that they should have more liberty and less stringent controls. They felt that they were capable of regulating their own conduct. They believed they should have a stronger voice in determining University policies and greater freedom to criticize. This attitude was particularly strong among the veterans. Student disturbances were not confined to the

Bowling Green campus and, even after they ceased here, they continued on other campuses. The student fight for greater liberty and more self government soon became nation-wide.

The demonstrations at Bowling Green and other institutions received wide publicity and awakened much criticism. An article in the *B-G News* of November 23, 1949, reported that President Prout, in addressing the Student Senate stated:

> Misconduct of students on the various state university campuses in Ohio is resulting in a great downfall of public confidence in what is going on in these institutions. This lack of confidence is developing into a feeling of animosity in the state legislature toward the state universities which is becoming a decided hindrance to these schools in obtaining sufficient state aid to meet operational costs.

Student morale remained low for the remainder of President Prout's administration. This was shown by a number of items in the *B-G News*. This paper reported, in its June 11, 1950 issue, that a member of the Student Senate charged that campus morale* was at an all-time low. President Prout denied the charge, but many students and faculty members believed it was true. Events in the years to follow seemed to confirm this belief.

Election of a New President

During the 1949-50 school year, President Prout informed the Board of Trustees that he would like to be relieved of the duties of president as soon as a suitable successor could be found. He asked that the search for a new president should be started at once, since he anticipated it would take at least two years and he did not wish to serve beyond that time. Following President Prout's request, the trustees, with President Prout's assistance, started the search. Their first step was to agree upon a list of qualifications which they thought the new President should possess. The list contained 11 items. Among these, in addition to high educational and administrative qualifications, they included the statements that he must be interested in athletics and fraternities, and must support present programs of good student conduct. The first of these statements reflected President Prout's interest in this field, while the second referred to the automobile and drinking regulations. The trustees also agreed on one other policy, although it was not included in the list of 11 items. This was to the effect that they would not consider any individual who was at that time a member of the University faculty or administrative staff.

After agreeing upon the qualifications they desired in the new President, the trustees asked for suggestions from the faculty, administrative officers, and friends of the University all over the country. In this way, they compiled a list of some 50 names. They then investigated a number of these candidates and had personal interviews with several, but failed to find one they wanted.

---

*This meant student morale.

Since the time they could devote to the problem was limited, they decided that they needed help. As a result, in May, 1950, President Prout, at the request of the Board of Trustees, appointed a faculty committee to cooperate with them in the search. At first, the trustees continued their own efforts but, finally, left all investigation of candidates to the committee.

The committee, as appointed by the president and approved by the trustees, included Martha Gesling, education; W. H. Hall, chemistry; L. A. Helms, economics; P. W. Jones, director, News Bureau; P. F. Leedy, English and librarian; F. C. Ogg, mathematics; J. R. Overman, mathematics (chairman); B. L. Pierce, business administration; and E. T. Smith, speech.

This committee considered over 100 names, investigated about 50 by correspondence, and made a thorough investigation of at least eight of the individuals. The latter investigations involved correspondence, personal interviews with references, and in most cases, a visit to the candidate in his present position. Most of these eight candidates also were invited to the campus by the trustees.

At first, it was not thought that there was any need to hurry the search, but, on April 2, 1951, President Prout informed the trustees (and the committee) of his desire to retire as of August 31, 1951. This meant that his successor had to be found and elected before that date. The committee now intensified its search, and the author, as chairman, was relieved of all teaching in order to devote his whole time to the search and investigation.

By the first of June, the committee had narrowed the field to three candidates, any one of whom it believed would make a good president for Bowling Green State University. The committee decided, therefore, to recommend all three to the trustees, and to leave the final decision to them. The trustees' choice was Dr. Ralph W. McDonald. The committee invited Dr. McDonald and his wife to appear before them at their meeting on June 2, 1951, to discuss the presidency of the University. After lengthy discussion, Dr. McDonald was unanimously elected. He agreed to assume the duties of the office on September 1.

One of the three men recommended by the committee was Dr. Ralph G. Harshman, at that time Dean of the College of Business Administration. His name was included for two reasons. In the first place, the committee thought he would make an excellent president. In the second place, it wanted to register a protest against the policy of eliminating all faculty and administration members from consideration. It is interesting to note that Dr. Harshman was destined to succeed Dr. McDonald in the presidency.

The committee, in its search, added a twelfth qualification to the 11 stated by the trustees. The first three presidents of Bowling Green State University had all been school superintendents whose service had been mainly in northwestern Ohio. The committee agreed that these men had given fine service, and that experience as a superintendent of a public school system was, at least in some respects, good preparation for a college presidency. The majority of the committee (it was almost unanimous) also believed that at this time in the history of Bowling Green State University, when it was just establishing itself as a University, it was imperative that the new president be a man with training and experience at the college rather than the public school level. The committee agreed that since Bowling Green was gradually becoming a cosmopolitan rather than a local institution, the new president should be chosen from outside the state. However, the committee also agreed that he should have some knowledge of (and be sympathetic to) the training of teachers, since this would continue to be a major function of the University.

Although the committee was almost unanimous in support of the above policies, some pressure was brought to bear to bring about the appointment of a school superintendent from northwestern Ohio. This pressure came from both inside and outside of the University. It became necessary for the chairman of the committee to inform the trustees concerning the committee's attitude and the policy it had adopted. The trustees then expressed themselves as being in accord with the committee's point of view. To the author, this pressure for the appointment of another public school administrator as President was evidence that some people, both inside and outside the University, still regarded Bowling Green as a teacher-training institution, rather than a university.

The man chosen by the trustees was, by both training and experience, well fitted to satisfy all points of view. Dr. Ralph Waldo McDonald was a graduate of Hendrix College (a small liberal arts college in Arkansas), with majors in English, economics, and mathematics. He received the M.A. and Ph.D. degrees from Duke University, with specialization in educational psychology, economics, and educational administration. In addition, he had one semester of study in law at the University of North Carolina. This last had been taken with no intention of becoming a lawyer, but because of its importance to an educational administrator. He had taught psychology and education at the University of North Carolina and at Salem College, Winston-Salem, N. C. At the time of his election, he was executive secretary of the department of higher education of the National Education Association. In this capacity, he conducted conferences and acted as a consultant on problems of university and college administration.

President Emeritus

After his retirement on August 31, 1951, President Prout became President Emeritus for life with certain assigned duties. Among the latter was the task of preparing a historical record of the outstanding and significant events of his administration. This task was never completed but a second duty, which was a labor of love, was faithfully performed as long as he was able. President Prout was a great lover of flowers and requested that he be given charge of beautifying the campus. For many years, his flower beds were points of interest. He supplied cut flowers to the University Union, fraternity and sorority houses, and for many University functions. He also delivered flowers almost daily to the faculty families residing near the campus. Often these were left on the doorstep early in the morning before the family was awake.

Summary of President Prout's Administration

President Prout inherited from his predecessor a strong, well-established College of Education, relatively new and smaller Colleges of Liberal Arts and Business Administration, and a still smaller graduate program. The institution had the name and the beginnings of a University, but was still regarded by the people of Ohio and the nation as primarily a teacher-training institution.

The principal tasks confronting President Prout were, therefore, the building of larger and stronger Colleges of Liberal Arts and Business Administration, and the development of a stronger graduate program. The accomplishment of these objectives involved the problem of building a strong faculty interested in other fields besides education. It also necessitated bringing about a change in the public image of the institution. World War II brought other problems, chiefly in the areas of faculty and housing. The accomplishments of President Prout's administration must be judged, mainly, in terms of its success in meeting and solving these problems.

Although seriously handicapped by the war, both the College of Liberal Arts and the College of Business Administration showed substantial growth in the last part of this period. The graduate program developed slowly, but as fast as physical facilities and faculty improvement permitted.

The quality and attitude of the faculty both showed improvement in the early years of this period, but both suffered badly during the war years. However, after the war ended, both again improved as rapidly as limited finances permitted. The change from a teacher's college to a University faculty was best shown by the vote on the report of the Committee on the Administrative Organization of Bowling Green State University.

There was also considerable evidence that the people of Ohio and the nation had come to look upon the Bowling Green institution as a University, in fact as well as in name. Although a few of the older residents of Bowling Green and northwestern Ohio still spoke of the normal, this was now the exception rather than the rule. Many of the public jumped directly from a normal to university image. In the intervening years, the name college was seldom used, except by students and faculty.

The author received evidence of the change in the national image of Bowling Green when he was serving as chairman of the committee in search of the new president. In investigating possible candidates, he interviewed a number of prominent men in education and other fields (from all over the United States) and found that Bowling Green State University was widely and favorably known. Occasionally, the comment was made that "I believe your institution started as a normal school," but the author does not recall a single individual (who knew anything about Bowling Green) who did not know that it was now a university.

Further evidence with respect to the new public image of Bowling Green State University is given by the change in the character of the student body during President Prout's administration. When he assumed office in 1939, almost all the students were from Ohio, a large majority from Wood County. There were none from foreign countries. In 1950-51 students came from 74 counties of Ohio and 30 states. Nearly 50 were from outside the continental limits of the United States.

The problems brought by World War II also were successfully met. It is true that the solution to these problems (both in the field of faculty and housing) were mostly temporary, but that is all that was possible because of financial and other limitations. In spite of these handicaps, some permanent progress was made in both these areas.

Another major development during President Prout's administration was the bringing of strong national sororities and fraternities to the Bowling Green campus. Some considered this development good; others doubted it. In the early years, when the college was small, the social needs of the students were largely served by all-college activities. As the enrollment grew, this was no longer possible and smaller groups were needed and were organized. Probably no one denied the need for such groups, but some felt that it could best be met by local groups, not necessarily entirely social in character.

No summary of the achievements of President Prout's administration would be complete without again referring to the question of faculty organizations. He inherited from his predecessors an undivided university faculty, which soon proved inadequate to meet the problems of three colleges and a graduate program. He left his successor an organization of three closely-knit, well-coordinated college faculties, each serving the needs of a particular college and the University as a whole. This was to prove a workable organization, and one that contributed greatly to the further development of strong Colleges of Liberal Arts and Business Administration.

Other achievements, during President Prout's administration, included: purchase of additional land, building an airfield and a golf course, establishing a radio station, building a temporary student union and planning for a permanent one, improving faculty tenure policies, establishing the faculty senate and council, strengthening the library and the graduate program, and establishing the ROTC and the AFROTC. In trying and difficult times, Dr. Prout kept the University on an even keel. He successfully met all problems as well as conditions permitted, and even achieved substantial gains in some areas. Probably no President could have done more.

CHAPTER TEN

The Administration of Ralph W. McDonald 1951-1961

ASIDE FROM THE CONTINUING need for up-grading the University, the major problems of President Prout's administration were the results of fluctuating enrollments—first up, then down, then up again. Probably the greatest of these problems were the shortages of both housing and faculty in the post-war years. These two problems continued to be major ones throughout most of President McDonald's administration, since President Prout had been able to find only temporary solutions, and enrollments continued to mount.

On-campus enrollment during President Prout's administration reached its highest point in 1949-50, when for the first semester it was 4,684. It decreased to 4,235 the next year, continued to drop slowly during the next three years. It reached its lowest point in 1953-54, when it was 3,221. These changes were only partly due to the steady decrease in the number of veterans in attendance. Another contributing cause was the fact that the University started to relieve the serious overcrowding in the dormitories, and thus reduced the number of rooming accommodations on campus.

This temporary drop in enrollments was most welcome, since it was possible to reduce the size of the faculty and to start rebuilding and increasing salaries. It also gave the University a few years in which partly to catch up with the housing shortages and to prepare for the increases to come. This breathing spell was well utilized.

After 1953-54, on-campus attendance started mounting again. Although the increase was not as sudden nor as spectacular as that which occurred following the end of the war, it was steady and substantial. The low of 3,221, for 1953-54, increased to 3,404 for the next year. After that it increased at the rate of approximately 500 students each year. It reached 6,229 for 1960-61, the last year of President McDonald's administration. Attendance would have increased much more rapidly during this period if it had not been for one circumstance; there were not enough rooms to house any additional students. Dormitory accommodations were increased (by building new dormitories) at the rate of about 500 each year. Enrollments increased by the same amount.

Bowling Green ceased to be predominantly a women's college in 1938-39, when the number of men exactly equaled the number of women. Except for the war years, the proportion of men continued to increase until 1950-51, when there were 41 per cent more men than women. With President McDonald's administration, the University entered a period of controlled enrollments. The controlling factor was, of course, the number of available rooms for men and for women. The trustees and President believed that the ideal situation would be to have approximately equal numbers of the two sexes, so they planned the building of dormitories with that end in view. The result was that, in the 1960-61 school year, there were 3,013 undergraduate men enrolled in the University and 2,888 women. This was approximately four per cent more men than women.

Enrollment by colleges in 1950-51 was: Education, 1,773; Liberal Arts, 1,146; Business Administration, 1,061; and Graduate School, 198. By 1953-54 the order was changed. Education still led with 1,381, Business Administration was second with 873, and Liberal Arts was third with 782. Enrollment in the Graduate School dropped to 151. In 1960-61 the corresponding figures were Education, 3,075; Business Administration, 1,221; Liberal Arts, 1,613; and Graduate School, 328.

Off-Campus Enrollments

Off-campus enrollments followed much the same pattern as those on-campus. A total of 545 students were enrolled in extension classes in 1951-52, but this number dropped to 421 by 1953-54. The decrease was largely due to the shortage of faculty for extension teaching. After 1953-54, enrollments rose slowly. The big increase started in 1956-57 as a result of the reopening of the University branch at Sandusky. This branch was started during President Prout's administration, but had to be discontinued. A second branch was opened at Mansfield in 1954, but it was transferred to Ohio State University in 1958. A third branch was opened at Bryan in 1957, another in Fremont in 1958, and another at Fostoria in 1959. In 1960-61, the last year of President McDonald's administration, off-campus enrollment was 675 in the branches, and 171 in extension classes offered elsewhere, for a total of 846.

Summer School Enrollments

During the last part of President Prout's administration, summer enrollments fell from a high of 1,688 in 1949, to 1,074 in 1951. Again, this decrease was due (at least partly) to the drop in the number of veterans. Early in his administration, President McDonald asked Dean Harshman to make a careful study of the whole problem of the summer school, and to prepare a new program. Dean Harshman, after working with the department chairmen, dean of faculties, and the President, proposed a number of changes which were gradually incorporated in the summer school program.

During most of President Prout's administration, the policy was to draw almost all of the summer school faculty from the members of the Bowling Green staff. Occasionally, a visiting professor was employed for the summer, but this was exceptional and usually occurred only when no Bowling Green faculty member was available. To make the summer school offerings more attractive, the new program proposed to add a number of instructors from outside the Bowling Green faculty. These were to be experts in their fields and individuals with a statewide or national reputation. This practice was started in the summer of 1952, and continued throughout President McDonald's administration. In 1952 nine visiting instructors were included in the summer faculty, and the number increased to 25 by 1961.

From time to time, prior to 1952, the University included one or more workshops, or special programs, in its summer offerings. It was now decided to increase substantially the number of these programs. Five were offered in 1951, 12 in 1952, and 27 in 1961. These special programs were planned mostly for teachers in service, and were keyed to the problems they met in their teaching. The 1961 list of special offerings included three institutes sponsored by the National Science Foundation.

During the last years of President Prout's administration, the summer school usually consisted of one term of eight weeks. Starting with the summer of 1954, this was changed to two sessions of five weeks each. In the summer of 1961, the last planned under President McDonald's administration, an extended session of nine weeks was started. This was for freshmen only. It was planned for high school graduates who were unable to secure admission for the fall semester. Since enrollments always decreased for the second semester, those who successfully completed this summer term could resume their college work at that time. Students with poor high school records also were encouraged to enroll in this session to test their ability to carry college work successfully.

Enrollment for the summer of 1952 was 998, and for 1953 it was 1,129. With the introduction of the new summer calendar in 1954, enrollment increased to 856 for the first term, 542 for the second, and 239 in the workshops and special programs, making a total of 1,637 for that summer. Enrollments continued to rise.

Housing Shortage

One of the most serious problems confronting the University, when President McDonald took office, was the serious shortage in housing. Many new buildings were needed (for classrooms and for student living) to replace the temporary structures and provide for increasing enrollments. In September, 1951, the University was housed in 16 academic buildings (three of which were temporary); eight large and 21 cottage-type dormitories (four of the large ones were temporary); and 11 other buildings (two were temporary). Several additional buildings were in the planning stage, but none was under construction.

New Dormitories

The most pressing need was for additional and better housing for both men and women. Two new dormitories were completed in 1955. These were the Alice Prout Residence Hall for women and Rodgers Quadrangle for men. The first of these was named in memory of the late wife of President Emeritus Frank J. Prout and the second for E. Tappan Rodgers, President of the Board of Trustees.

Founders Quadrangle was completed in 1957. It consisted of four separate but connected residence halls for women. These halls were named Treadway, Harmon, Lowry, and Mooney, in memory of men who had been prominent in securing the passage of the 1910 legislation establishing the Bowling Green Normal School. Judson Harmon was Governor of Ohio at that time; John Hamilton Lowry sponsored the legislation in the Ohio House of Representatives; Granville W. Mooney was speaker of the House; and Francis W. Treadway was Lieutenant Governor.

A new dormitory for men was completed in 1960, and named Conklin Quadrangle, in honor of Arch B. Conklin, Emeritus Dean of Students. With the completion of this quadrangle, the University had permanent (and excellent) housing accommodations for almost 5,000 students. A large new residence center for women consisting of three separate halls was also under construction in 1961. It was completed in 1962, and was named McDonald Quadrangle in honor of President Emeritus and Mrs. Ralph W. McDonald. The 1,221 women accommodated in this quadrangle raised the number of student housing accommodations on campus to over 6,000 students.

One other residence hall was in the planning stage. This was to include four separate residence units housing 350 students each, radiating like spokes of a wheel from a building at the hub, which was to contain a central kitchen, dining rooms, snack bar, and recreation rooms. This building was not completed until 1964, but plans were under way and, on July 22, 1961, the trustees named it Harshman Quadrangle, in honor of Dr. Ralph G. Harshman, who had just been elected President to succeed Dr. McDonald.

An addition to Kohl Hall, the first dormitory for men, was also being planned. This was completed in 1962, and added 180 more beds for men. Plans also were under way for a new dining hall, to replace the old, wooden Commons. This was finished in 1963.

All but one of the temporary buildings, brought in during the war, disappeared from the campus before the end of President McDonald's administration. The Psychology Building was removed in 1961, and the Gate Theater was torn down in the same year. On June 11 of that year, the trustees authorized the burning of 12 apartment buildings, which had been obtained from the Federal Public Housing Authority in 1949. No buyer could be found and it would cost too much to tear them down, so it was decided to burn them. This was done during a fire school supervised by Northwest Ohio Firemen's Association and the state fire marshal. The only temporary building that remained was the old Commons, which was torn down in 1962.

The Sale of Bonds

Kohl Hall, built in 1939, was financed by the sale of revenue bonds. A court decision prevented the sale of such bonds on the open market until 1954. However, during the period from 1939 to 1954, the University issued privately a number of revenue bonds. These were sold to banks, fraternal orders and individuals, but no sizable issues could be sold under such conditions. After years of research and changes in enabling legislation, bond council approval was given, and open market sales started in 1954. Alice Prout Residence Hall, Rodgers, Conklin, and McDonald Quadrangles, and the University Union all were financed in this way.

The right to sell bonds on the open market has been vital to the expansion of the state-supported universities of Ohio, since it has enabled them to add dormitories and other revenue-producing facilities without the use of tax funds. Bowling Green State University can be justly proud that it led this long fight. Its business manager, Ervin J. Kreischer, never ceased his efforts until the fight was won.

During President McDonald's administration, six buildings, costing a total of over $16 million, were built by the sale of bonds. Three others, costing over $9 million, were either under construction or planned. This brought the total cost of locally financed buildings (completed, under construction, or planned) to over $25 million, all without cost to the taxpayers of Ohio.

New Academic Buildings

Residence halls were not the only buildings constructed during President McDonald's administration. State appropriations were used to build four new academic buildings, add to a fourth, and remodel two old buildings. The first new building was the Hall of Music, completed in 1957. Two others were finished in 1959. These were the Home Economics Building and South Hall. The latter houses the Departments of Psychology, Sociology, and Speech. The last new building was Memorial Hall, completed in 1960. This building was named in honor of all Bowling Green State University students who have given their lives serving our nation in the armed forces. In addition to providing offices and classroom facilities for health and physical education and ROTC, it contains a large combination assembly hall and basketball floor.

Two old buildings were remodeled in 1958 and 1959. The first of these was the Elementary School building. Starting with the 1955-56 academic year, this school, which had been maintained by the University since 1914, was taken over by the Bowling Green city school board. In September, 1958, the campus elementary school was discontinued, and the building was converted for use as classrooms by the Education Department. The abandonment of the University-maintained training school was the result of two causes: (1) it was too small to be of any real use as the University was now using not only all of the schools of Bowling Green, but many others in northwestern Ohio, and even farther away; and (2) the building was needed for the use of college classes. The change also was in line with the experience of other teacher-training institutions, most of which were abandoning (or had already abandoned) their on-campus training schools. Those that survived were used mainly for experimental purposes. After the completion of the new Home Economics Building, the Practical Arts Building was remodeled to house the College of Business Administration.

At their meeting on September 11, 1959, the trustees renamed the first of the remodeled buildings Hanna Hall, and the second, Hayes Hall. The first was in honor of Mrs. Myrna Reese Hanna, the first woman to be elected to the General Assembly from Wood County, and joint author (with Senator Van Everett D. Emmons), of the 1929 bill changing the status of the Bowling Green and Kent institutions from normal school to college. Hayes Hall was named in honor of Rutherford B. Hayes (nineteenth President of the United States) and his wife, Lucy Webb Hayes. A large addition to the Chemistry Building also was completed in 1960, and the entire building was named Overman Hall, in honor of the author of this history. This building provides facilities for chemistry, physics, geology, and mathematics.

Two other buildings and improvements were either under construction or in the planning stage. These were an addition to the Fine Arts Building, completed in 1962, and an administration building, completed in 1963. The latter is a 10-story structure, which completed the enclosure of the inner campus on the west. With the opening of the new Administration Building, the former one was renamed University Hall.

The construction of a high-rise building evoked considerable criticism as many thought it overshadowed and dwarfed the older buildings. However, after completion, most of the criticism died out. Some even thought that it improved the appearance of the campus, which had previously looked flat and appeared to be in a depression. The new building seemed to correct this impression. President Williams, the first President of the University (who had been raised in the hills of southern Ohio), often spoke of the flat appearance of the Bowling Green campus, and said even one small hill would be worth a million dollars. Now, after many years, the University had a hill.

Regardless of appearance, the growth of the University made the erection of taller buildings necessary. In no other way was it possible to save a small, open inner campus, and at the same time keep the main administration and academic buildings within easy walking distance of each other. A new Library, nine stories high, and other high-rise buildings being planned, should improve further the appearance of the campus by supplying more hills to lend variety to the old, flat, monotonous skyline.

During President McDonald's administration, a new little theater was constructed, to take the place of the old Gate Theater. This was accomplished by remodeling the large room under the main auditorium in University Hall. This room had an interesting history. First, it was the college gymnasium and as such was the scene of many exciting and noisy basketball games. The noise was increased by the low ceiling which also greatly handicapped the visiting teams. Their loop shots usually hit the ceiling, whereas the Bowling Green team knew that such shots were impossible and attempted none.

After the building of the men's physical education facility, this room was remodeled. As the Recreation Hall (usually called Rec Hall), it became the scene of many college dances and other social gatherings. Later the shortage of large lecture rooms caused this room to be converted to this use. Now it was to assume a new (and final?) role as a little theater. On March 11, 1961, the trustees voted to name this new room (when remodeling was completed) the Joe E. Brown Theater. This was in honor of the veteran actor who is a native of northwestern Ohio and who had, on a number of occasions, appeared with and advised University play-production groups.

Even with the new buildings completed by 1961, and those under construction or being planned, the physical plant at Bowling Green State University was still inadequate to accommodate all of the students who applied for admission. The 1961-62 catalog (and subsequent ones) carried the following statement:

> It is necessary for the University to limit the admission of students because residence halls and classroom facilities, despite rapid expansion of the physical plant, are insufficient to accommodate all of the thousands of new students who apply each year.

Campus Improvements

By the end of President Williams' administration, the original campus of 82½ acres had grown to 105 acres, and it was anticipated that no additional purchases would be necessary. However, during President Prout's administration, conditions changed, and the President and trustees established the policy of buying more land whenever it became available, provided the money could be obtained. During President Prout's administration, the campus grew from 105 acres to 152 acres in the campus proper, plus 120 acres at the airport, for a total of 272 acres. This policy of buying additional land to meet the future needs of the University continued, at an accelerated pace, during President

McDonald's administration. By September 1, 1961, the campus proper had grown to 611 acres, plus the 120 at the airport, a total of 731 acres. In addition, negotiations had been started for the purchase of additional land for a new stadium.

In this connection, it is interesting to recall the statement from the first catalog:

> The campus of eighty-two and a half acres affords ample space for agricultural experiments, school gardens, and nature study experiments.

Obviously, no one at that time (1915) even dreamed of the growth that was to come.

Although several new buildings had been built, and a number of other changes made, the campus of Bowling Green State University looked about the same in the spring of 1959 as it did in 1918, after the old mall and the circle were constructed. However, all this was changed in the summer of that year. The old walks and streets were removed and (to quote the March, 1959, catalog):

> New walks were laid in a pattern most convenient for walking from building to building, the entire area was seeded in grass, and trees and shrubbery were planted. . . . The area is now quiet and really beautiful, free from vehicular trafffic, and conducive to a better atmosphere for living and learning.

The change in the appearance of the campus was so radical that it aroused considerable criticism, particularly from older graduates. With the passage of time, these criticisms have gradually died out and almost everyone now agrees that the new look is much more attractive than the old. As one faculty member remarked, "It looks like a college campus for the first time." The appearance of the campus was to be improved further with the removal of the old stadium, the completion of the new Library and other buildings, and the extension and landscaping of the open spaces. The old handicap, imposed by the grouping of the original buildings around a small circle, will finally be largely overcome.

Other campus improvements during this period included additional parking areas and extensive additions to the underground tunnel system which carries electricity, water and other services to the University buildings. Total campus improvements (exclusive of new buildings and the purchase of land) during President McDonald's administration amounted to over $1.25 million.

Cost of Buildings and Improvements

The total cost of all new buildings, and additions to and remodeling of old buildings financed by state appropriations, amounted to almost $7 million. This included buildings under construction and being planned. If we add this amount to the $1.5 million for campus improvements, and over $25 million for locally financed construction, we reach the staggering total of almost $35 million of campus improvements finished or started during the 10 years of President McDonald's administration. It is interesting to compare this amount with the original appropriation of $150,000 made for the 1911-13 biennium, and with the fact that it was understood at that time that an additional appropriation of $100,000 would be sufficient to take care of the needs of the new institution for many years. Truly, no one could at that time foresee the future.

Trustees

From the early 40's to the middle 60's there were few changes on the Board, since four men served throughout the entire period. These were: E. T. Rodgers, Tiffin, 1923-28, 1943-61; Alva W. Bachman, Bowling Green, 1944-64; Carl H. Schwyn, Cygnet, 1945-65; and James C. Donnell, II, Findlay, 1946-65.

The devotion and the services of these men, both individually and as a group, cannot be overestimated. The encouragement and help they gave to three presidents were a very large factor in the development of Bowling Green State University during this period of over 20 years. Unfortunately, Mr. Rodgers is now deceased, but the other three men are still rendering valuable service to the University, even though they are no longer trustees.

Upgrading the Faculty

When President McDonald took office in September, 1951, everyone connected with the administration of the University (trustees, president and faculty) was determined to continue the growth in quality and standing which had started during the previous administration. It was evident to all that the first need, and the greatest, was to improve the educational qualifications of the faculty. We have noted the serious dilution of the teaching staff which had taken place after the war. Whereas, in 1940-41, almost 65 per cent of the faculty held doctor's degrees, by 1950-51 the figure had fallen to 22 per cent. In the same year 27 per cent of the teaching staff were at the rank of instructor, and many others were on temporary appointments. Obviously, something would have to be done about this situation before Bowling Green could become a strong university.

If the author had not already been aware of this situation, it would have been brought to his attention during the search for a new President. Almost every candidate he interviewed raised the following questions:

Can anything be done about the faculty situation?, If I come to
Bowling Green as president, would the faculty and trustees support
me in a campaign to improve the faculty?, Can Bowling Green
get sufficient funds to raise faculty salaries to the level of other comparable institutions?

Before accepting the presidency, President McDonald asked similar questions of the Board of Trustees. He received their assurances that they would back him fully in any measures needed, including large increases in salaries. They also assured him that they thought it would be possible to obtain sufficient funds to cover these increases. It was only after receiving these assurances that President McDonald agreed to come to Bowling Green.

Just before the end of President Prout's last year, the author had been appointed to the newly created office of Dean of Faculties. Immediately after accepting the presidency, President McDonald approved this appointment and informed the author that the problem of building a faculty to meet the needs of a strong and growing university would be his (the author's) first task and responsibility. The new President promised that he would find enough money to pay the new and improved staff. The author hoped he could keep this promise, but was somewhat skeptical because of many years of experience with low salaries and inadequate state appropriations. Events were soon to show that this skepticism was unwarranted, since the President more than kept his promise.

The faculty could be improved in one, or more, of three ways: (1) by dropping some members who were not on tenure, and did not have the required qualifications, or the ability or desire to acquire them, (2) by encouraging other and promising individuals to increase their qualifications by further graduate study, and (3) by employing new members with the highest obtainable qualifications. The first of these methods proved to be the quickest and the easiest to carry out. As we have noted previously, most of the individuals in the first group had been hired on a temporary basis to meet an emergency. They had accepted appointments with the understanding that they would be terminated when the emergency was over. They were sorry to leave the University, but suffered no hardship as their college experience enabled them to secure new positions usually better than the ones they had previously held.

A number of promising individuals, not on tenure, were granted leaves of absence, to continue graduate work. Several of these eventually earned their doctor's degrees and returned to the University to become valuable members of the faculty. The author's greatest difficulties were with a few faculty members, already on tenure, but without a doctor's degree. The younger members of this group were encouraged to continue graduate work, either by summer study or by taking leaves of absence. Many willingly responded to this encouragement, but considerable pressure had to be applied to others.

The methods used to encourage further study will be discussed later. That they were effective is shown by the fact that, of the indivduals who were encouraged to take further graduate study, 22 eventually earned a doctor's degree. Most of these are still valued members of the University faculty.

Faculty Salaries

Although salaries increased during the latter part of President Prout's administration, they were still too low. For the year 1951-52, the median salary was $4,800 for the full professor, $4,200 for an associate professor, $3,700 for an assistant professor, and $3,300 for an instructor. When school opened in the fall of 1951, one of the first tasks the new President assigned the author was to work out a salary schedule for the following year. He stated that he was doing the same thing, and we would compare our proposals.

Up until this time Bowling Green had never had a real salary schedule. It is true that each year the President informed the deans of the range of salaries for each faculty rank. These figures were determined by the existing salaries (plus any individual increases), and by what the President and deans thought it would be necessary to pay in order to secure competent additions to the faculty. The relationship between salary and educational qualifications was not very close. Salaries and increases in salaries usually depended upon reputation as a teacher and length of service more than any other factors. Now President McDonald proposed to base the new schedule for each rank upon educational qualifications alone.

The proposed schedule, drawn up by the author, was a compromise between what he thought the salaries should be, and the amount of money he thought would be available to pay them. Since the next year would be the second of the biennium, there would be no increase in state appropriations. The resulting proposal called for higher salaries than the author thought could possibly be paid. It was intended as a set of goals to be realized when future appropriations permitted.

The first thing the President did, when he met with the author to discuss salaries, was to hand him a copy of the schedule he had prepared. One glance was enough to show that the figures were so much higher than his own proposals that the author decided not to submit his schedule, if he could avoid it. His first comment was that the proposed salaries were satisfactory, if funds were available. The President replied that most of the money needed for the raises would have to be found by reducing the size of the faculty. He thought this would be possible, since enrollment was decreasing. If, however, this did not prove sufficient, he promised to find any balance needed by economies in other areas.

The author agreed to the President's plan, although, at the time, he did not see how such a decrease in the size of the faculty could be accomplished. The college deans and the author spent many hours together going over the faculty list and pruning wherever possible. The first step was to drop all individuals on temporary appointments, except a few who should be encouraged to continue graduate study. The next step was to consider other faculty members not yet on tenure, and to eliminate all who could be spared among those with the least promise for the future. Other faculty members, even including a number on tenure, were encouraged to take leaves of absence for further graduate study. The net result was a reduction of approximately 30 in the number of faculty members and a saving of almost $100,000 in salaries.

Since the salary schedule for 1952-53 (and the similar ones that followed) played such an important role in President McDonald's administration, it is necessary to give it in full. Salaries for each rank were based upon educational qualifications and, in order to have a concrete, standard measure that could be applied to all individuals, these qualifications were measured in terms of graduate degrees. One of the primary purposes of the schedule was to encourage further graduate study on the part of those who did not have a doctor's degree. Therefore, salary differentials were provided for individuals who were continuing their graduate study. The faculty was divided into three major groups. Two of these groups were each divided into two sub-groups. These divisions were as follows:

I. Those having Ph.D. degree
II. Those having master's degree, plus at least 30 semester hours
    A. Those now working systematically toward the doctorate
    B. Those not now working for higher degree
III. Those having master's degree and less than 30 hours of additional work
    A. Those working systematically toward the doctorate
    B. Those not now working for higher degree

The maximum and minimum salaries for each rank and each of the above groups, and the minimum increase over 1951-52 salaries are given in the following table:

Rank	Salary Schedule (1952-53)	Minimum Increase
Professor		
I	$5,500—7,000	$800
IIA	4,800—5,300	400
IIB	4,300—4,800	300
IIIA	4,300—4,800	300
IIIB	4,000—4,300	200
Associate Professor		
I	4,800—6,000	600
IIA	4,400—5,000	300
IIB	3,900—4,500	200
IIIA	3,900—4,500	200
IIIB	3,600—4,300	100
Assistant Professor		
I	4,400—5,200	500
IIA	3,800—4,800	300
IIB	3,600—4,300	100
IIIA	3,600—4,300	200
IIIB	3,400—4,000	100

Instructor

I	$4,000—4,800
IIA	3,400—4,400
IIB	3,200—3,900
IIIA	3,200—3,900
IIIB	3,000—3,700

The median salary for a full professor was increased from $4,800, which it had been in 1951-52, to $6,000 in 1952-53, or an increase of almost 25 per cent. The corresponding figures were from $4,200 to $4,800, or 14 per cent, for an associate professor; from $3,700 to $4,000, or 8 per cent, for an assistant professor; and from $3,300 to $3,500, or 7 per cent, for an instructor. All this was accomplished without any increase in revenues. In fact, even with these raises, the total faculty cost was less in 1952-53 than in 1951-52.

Although the majority of the faculty members were more than pleased with the new schedule, there were some who were afraid the emphasis on educational qualifications (as measured by higher degrees) would work to their disadvantage. These individuals fell into two groups. The first was composed of those who did not have the Ph.D. degree and were either too old or unwilling to renew their graduate study. In the second group were faculty members in specialized departments such as art and music. Both groups argued that the Ph.D. degree should not be used as the sole proof of the highest level of professional attainment. The first group wanted outstanding teaching ability and length of service included. The second thought that, in their fields, other qualifications such as artistic ability and production were more important than the Ph.D.

The administration pointed out that these other factors were used in determining an individual's salary within the range for his rank and group. This failed to satisfy completely the discontented, since the fact remained that individuals without the Ph.D. degree could never, under the schedule, attain the highest salary level. President McDonald admitted the validity of some of these arguments, and hoped that the time would come when other factors (besides the Ph.D.) could be given greater weight. However, since the accrediting bodies used the percentage of Ph.D.'s on the faculty as the chief measure of its qualifications, it was necessary for a few years, at least, to concentrate on this one factor. No one could really deny this, since less than 22 per cent of the faculty, at this time, had doctorates.

In spite of the admitted weakness in President McDonald's salary policies, including overemphasis on the Ph.D., it must be admitted that they were outstandingly successful in accomplishing the ends for which they were intended. They encouraged 22 members of the 1951-52 faculty to achieve the Ph.D. degree. In fact they did more than encourage this, since the resulting increases in salary were, in many cases, sufficient to pay, in a few years, for the cost of the graduate study. Furthermore, the salary levels were high enough

to enable Bowling Green to attract new faculty members of the highest qualifications, when there was a shortage of such individuals. The best evidence of
this is the fact that the 22 per cent of the faculty holding doctorates was raised
to 61 per cent by the end of President McDonald's administration. In addition,
a number of other members of the faculty were in the last stages of their
doctoral work.

At the end of President Prout's administration, salaries at Bowling Green
State University were lower than at any of its three sister universities. This
situation was completely changed during the first years of President McDonald's administration. On July 29, 1955, the President reported to the trustees
that, during the preceding four years, Bowling Green salaries had been brought
from the bottom to the top of the Ohio institutions and to a level close to the
average salaries paid in the leading universities of the country. He also reported that the higher salaries being paid at Bowling Green State University
had become a matter of concern on the part of the other comparable state
universities of Ohio, and that the presidents of these universities had suggested
that, as a matter of cooperation, the salaries at Bowling Green be held in line
with those paid at Kent, Miami and Ohio Universities.

The trustees' reaction to this suggestion was that, while they recognized the
importance of cooperation with the other universities, they also recognized the
right and the responsibililty of each of the state universities to operate in accordance with policies and plans considered best by its own governing board
and administration. It, therefore, decided unanimously, as a matter of policy,
that the President should establish and provide salaries at as adequate a level
as could be arranged within the available funds.

That President McDonald followed the policy approved by the trustees
is proved by the faculty salaries for 1961-62, as shown below:

Rank	Maximum	Minimum	Mean
Professor	$15,000	$9,200	$12,344
Associate Professor	12,000	7,364	10,321
Assistant Professor	11,000	7,000	8,919
Instructor	8,700	4,800	6,784

The above maximums were, in all cases, over double the corresponding ones
in 1951-52, and the increases in the minimums were almost as great. In fact,
the minimum salary in each rank, in 1961-62, was approximately 50 per cent
more than the maximum in 1951-52. Salaries in other comparable institutions
also increased in this decade, but not to this extent.

Increases in salaries during President McDonald's administration did not
result entirely from increased state appropriations. A large part of the funds
used for this purpose came from changes in the University's internal operations
and from better financial management.

Faculty Tenure

A new statement of tenure policies was approved by the Board of Trustees on November 28, 1953. This embodied several changes from the former policies which had been in force since 1944. During President Prout's administration, it was necessary to make a number of temporary or term appointments. Although such appointees were always informed that the positions were temporary and could be terminated without notice, the terms of the appointment were not always in writing. This resulted in misunderstanding in one case. The new statement, therefore, defined two kinds of appointments, term and regular, and provided that a term appointment should be for a specified period of time and should terminate at the end of that period, without the necessity of any notice. It also provided that the precise terms of any appointment should be stated in writing, with copies in the hands of both the appointee and the University.

Other important changes had to do with probationary periods for regular appointees. Under the former policies, all full professors were on tenure and any promotion to a higher rank gave tenure. The new policy provided for a five-year probationary period for all ranks above instructor (including full professors) and required that, in case of promotion, the faculty members' total probationary period should be that specified for his new rank.

A new feature of the 1953 tenure policies was granting credit for prior full-time service in other accredited colleges or universities. However, it stipulated that the probationary period should,

include full-time service on the faculty of Bowling Green State University of four years for an instructor, three years for an assistant professor, three years for an associate professor, and two years for a professor.

Although the disturbances at the close of President McDonald's administration were partly the result of a question concerning tenure, they were not caused by any defect in the tenure policies themselves, but by failure to follow the provisions of these policies.

Departments and Courses

The undergraduate program was well-developed by the end of President Prout's administration. As a result, there were relatively few changes in departments during the period from 1951 to 1961. The changes that did occur were mostly minor and in the nature of reorganization of existing departments, rather than the addition of new ones. Only three new departments were added. These were Departments of Accounting, Air Science, and Geology. Air Science came as the result of the AFROTC established in 1952-53. Accounting was separated from Business Administration, and Geology from the old Department of Geography and Geology. Two departments were discontinued by combining with a third. These were Engineering Drawing and Graphic Arts, which were put under Industrial Arts (where, by the way, they had formerly been). In 1951 the Foreign Language Department offered five languages: French, German, Latin, Portuguese, and Spanish. During this period, Portuguese was dropped and Russian added.

Early in President McDonald's administration (and under his leadership), the deans of the undergraduate colleges and of the Graduate School undertook, with the department chairmen, a critical study of all course offerings of the University. The catalog in 1951 contained courses that were seldom offered and others, which, when offered, attracted too few students. The first result of this study was to reduce the number of courses by eliminating all deadwood. This was followed, as enrollments grew and finances permitted, by another period of growth and reorganization, on the graduate as well as the undergraduate level.

New Undergraduate Schools

At their meeting of October 19, 1960, the trustees authorized the President to plan for and, when ready, to establish three new schools. These were a School of Journalism in the College of Business Administration, a School of Music in the College of Education, and a School of Applied Science (engineering) in the College of Liberal Arts. The first two were established in 1961, but the last is still not in existence.

Graduate Programs

The master's programs in the Graduate School were greatly strengthened during President McDonald's administration. In the early years several major fields were discontinued because of low enrollments or inadequate facilities, or both, but later most of these were restored and others added. By 1961 a candidate for the master's degree could major or minor in any one of 16 fields and minor in any one of five more. Other departments were planning graduate programs, and four more major and two more minor areas were added the following year. As a result of these expansions almost every department of the University was involved in one or more graduate programs.

The greatest development in the graduate field came in 1960. At their meeting held on October 19, of that year, the trustees authorized the President to start programs leading to the Ph.D. degree in biology, education, English, and speech. It was specifically stated that this action was not to be interpreted as an authorization to start these offerings at once, but was only an approval for the administration to begin planning such programs to be offered whenever faculty and facilities became adequate. The only one of these to be started under President McDonald's administration was the Ph.D. program in English. However, President McDonald did not have the pleasure of conferring the first doctorates granted by Bowling Green State University. This event did not come until January 25, 1963, when Walter C. Daniel and Linda (Welshimer) Wagner received Ph.D.'s in English. This was the last in a series of significant events in the development of the University: the first bachelor's degree in 1917, the first master's degree in 1936, and the first doctorates in 1963.

The University Library

We have seen the modest start of the University Library in 1914, in one small room in the basement of the old Methodist Church, across from the Armory. In 1915, the books were moved to the new Administration Building (now University Hall), and housed on the third floor in the rooms now used as a language laboratory. The lack of foresight as to the future development of the institution is well shown by the fact that this suite of rooms was intended to be the permanent location of the Library.

However, the book collection soon outgrew these quarters, and in 1927 the Library moved into a separate building. This building was larger than the Library needed at that time. For a number of years, the top floor was used for classrooms and housed the English Department. Even after some of these classrooms were converted into stacks in 1948, the Library again outgrew its quarters, and an addition was built in 1950-51. Still more space on the third floor was converted into a study area, when the Political Science Department vacated the space. It was planned, at that time, to enlarge the building further by constructing a second wing to the south. It was soon evident, as the University continued to grow, that even this would be inadequate, so the decision was made to build an entirely new Library. This Library was completed in 1967.

The growth of the book collection in the University Library, which began under President Prout's presidency, continued at an accelerated pace during the administration of President McDonald. This growth was not only in the number of volumes, but even more in their quality. Particular attention was given to building a library adequate to the needs of the students in the University's developing graduate program. Even measured in terms of the number of volumes alone, the growth during this decade was impressive. The total number of books and documents almost doubled from 188,000 in 1951, to more than 330,000 in 1961. In the same period, the number of periodicals received regularly increased from approximately 725 to over 950.

This development was made possible by the fact that the funds available for the purchase of books (which had been totally inadequate during President Prout's administration) were substantially increased during the 1950's. This increase enabled the librarian, Paul F. Leedy, to make great progress in building a collection of books and other source materials to meet the needs of the expanding undergraduate and graduate programs. In this, he was supported and aided by the President of the University, the Faculty Library Committee, and the department chairmen.

Research

Even in the early years of Bowling Green State Normal College, in spite of very heavy teaching loads, several members of the faculty were writing and publishing. However, for many years, the emphasis was on teaching, rather than research and scholarly productivity. This situation remained unchanged throughout all of President Williams' presidency.

President Prout had a somewhat greater interest in promoting research and some progress was made during his administration. In 1939-40 the faculty Committee on Research was appointed. It did much to encourage scholarly productivity by the faculty. However, the faculty still was handicapped by heavy teaching schedules and lack of financial support. This situation did not change materially before 1951.

Under President McDonald, greater emphasis was placed upon research. Scholarly productivity, as well as teaching ability, was considered in hiring new faculty members, and in determining salary increases and promotions. More money was available to support research projects. Teaching schedules were reduced to make it possible. Previously, the standard teaching load had been 15 class hours a week, although schedules frequently reached 16 hours and even higher. Under President McDonald, the standard load was reduced to 12 hours a week, and faculty members engaged in research often were given still lighter loads. The result of all these factors was a great increase in the scholarly production of the faculty. At the time of the golden anniversary celebration, in 1959-60, a survey was made which showed over 100 books and articles published in the two years preceding, and approximately 50 more either submitted for publication or in progress. These were in addition to a number of artistic productions in both music and art.

Administrative Officers

The administrative staff and organization of the University had failed to keep up with the rapid growth after the end of the war. One of the first acts of the new President was to issue a statement describing a new and expanded administrative organization. This was presented to the faculty at a meeting held on September 12, 1951, and later distributed in mimeographed form. In the main the new organization was based on the recommendations of the Committee on the Administrative Organization of the University, which had been approved by the Senate and faculty. The report of this committee was discussed in the preceding chapter.

The main features of the new organization were the establishment of new administrative offices and several administrative councils. The principal new offices were those of Dean of Faculties and Dean of Administration. These were created at the end of Dr. Prout's administration, with the approval of the new President, but did not go into effect until September, 1951. These two new offices were of equal rank and both reported directly to the President.

President McDonald's report to the faculty stated:

The Dean of Faculties . . . will have the chief administrative responsibility for the academic program of the University.

The title of this position was later changed to Provost. The Dean of Administration, in addition to assisting the President in his general administrative functions, was responsible for the administration of all non-academic operations of the University relating to student life and welfare, beginning with the student's application for admission and ending only with his graduation and placement.

A number of other new administrative offices also were established during the first year of President McDonald's administration. The most important of these (for the administration of the academic program) were assistant deans in each of the three undergraduate colleges. These assistants were badly needed, since the administrative load had become too heavy for one individual to carry. This was particularly true in the Colleges of Liberal Arts and Education, and was rapidly becoming so in the College of Business Administration. Other administrative positions created during this decade were those of Secretary of the Faculty, Director of Residential and Plant Operations, and several administrative assistants to the President.

No new administrative officers were brought into the University during President McDonald's term in office. There were, however, a number of new offices, new titles, and considerable shifting from one position to another. Several appointments were made at the end of the previous administration. These were Ralph G. Harshman, Dean of Administration; James Robert Overman, Dean of Faculties; and Benjamin L. Pierce, Dean of the College of Business Administration.

In 1952-53 John W. Bunn was appointed to the new position of Director of Residential and Plant Operations. Mr. Bunn joined the staff in 1939 as Assistant Registrar. Later he became Registrar, and still later, served the University in a number of different capacities. The last of these was assistant to the Dean of Administration. In 1953 Lloyd A. Helms was appointed to the newly created position of Secretary of the Faculty. The next change came in 1954, when the author resigned as Dean of Faculties to return to teaching. No successor was appointed at this time.

The year 1955-56 saw a general reorganization of the administrative staff, but brought only two new individuals. The first of these was Elden T. Smith, chairman of the Speech Department, who was made Director of Student Life and Services. This title was later changed to Dean of Students. Dr. Smith, although he had made an outstanding record in developing the Speech Department, always had a great interest in the larger problems of University administration, and had served on many important committees.

In the same year, Dr. Harshman's title was changed to Vice President, and Kenneth H. McFall became Provost. This latter was a new office created to take the place of the discontinued Dean of Faculties. This set off a chain reaction. Emerson C. Shuck became Dean of the College of Liberal Arts, and Lloyd A. Helms became Dean of the Graduate School. In the same year (1955-56), Herschel Litherland resigned as Dean of the College of Education, and was succeeded by John E. Gee.

Another change came with the 1960-61 school year, when Dr. Harshman retired from the vice-presidency to return to teaching and Dr. McFall succeeded him as Vice President. The office of Provost was discontinued, only to be revived a year later. Dr. Harshman's return to teaching also was destined to be short. The same year (1960-61), brought the second new face to the administrative staff, when Dr. Pierce retired as Dean of the College of Business Administration and William F. Schmeltz, chairman of the Accounting Department, was appointed as his successor.

The building of a well-organized and efficient administrative organization was one of President McDonald's major contributions to the University. He was very fortunate in the fact that the individuals who were to man this organization were already on the staff.

Administrative Councils

The faculty and the Committee on Administrative Organization of the University had feared that the change from a single University faculty to separate college faculties might result in a loss of the unity that had been the chief strength of the old faculty organization. To prevent this, the committee had recommended the creation of a series of policy-forming councils. President McDonald shared these fears and established three councils. These were the Academic Council, the Council on Student Affairs, and a re-vamped Executive Committee.

The Academic Council was comprised of the Dean of Faculties as chairman, the Dean of the Graduate School, the three deans of the undergraduate colleges, the Dean of Administration, and three teaching faculty members, one to be elected by each of the undergraduate college faculties. The President of the University was also an ex-officio member of the Council.

The President defined the functions of the Academic Council, as follows:

(It) will review all major decisions on academic policy that arise from the respective colleges, will consider any additional matters related to curriculum and instruction . . . and will formulate definite recommendations for the academic policy of the University . . .With the approval of the Dean of Faculties, the recommendations of the Academic Council will be transmitted to the President.

The Council on Student Affairs was comprised of the Dean of Administration as chairman, the Director of Admissions, the Dean of Students, the Dean of Women, the Counselor of New Students, the Dean of Faculties and three teaching faculty members, one to be elected by each of the undergraduate college faculties. The President of the University and the President of the Student Council also were ex-officio members. A year later, four student members (one from each class) were added. The President's outline stated:

> The Council on Student Affairs will consider any and all matters of University policy related to student life and will make recommendations for University policy in this area . . . With the approval of the Dean of Administration, the recommendations of the Council on Student Affairs will be transmitted to the President.

The Executive Committee had, for many years, been (with the President) the chief policy-making body of the University. Under the new plan, its title was changed to Executive Council, and it was defined as an institution-wide, policy-developing agency for any matters that did not come directly under the responsibility of either of the other two councils. Its membership had, in the past, included only administrative officers of the University, but it was now enlarged to include the business manager and three teaching faculty members to be elected by the three undergraduate faculties. From the start, there was considerable confusion as to what questions were to be considered by this Council. As a result, it was dropped in 1955-56.

In September, 1955, the President announced a number of revisions in the administrative organization. The chief feature of this announcement was the identification of five major areas of administration, each with an administrative head. These were: (1) the Academic Area under the Provost, (2) the Area of Student Life and Services, under the Director of Student Life and Services, (3) the Area of Financial Administration under the Business Manager, (4) the Area of Residential and Plant Operations, under the Director of Residential and Plant Operations, and (5) the Area of Public Relations under the Vice-President. The latter officer also continued to serve as the assistant and consultant to the President on all matters related to the development of the University.

University Senate and Faculty Council

The new administrative organization made it necessary to revise the constitution of the University Senate, which had been adopted in 1949. Early in President McDonald's administration, the Senate appointed a committee to study this problem and to propose a new constitution. After discussion and some amendments by the Senate, the recommendations of this committee were approved by that body and by a vote of the entire faculty. The new constitution was approved by the Board of Trustees at its meeting on June 5, 1953, and became the official charter of the University faculty.

The new charter differed from the 1949 constitution in several ways. One of the chief criticisms of the latter documents was that it deprived the faculty members, who were not also members of the Senate, of the opportunity to discuss and become fully informed concerning University problems and policies. It is true that it provided that complete minutes of the Senate should be sent to all faculty members, but this was not thought to be enough. President McDonald was aware of this situation and, in his 1951 outline of the new administrative organization, stated that there were a number of other problems that should receive early attention. Among these, he mentioned the role of the general faculty in university administration.

As a result of these criticisms, the new charter included provisions concerning the University faculty, composed of all full-time employees of the University holding faculty rank. This faculty was to meet with the Senate and have the right to participate in its discussions.

The organization and functions of the University Senate remained much the same as before, but membership was somewhat more restricted. Whereas the previous constitution of May, 1949, included assistant professors who were members of the Senate before March, 1949, the new charter confined the membership to professors and associate professors who had attained permanent tenure. The new charter stated:

> Broadly defined, it shall be the function of the University Senate to increase the effectiveness of the University Faculty by providing a smaller body composed of those members who, because of the amount and quality of their preparation and service, as evidenced by appointment to higher academic ranks, are best qualified to act for the Faculty.

In addition to its former duties of studying University problems and making recommendations to the administration, the Senate was designated by the charter to elect certain members of the three councils and certain faculty members to standing committees.

The new charter retained a Faculty Council to act as the executive committee of the University faculty and Senate. The Faculty Council also was to plan the agenda for the meetings of these bodies. The members of the Council, as provided in the 1953 charter, were the President of the University as presiding officer, the Dean of Faculties, the Dean of Administration, and six faculty members, three elected by the Senate and three by the undergraduate college faculties.

The newly organized Faculty Council, at its first meeting in the fall of 1953, approved the appointment by the President of the University of a secretary of the faculty who would also serve as secretary of the Faculty Council. This appointment was to be made from the elected faculty members of the Council, and Lloyd A. Helms, Professor of Economics, was the first appointee.

The faculty charter was revised in 1954 and again in 1956. These revisions were largely the result of changes that had taken place in the administrative organization of the University. In 1954 (with the resignation of the author), the position of Dean of Faculties was discontinued. A year later, a similar office was established with the title of Provost. At the same time, the title of Dean of Administration was changed to Vice-President. The Executive Council (as we have noted) was discontinued in 1955-56, and the Faculty Council was enlarged. The new Council was composed of the President of the University as chairman, the Secretary of the Faculty, the Vice-President, the Provost, and nine faculty members. Six of the latter were elected by the Senate, and the rest by the three undergraduate faculties.

During the latter part of President McDonald's administration, the University faculty and Senate, and the Faculty Council, became relatively inactive and seldom met. This was due largely to the failure of the Council, which was the executive committee of the other two organizations, to function effectively. One reason for this was the fact that the charter made the President of the University the chairman and gave no specific authority to this body to act on its own initiative. It is true that the charter did provide for a chairman pro tem, selected by the elected members. This officer was to preside in the absence of the President. The chairman pro-tem also was to be responsible, with the President, for planning the agenda of Council meetings, and for doing everything possible to render the work of the Council more effective. This last provision was certainly broad enough to have enabled the chairman pro-tem to call meetings and plan agendas on his own initiative. However, this was not done, and the Council, Senate, and faculty met less and less frequently.

There was another and more general cause for the faculty's loss of interest in the Senate. This was the fact that the faculty had grown too rapidly. In 1961 almost half the members had been on the staff for five years or less. This was too large an increase in too short a period to enable the faculty really to get acquainted and to learn to work together. This rapid growth had another effect. Since membership in the Senate was confined to professors and associate professors who had attained tenure, approximately two-thirds of the faculty were not members. As a result, the Senate no longer represented the majority of the faculty. The newer members felt that they were discriminated against, and were only second-rate faculty members. This was unfortunate at this time, since the majority of the newer faculty members were well-trained, capable, ambitious, and anxious to contribute to the development of the University.

The failure of the machinery for faculty participation in University administration was undoubtedly the greatest weakness in President McDonald's administration, and was one of the principal causes of the events that finally led to his resignation. The machinery was there and, in spite of all its weaknesses, it could have been made to function effectively. The blame for its failure to do so must be shared by the administration and the faculty. The faculty did finally make the attempt to remedy the situation. In April of 1961, the Senate met as the result of a faculty petition, and appointed a committee to draw up a constitution for a new Senate, with its own executive committee, to serve as a free deliberative body with the right to determine its own agenda.

The events that followed and which finally led to President McDonald's resignation might have been prevented, if these proposed reforms had been incorporated in the 1956 charter. Similar provisions had been included by the committee that drew up the original draft of the 1956 charter, but they had been removed before it was approved by the President and trustees.

Student Government

Student government underwent a number of changes during these years. The newly formed Council on Student Affairs, which included four student members, became the principal forum for the expression of student sentiment, and the Student Senate diminished in importance and effectiveness. In addition to serving on the Council on Student Affairs, students participated in the administration of most student activities through membership on many other committees. The catalog of February, 1954, stated:

> The Student Court is vested by the Board of Trustees with judicial authority in student traffic violations and other cases by authorization of the President of the University.

In 1959 a new Student Body Organization was formed including executive officers, a student cabinet, a student council, and the student court. The purpose of this organization, according to the 1959-60 catalog, was as follows:

> . . . to provide students with wide opportunities for responsible participation in the government of the University community and to give the University the advantage of student deliberation and experience in arriving at the soundest possible policies and practices with respect to matters which relate directly and uniformly to all students enrolled at the University.

This organization was quite active in trying to control and direct the student demonstrations of 1961, although it was not responsible for their outbreak.

Fees and Expenses

The cost of a year at Bowling Green State University continued to rise during the decade from 1951 to 1961. The registration fee, which had been $45 a semester in 1951-52, was $100 a semester in 1961-62. The miscellaneous fees (activity, health, library, University Union, etc.) which totaled $29.50 a semester in 1951-52, were replaced by a single incidental fee which was $100 for the same period. Thus total fees (for residents of Ohio) rose from $75.50 to $200 a semester. The nonresident fee, which was $37.50 a semester in 1951-52, had increased to $175 for the same period by 1960-61. This was in addition to the registration and incidental fees.

Charges for board and room also increased from $189 a semester in

1951-52 to $350 in 1961-62. The 1951-52 catalog estimated the total necessary cost of study at Bowling Green State University (for a resident of Ohio) at $291.50 a semester, or approximately $600 for a year. The 1961-62 catalog gave no estimate, but, on a similar basis, the total cost was approximately $600 a semester, or $1,200 a year. This represented an increase of 100 per cent. Costs at Bowling Green were now comparable to those at other state-supported universities in Ohio.

The increase in the cost of a year at Bowling Green State University resulted from several factors. Charges for board and room had to be raised, because of the expense of building new dormitories and the increased cost of food and services. Fees had to be increased because state appropriations were not sufficient to cover faculty salaries, employees' wages, and other educational expenses. The General Assembly, in considering the budget requests of the state universities, insisted that fees at Bowling Green be put on the same level as those at the other state-assisted universities.

There was another reason in addition to those mentioned above. This was a radical change in the attitude of the administration of the University. President Williams, the first president, wanted to furnish a good college education at the lowest possible cost. President McDonald, on the other hand, put the emphasis on quality. However, because of good financial management, costs at Bowling Green State University continued to compare favorably with those at other state universities.

A New Alumni Association

During President Prout's last years in office, a number of differences concerning policies and functions rose between the Alumni Association and the administration of the University. These continued and became even worse during the first part of President McDonald's term of office. Finally, President McDonald appointed a Committee on Alumni Organization and Relationships to study the problem and make recommendations. This committee was composed of Frank J. Prout, President Emeritus of the University; Elden T. Smith, Director of Student Life and Services; Florence Currier, Dean of Women; Lloyd A. Helms, Secretary of the Faculty; Ralph G. Harshman, Vice-President of the University; and six alumni members. After considerable study, the committee recommended the formation of a new alumni group and proposed a constitution. This constitution was approved by the Board of Trustees on February 8, 1957.

At first the new organization was opposed by the old group, which had incorporated under the title of Bowling Green State University Alumni Association, Inc. Finally, however, in the interests of peace and the future development of the University, the old group decided to dissolve in favor of the new.

Organizations and Activities

Bowling Green State University always held the philosophy that a college education should provide for the social as well as for the mental development of its students. To this end, the University, from its beginning as a normal school, always provided a wide range of social and cultural organizations and activities at a minimum expense to the student. This policy was continued under President McDonald.

The catalog published in March, 1961, contained the following statement:

Studies come first, always, but they are not the whole of a college education. While a college career should most certainly mean intellectual development, it should also be the means for further social and personal development.

To this end Bowling Green State University provides an extensive social and cultural program. While the program includes parties and dances, it goes much further by giving the students a great range of opportunities for experience in working with others (and), in assuming leadership for student activities.

Cultural opportunities expanded. The same catalog March, 1961, contained the statement:

Students have an opportunity to hear noted musicians, symphonic orchestras and bands, lecturers and actors brought to the University each year through the Artist Series . . . In addition, the Department of Music provides a series of faculty and student recitals and concerts, the Department of Art sponsors a number of exhibits . . . and other departments and divisions . . . present cultural and informational programs.

Honorary, Departmental and Social Groups

The number of honorary, departmental and other student organizations increased during this period. The March, 1961, catalog listed 27 honor societies, 22 of which were national. In addition, it listed 44 departmental and other voluntary student organizations, 16 of which were national and 28 local.

The number of fraternities and sororities also increased. At the end of this period there were 11 sororities and 17 fraternities on campus. All of these, except one men's group, were national.

Speech, Publications, and Music Activities

The number of student activities, in connection with the instructional program of the University, also expanded. Students in the Speech Department received valuable experience in managing a radio station, in forensics and in dramatics. Student staffs, under the supervision of the Journalism Department, published the *B-G News,* twice a week and *The Key,* annually. The Music Department sponsored three choruses, two bands, the University Symphony Orchestra, two smaller orchestras, and several other vocal and instrumental ensembles.

Intramural and Intercollegiate Athletics

The Health and Physical Education Department, in addition to conducting the required courses for freshmen and sophomores, offered a wide variety (approximately 40) of intramural sports open to all students. It also carried on a program of intercollegiate athletics with teams in football, basketball, golf, tennis, swimming, track, cross-country, and hockey. Women's hockey and swimming teams competed with teams from other colleges and universities.

Bowling Green State University withdrew from the Ohio Athletic Conference during President Prout's administration. It continued to schedule games independently until 1952, when it joined the Mid-American Conference. The other members of this conference are Miami University, Ohio University, Kent State University, the University of Toledo, Western Michigan University, and Marshall University. Since joining, Bowling Green has won six championships in football, three in basketball, six in swimming, three in wrestling, and one each in golf and tennis.

There may be some difference of opinion, among educators and the public, about the place of an athletic program in the scheme of higher education. However, there can be no doubt about the role that athletics have played in the development of Bowling Green State University and in the gaining of national recognition. The latter point was deeply impressed upon the author when he was investigating possible candidates for the presidency of the University to succeed President Prout. One of the things that all of the men interviewed knew about the Bowling Green school was the fact that it had a strong basketball team and, in a few cases, this was the only thing they knew.

It is interesting to note how the educational and athletic development have closely paralleled each other, and it is sometimes hard to tell which was the cause and which the effect. In the early days the normal school was not considered worthy of membership in either the Ohio College Association or the Ohio Athletic Conference. As a result, its athletic teams had to seek competition elsewhere and, together with several other schools in somewhat the same position, to form a new conference. As the institution grew, both educationally and athletically, it was admitted to both of the above bodies, but was for a number of years the underdog in each. As time went on, Bowling Green rose to leadership in both organizations. Eventually, its athletic teams became too strong for the other members of the Ohio Conference and Bowling Green was again forced to seek stronger opponents. Finally, it joined the Mid-American Conference. This organization is now recognized as one of the strongest in the country, and Bowling Green is recognized as one of the strong state institutions of higher learning.

No discussion of the athletic program would be complete without the mention of several outstanding coaches.

Warren E. Steller contributed much to the development of the physical education program, both as an instructor and as a coach, particularly of football and basketball. During the 10 seasons he coached football (1924-34), his teams won 40 games, tied 19 and lost 21. His record was just as impressive in baseball, which he coached in 1925 and from 1928 to 1959. During that time, his teams won 217 games and lost 139. The baseball diamond is named in his honor.

In 1941 Robert H. Whittaker became head football coach and served for 14 years. He coached the track teams from 1941 to 1948, and again from 1956 to 1960. His football teams won 66 games, lost 50 and tied 8. In track his teams won 77 meets and lost 40. The new track is named in Mr. Whittaker's honor.

Harold W. Anderson came to Bowling Green in 1942 as head basketball coach, and his teams soon won national fame. They were invited to the National Invitational Tournament five times in six years and won three Mid-American championships. He is one of five major college coaches whose teams have won more than 500 victories. His all-time record (including his career before coming to Bowling Green) was 504 wins to 226 losses. In 1961 Harold Anderson was elected by the Helms Athletic Foundation to its Basketball Hall of Fame. The basketball court in Memorial Hall is named in his honor.

In 1955 Doyt L. Perry, a graduate of Bowling Green State University and a former football star, returned to his alma mater as head football coach. During the 10 years he served in this capacity, his teams made a record that brought him national recognition as one of the outstanding coaches of the country. His teams made the phenominal record of 77 wins, 11 losses and 5 ties. In 1965 Mr. Perry gave up his coaching duties and succeeded Harold Anderson as Director of Athletics. The new University stadium is named in his honor.

The 1960 football season was saddened by a tragic accident. On October 29 of that year, the Bowling Green Falcons defeated the California State Polytechnic Mustangs by a score of 50-6. The celebration, however, was soon ended, when the plane which was to take the Polytechnic team home to California crashed on takeoff from the Toledo Express Airport. Twenty-two were killed; 16 of these were members of the Cal Tech team. As soon as they recovered from the stunning shock, students at Bowling Green State University and the University of Toledo, as well as citizens of Bowling Green and Toledo, rallied to the aid of the survivors, and rendered them every assistance possible, financial and otherwise.

Golden Anniversary

During the 1959-60 school year, Bowling Green State University celebrated the golden anniversary of its founding. The program started at a keynote luncheon on homecoming day, October 10, 1959, with an address by President McDonald. This was followed by a series of five symposia throughout the year, on the humanities, business and education, the social sciences, science and mathematics, and education. Nationally known scholars and business leaders participated in these symposia. All were well attended by faculty, students, alumni, and friends of the University.

The anniversary events ended with a convocation on May 19, 1960, on the fiftieth anniversary of the day on which the act creating the University was signed. The speakers at the convocation were Michael V. DiSalle, Governor of Ohio, and Harlan H. Hatcher, President of the University of Michigan.

Automobile Regulations

At the end of President Prout's administration, male students could obtain permits for the operation of an automobile in Bowling Green, if they could establish a just need. Unmarried women students, however, could not secure such a permit. All this was soon changed. The catalog published in February, 1954, contained new regulations which permitted the operation of an automobile by any student regardless of sex, or of need. The only requirements were approval of parents or guardian, payment of a fee, possession of a driver's license, and evidence of paid-up insurance.

The above regulations remained unchanged during the rest of President McDonald's administration. The catalog of March, 1961, contained the following statement:

> The University recognizes that the use of automobiles is a part of the daily living of most Americans, and considers it a part of a student's education that he develop habits of responsible citizenship in this respect . . . (Therefore) the University permits any student to bring his automobile to the campus, if he and his parents feel that it is desirable for him to do so.

Drinking Regulations

The liberalization of the rules to permit any student to operate an automobile removed one of the principal causes of student unrest, which existed at the end of President Prout's administration. However, another source of strong discontent remained. This was the University's policy on drinking by students. The restrictions on the use of automobiles were lifted, but the regulations concerning the use of alcohol became more stringent.

The rules at the end of President Prout's administration simply stated that any student convicted of drunkness was eligible for dismissal from the

University. No change was made until 1953-54. The catalog announcements for that year defined possession or use of alcoholic beverages on the University campus, or on property owned or rented by the University, to be automatic withdrawal from the University, and stated that the student would be dropped from the University immediately.

The catalog published in February, 1957, extended the prohibition against the possession or consumption of alcoholic beverages to include "in connection with any event or activity engaged in by a University organization." It also stated that a student's being under the influence of alcoholic beverages was considered in violation of University regulations and would subject the student to dismissal. The effect of these two additions to the previous regulations was to extend the prohibition to off-campus as well as on-campus drinking.

The final changes came with the 1959-60 catalog which stated:

> Drinking of alcoholic beverages while a student is under the jurisdiction of the University is considered contrary to good citizenship in the University . . . The University expects each student to refrain from drinking alcoholic beverages in any form. Violation of this policy . . . may lead to dismissal.

This same catalog also stated that any student assisting in the transportation of alcoholic beverages in any form to an event or activity engaged in by a University-recognized organization would be immediately dismissed.

These regulations have been discussed here at some length, because of the bearing they had upon the unrest that broke out in student demonstrations toward the end of President McDonald's administration. These regulations were strongly resented by many members of the student body. This resentment was a major cause of the events that led to President McDonald's resignation in June, 1961.

Student Demonstrations

The first student riot occurred in 1949 during President Prout's administration. A similar disturbance took place early in the morning of Friday, May 24, 1957. The chief cause of the earlier riot was the resentment of the students against the strict regulations concerning the use of automobiles and alcoholic beverages. By 1957 the automobile restrictions were much more lenient, but those on the use of alcoholic beverages had become even more stringent.

Early in May of 1957, two fraternities were disciplined for serving alcoholic beverages at off-campus social events. This action was supported by the Interfraternity Council and by an editorial in the *B-G News*. No disturbances occurred at the time. However, at one o'clock in the morning of Friday, May 24, a torchlight demonstration started on campus protesting the action taken against these fraternities. About 300 students participated and, after touring the campus, congregated on East Wooster Street in front of the President's home. Since this street was also U. S. Highway 6, the crowd caused a traffic jam which soon extended for over half a mile. University police and city police, city firemen, sheriff's deputies, and state highway patrolmen were soon on the scene, and a series of fights started in which several received minor injuries. Finally, the traffic jam was broken by driving several large trucks through the crowd. By 3 a.m., the crowd dispersed and order was restored.

Although there were no other disturbances for several years, student unrest continued. The next outbreak occurred on Sunday, March 26, 1961, and was apparently unpremeditated. It started with a water fight on Fraternity Row, but a crowd gathered and finally moved to Wooster Street in front of Founders Quadrangle. Traffic on U. S. 6 was again blocked, and the state highway patrol had to disperse the crowd. No serious violence occurred, and the B-G News of March 28 called it an outbreak of spring fever.

Apparently, it was more than spring fever, since on the same day the B-G News article was published, the students staged a strike. Although a majority of students attended classes, a large number congregated on the campus in front of the Union and built bonfires to keep warm. The crowd was orderly and was addressed by a number of speakers from both the faculty and the student body. Some speakers urged the students to return to classes; others advocated continuing the strike. The number of absentees from classes gradually diminished, but the strike (and the demonstrations) continued until stopped by the spring recess, which started at noon on March 29.

During the demonstrations, students carried signs stating a variety of grievances, but no one seemed to know exactly what the strike was about. The Student Council held a hasty meeting to draw up a statement, but were unable to reach an agreement immediately. A committee was appointed, and made its report to the Student Council. On April 13, the Council issued a set of resolutions containing five grievances. The first of these concerned an automobile regulation which they claimed caused a person to be punished twice as a direct result of a single offense. The second complaint related to administrative attitudes. The Student Council stated that the attitudes and the actions of certain members of the University staff had kindled ill feelings among the student body. The third grievance concerned the alleged administrative censorship of the B-G News. The council asked that the "student editor's opinion on news editing and coverage . . . should be final with the advice of, not the consent of, the B-G News Director." The fourth resolution called for a revision of the rules governing class attendance. This included the recommendation that "the number of permissable, unauthorized class absences . . . be increased to twice the number of credit hours per course." The final grievance was against the regulations governing the conduct of women students. The Council pointed out the rules concerning men's calling hours, clothing and the disciplining of "women engaged in improper social behavior (petting) in front of residence halls" needed to be changed.

As in the 1957 disturbance, the rules concerning the use of alcoholic beverages were not included in the list of grievances. In spite of this, as was true in

1957, the newspapers and the general public still thought the drinking regulations were a major cause of student unrest. However, the fundamental causes were much more general and more basic than the use of alcohol or the five grievances enumerated by the Student Council. They were to be found in the changed character of the student body, and in the changed attitudes and standards of the public. In the early days, the students at Bowling Green came largely from families in which discipline was rather strict. The children took this as natural, and the parents wanted it continued in college. Their attitude was much like that of the father who told his boy, "If you get a whipping in school, I'll give you another when you get home." Social drinking was unknown in these families, and the parents wanted it prohibited in college. One reason that Bowling Green was chosen as the site of the new normal school was the fact that it was dry at that time.

By 1949, and to a greater extent by 1957 and 1961, all this had changed. The student body was now more cosmopolitan, and a fairly large percentage came from larger cities and from higher-income families. Standards had also changed. Family discipline was, in general, less strict, and the children were given much greater liberty. In many families, social drinking was a matter of course. When the children from these homes entered college, neither the parents nor the children could see any reason why they should not continue to have the same liberty to which they were accustomed.

The desire of students for greater freedom in all ways, and their demand for a larger voice in controlling not only their own conduct, but the administration of the University as well, was not confined to the Bowling Green campus. This is shown by the occurrence of similar (and often more serious) student demonstrations throughout the country. The distrubances at Bowling Green were undoubtedly influenced by the national movement.

By the end of President McDonald's administration, many members of the faculty sympathized with the students' desire for greater freedom, even if they did not approve of the means they used in attempting to achieve this end. Even those who (as a matter of principle) believed the University should act in loco parentis, and impose rather strict regulations on student conduct, were beginning to doubt if such controls could be enforced much longer, in light of the public's attitude and the growing size of the University.

Faculty Morale

Faculty morale, in spite of the low salaries, was high at the end of President Prout's administration. After many years, and many attempts, the faculty had finally achieved unity of purpose, loyalty to the University (rather than to the teachers' college alone), and faith in its future as a strong, multiple-purpose state institution of higher learning. Most of its members were eager to share and participate in the future development which they foresaw.

This high morale continued during the first years of President McDonald's administration, since the faculty could see the great progress that was being made toward the realization of their hopes for the future. Faculty morale was strengthened further by very substantial immediate increases in salaries and promises of more in the future.

Unfortunately, a number of factors brought on a lowering of this morale before the end of President McDonald's term. Perhaps the most important of these was the rapid change in personnel, which was the unavoidable result of the up-grading of the faculty by weeding out the less qualified, and adding new members with better training. Of the 254 members of the teaching faculty in 1961, 147, or 58 per cent, joined the staff after 1951, and 113, or 45 per cent, after 1955. Put in a different way, over half of the faculty in 1961 had been at Bowling Green for less than 10 years, and almost half for less than five. This was too great a change in too short a time for the faculty to achieve a new unity and develop strong loyalties. Possibly greater efforts toward these ends could have been made by both faculty and administration, but, in any case, five (or even 10) years were too short a period.

There was a second, and very important cause of the lowered morale. This was the rapidly growing demand, by college faculties, for greater liberty, and for increased participation in the formation and administration of University policies. This paralleled the similar movement among students, and, like the student movement, was nation-wide in its scope. The administration of Bowling Green State University from the beginning was from the top down. The Act of May 10, 1910, which created the two new normal schools, gave the Boards of Trustees in connection with the presidents, the authority to employ a faculty, provide a course of study and proper equipment, and fix rates of tuition. Subsequent acts, changing the names and scopes of the two institutions, made no change in this respect. The only authority given to the faculty, by law, was the provision in the Act of March, 1929: "On the recommendation of the faculty, the board of trustees may confer . . . honorary degrees." In practice the trustees of the Bowling Green institution delegated much of their authority to the President, but at no time, prior to 1951, was there any delegation of specific powers to the faculty.

Under President McDonald's administration, the faculty had a much greater part than ever before in determining University policies. This was the result of faculty membership on the important councils, which we have already described. The University faculty and Senate furnished further opportunities for study, discussion, and recommendations concerning matters of policy and administration. Imperfect as it was considered to be by some faculty members, the fact remains that the machinery existed for greater faculty participation in, and contributions to, the administration of the University. The machinery existed, but it was not fully used. The responsibility for this situation lay as much with the faculty as with the administration. One important factor was the lack of proper communication between faculty and President.

Faculty Petitions

The resentment of a number of faculty members against what they considered to be a one-man administration was, without question, the major cause of the events that led up to President McDonald's resignation. Signs of faculty unrest had existed for some time, and some of the faculty, apparently, were only waiting for a good opportunity to voice their grievances and demands. This opportunity came in the spring of 1961, when the administration announced that a faculty member in the last year of his probationary period would not be re-employed for the following year. This action of the administration led to a series of petitions from the faculty. Some of these supported the President, but others asked the administration to rescind its action, and to employ the faculty member for the following year, thus giving him tenure. Those who signed the latter petitions claimed that the action of the administration violated the University tenure regulations, both in spirit and in fact. This controversy is too recent, and the emotions aroused on both sides were too violent, to make it possible to judge fairly the merits of this dispute, or of the particular case that triggered the explosion. The important fact is that it was one of the major causes of the events which followed.

President McDonald Resigns

At the meeting of the Board of Trustees held on June 24, 1961, President McDonald submitted his resignation as President, to take effect on September 1, 1961. At the same meeting, President McDonald recommended that Dr. Ralph G. Harshman be appointed acting president, effective September 1. The trustees accepted the resignation and recommendation, and Dr. Harshman was duly elected.

Dr. Harshman was well-qualified for the position to which he was elected, and was also well-acquainted with the problems confronting the University. He had been on the faculty since 1936, Dean of the College of Business Administration from 1937 to 1951, and Dean of Administration and Vice President for a number of years. The University was indeed fortunate to have an individual of Dr. Harshman's ability and experience to take over the presidency in this emergency. At the time of President McDonald's election in 1951, the faculty committee recommended three individuals to the trustees, and one of these was Dr. Harshman. He was eliminated at that time, since the trustees had adopted the policy of considering no member of the faculty for the presidency.

Summary of President McDonald's Administration

The building of a great university requires the cooperation of all concerned: the governing body, the president and administration, the faculty, and the students, all working toward a common end and with full respect for, and faith in, each other. This united effort did not exist at the end of President McDonald's term in office. In all other respects, however, his administration was an outstanding success.

The growth and development of the University in the brief span of 10 years was truly remarkable. On-campus enrollments grew from 4,235 in 1950-51 to 6,229 in 1960-61, and would have increased much more, if dormitory space had been available. Off-campus services also increased. The branch at Sandusky was re-opened, and new branches were started in Bryan, Fremont and Fostoria. Summer school offerings were increased, and made more varied and attractive. As a result, summer attendance rose from 1,074 in 1950-51 to 4,751 in 1960-61.

The faculty grew more in quality than in size. In 1950-51 the full-time teaching faculty numbered 233. In 1960-61 the corresponding number was 252. Only 22 per cent of the full-time teaching faculty held the doctor's degree in 1950-51, while in 1960-61 the figure was 61 per cent. The increase in faculty qualifications was paralleled by an even greater increase in faculty salaries. Whereas, in 1950-51, salaries at Bowling Green were the lowest of any of the four sister-institutions, by the end of the 1954-55 school year, they were the highest. They were so high, indeed, as to be embarassing to the other institutions. Many, including the author, regard the increase in faculty qualifications and salaries as the greatest service of President McDonald's administration to Bowling Green State University. Certainly a strong university is impossible without a strong faculty, and a strong faculty can not be built and maintained without a salary scale high enough to attract and keep well-qualified and outstanding faculty members.

Another of President McDonald's great contributions was the building of an adequate administrative staff, and the creation of an effective administrative organization. In no area was this more needed than in that of finances. During President Prout's administration, systematic planning of expenditures had often been impossible. He was faced with a series of emergency needs often without the necessary funds to meet them. This had forced a policy of robbing Peter to pay Paul. By the time President McDonald assumed office, the sudden emergencies were mostly over, and it was possible to set up an organization and plan for more systematic and efficient administration of the University finances. President McDonald was unusually well qualified to perform this task, but it was so large that, even with the able assistance of Ervin J. Kreischer, business manager, it occupied a great deal of his time and thought. This probably was one factor that caused him to lose touch with the faculty.

We have noted that the organization for the administration of the academic and student personnel programs was seriously understaffed when President McDonald took office, and that one of his first acts was to approve the appointment of a Dean of Faculties and a Dean of Administration to head these two areas. At the same time, assistant deans were appointed to relieve the deans of the three undergraduate colleges of part of their heavy loads. The machinery for faculty participation in University administration was also improved by the creation of the policy-forming councils and revisions of the faculty charter. It is true that most of these changes had been either made, or recommended, before President McDonald took office, but they received his approval and support. The failure of some of this machinery to function as effectively as had been hoped was not entirely the fault of the President.

Great progress also was made in the instructional program of the University. The undergraduate offerings were refined and extended, and Schools of Journalism and Music were started. The Graduate School was greatly strengthened and a Ph.D. program was started. As a necessary aid to the development of the academic program, library facilities were improved both in quality and in size. The number of books and documents almost doubled, from 188,000 in 1951 to more than 330,000 in 1961.

The growth in the fields summarized above was paralleled by a similar growth in physical facilities. During this decade the last of the temporary buildings of the war and post-war years were removed, or destroyed. Eight new buildings and an addition to one old building were constructed. Two other buildings were completely remodeled. One other building was under construction and four more were being planned. Major campus improvements were made, both above and below ground, and approximately 600 acres were added to the campus. The total cost of all these physical improvements was approximately $35 million. This development of the physical plant was, to many, the most important growth of the decade from 1951 to 1961. At least it was the obvious and most spectacular development. By the end of this period, the very serious shortage in housing that existed at the end of President Prout's administration had been overcome. This, alone, was major achievement.

Other, somewhat less important, accomplishments could be listed, but these are enough to show that during the 10 years of President McDonald's administration, the University made greater progress than in any previous decade.

The best way to know any man is by his deeds, and President McDonald's have already been told. However, in order really to understand President McDonald's administration, its many achievements, and the disturbances at the end, it is necessary to know something of his personal characteristics. Since he became a controversial figure, anything that is written here will be criticized, and some may accuse the writer of prejudice. All that the author can say is, "This is the man as I knew him."

First and foremost, President McDonald was a man of principle. He decided all questions in terms of what he considered to be right or wrong. The question was always, "What is right?" and never, "What is expedient?" or "What is good public relations?" He was incapable of compromise where principles were involved. One illustration of this was his attitude toward the American Association of University Women. During Dr. Prout's administration, Bowling Green State University and its women graduates had been interested in obtaining the approval of this organization. Apparently negotiations were nearing a successful conclusion at the time President McDonald assumed the presidency. However, the picture soon changed and negotiations were dropped, since President McDonald felt that the AAUW should not act as an accrediting agency. Great pressure was brought to bear to induce him to modify his position, but he did not change. It was very bad public relations, but it was a matter of principle.

President McDonald was highly capable, and was justifiably confident in his own ability and judgment. This led many to feel that he was intolerant of the ideas of others and that he could never be convinced that he was wrong. The author did not find this to be the case. President McDonald did not like yes men, but respected and relied on those who had ideas of their own and were willing to fight for them. He was a hard man to convince, but he could be convinced, but only by cold reason and logic.

He was a perfectionist and a man of the highest standards. Good was never enough; he demanded the best. His ambition for Bowling Green was not that it should become one of the best, but the best. He was not satisfied with bringing faculty salaries at Bowling Green to a level with those of the other state institutions; he wanted them to be the highest. He succeeded in this, but at the expense of much criticism from the other schools.

Last, but not least, President McDonald was a hard worker, and put in incredibly long hours. It is often said of a man that his work comes first. With President McDonald it did not come first, but first, last, and all the time. While at Bowling Green he had no other interests. All his time and all his thoughts were devoted to the betterment of Bowling Green State University. The term dedicated has been greatly overworked, trite, and often meaningless, but it accurately describes President McDonald. His life while at Bowling Green was truly dedicated to the betterment of the University.

Unfortunately these qualities, while they enabled him to make remarkable contributions to the University, did not serve to make him popular with students, faculty, citizens, or with the presidents of the other state universities. He did not court popularity and he did not win popularity. He built a university. The few who really knew him discovered that he had great personal charm and human warmth, but unfortunately he was too busy to show this side to many.

CHAPTER ELEVEN

The Administration Of Ralph G. Harshman 1961-1963

EACH PRESIDENT of the institution now known as Bowling Green State University was confronted, upon assuming office, with a different set of problems. In the case of President Williams, it was the task of building an entirely new institution. With President Prout, it was the strengthening and developing of the programs already started, and the meeting of the many problems arising during the war and post-war periods. To President McDonald fell the tasks of expanding, improving and systematizing the business and educational administration, strengthening the academic program, building a faculty of real university caliber for graduate and undergraduate instruction, raising faculty salaries to a level high enough to make this possible, and gaining national recognition of Bowling Green as a strong and rapidly developing state university.

President Harshmann's tasks were two-fold. In the first place, he had to carry on and develop the existing programs and operations, and to do this in such a way as to prevent any serious interruptions or delays. This in itself was a tremendous task, but it was not all. As we have seen, for a variety of reasons, both faculty and student morale were at an all-time low at the end of President McDonald's term in office. The new President, therefore, had the task of building a new spirit of cooperation, and a renewed pride in the University, faith in its future, and confidence in its administration.

Trustees Committees

The members of the Board of Trustees were, by this time, fully aware of the serious problems confronting the University with respect to faculty and student morale. As a result, at their meeting on June 24, 1961, they appointed an Advisory Committee of three men to make a study of student, faculty and administrative relationships. The members of this committee were from outside Bowling Green, and were well known in the field of higher education. On September 23 of the same year, this committee submitted two reports, one for the press, and one confidential and not to be published.

192

After receiving and studying the reports of the Advisory Committee, the trustees on November 3, 1961, authorized the appointment of three committees, a Faculty Study Committee, a Committee on Student Affairs, and a Committee to Screen Presidential Candidates. The first two committees were to study and make recommendations concerning the improvement of faculty and and student government and relationships. The third committee was in recognition of the fact that Dr. Harshmann was approaching retirement age, and all concerned, including Dr. Harshman, felt that the search for his successor should start immediately.

The Faculty Study Committee

At first, this committee was composed of 11 faculty members. Later, due to the resignation of one member from the faculty, this number was reduced to 10. In addition, five subcommittees were created to study different phases of the general problem. Each of these subcommittees consisted of two members of the central committee, plus three or more elected from the faculty at large.

This committee submitted its final report to President Harshman on February 1, 1963. At its meeting held on October 4, 1963, the Board of Trustees, on the recommendation of the new President, Dr. William T. Jerome, III, gave general approval of this report, without binding itself to accept all of its details. Since the work of this committee was carried out during Dr. Harshman's administration, with his support and cooperation, the major features of its report are summarized in this chapter.

Reasons for Faculty Discontent

Years of experience as a college teacher and administrator have led the author to believe that a certain amount of faculty unrest is both normal and beneficial. However, by the end of President McDonald's administration, faculty discontent had gone far beyond this stage, and had reached a point that seriously endangered the immediate future of the University.

This situation was undoubtedly due to a number of causes, but by far the most important was the feeling that the administration of the University was too highly concentrated in the office of the President. This concentration was a natural result of the history of the University. In the beginning, when the institution was very small, the President was largely a one-man administrator. There was no actual delegation of power and authority, although there was a great deal of informal consultation and discussion with both individual faculty members, and with the faculty as a whole. As the institution grew, there was less and less of this informal participation. From time to time, as we have seen, additional administrative officers were appointed, various committees and councils were organized, and machinery was set up which was intended to give the faculty a greater opportunity to participate in the discussion of University policies and administrative functions. Although all of these brought about some decentralization, the government of the University still remained largely in the hands of one man, the President.

During President McDonald's administration, with the addition to the faculty of many members, a large number of whom were from institutions with greater decentralization of power, there was a growing conviction that Bowling Green State University was too large for any one man to administer, and that future development demanded that the abilities of the entire staff be used in policy-forming, in planning, and in administration. Considerable progress, as we have seen, was made in this direction during President McDonald's term in office, including the inauguration of faculty councils and the adoption of a new faculty charter. However, as we have also seen, these had failed to bring about the degree of decentralization that many faculty members regarded as both desirable and necessary for the future development of the University.

Report of Faculty Study Committee

In the introduction to its report, the committee stated nine guiding principles which they had followed in its preparation. Two of these dealt with the decentralization of administrative functions. These were as follows:

> That there must be within the university organization clear delegation of authority to area administrators, deans, department chairmen, and others, to exercise powers commensurate with their offices, functions, and duties; this means, in effect, that there must be decentralization of authority in the decision-making process to the level closest to problems as they arise.

> That in a mature, well-run university, much of the academic administration, from the department level, to the level of the academic deans, and to the Office of the Provost should be conducted in orderly fashion without much direct involvement of the Office of the President.

A second principle was stated as follows:

> That faculty participation in the process of screening and evaluating key administrative personnel is fundamental to good faculty-administration relations in a mature university.

We have already seen that the faculty was asked by the Board of Trustees to participate in the evaluation and selection of a new president at the time President McDonald was chosen for that office. The faculty for a number of years had had some part in the selection of department chairmen, and the committee felt that such procedures should be extended to all key administrative personnel.

Some of the most important recommendations of the committee had to do with the University Senate. In the past, membership in this body depended upon rank or office, and its functions were largely confined to studying, discussing, and advising. Throughout most of its history, the President of the University was the Senate chairman. The committee report contained the following statement:

> In this report, a definite stand is taken that a Senate shall be organized as a body to represent the faculty and to include specified administrative officers, for the purpose of policy making in certain limited areas . . . and for the further purpose of making studies and offering recommendations to administrative officers and the Board of Trustees on any matters germane to the academic welfare of the institution and the faculty.

The committee report listed eight specific areas in which the Senate should have power to frame policy, and stated that studies and recommendations may be made on the request of the administration or any full-time faculty member.

It was recommended that membership in the Senate should no longer depend entirely on rank or office, but that the faculty members should be elected by the faculties of the Graduate School and of each of the undergraduate colleges. The majority of the committee believed that this change would result in greater efficiency and interest by reducing the size of the body, and by confining its membership to faculty members better qualified for and more interested in the overall problems of the University.

For many years, the faculty had felt the need of some recognized and approved method of communication with the Board of Trustees. On two occasions, in the history of the institution, the Board had asked for faculty cooperation. The first of these was when it asked President Prout to appoint a faculty committee to work with the Board in choosing his successor. The second was the appointment of the three faculty committees on November 3, 1963, and this had followed the confidential report of the Advisory Committee.

The faculty seldom took the initiative in communicating with individual trustees, or with the Board as a whole, and it did so only in emergencies, and with a feeling that it was highly irregular and might even be dangerous. On a few occasions, requests for a hearing before the Board were refused. One of these was when the question of a successor to President Williams was under consideration. The first time (as far as the author knows) that representatives of the faculty were invited to meet with the trustees to discuss University problems was at the end of President McDonald's term in office, after the faculty had resorted to petitions, and had requested a hearing.

Obviously some better and approved method of communication was needed. To meet this need the committee recommended that:

> When deemed advisable, the Senate may . . . address . . . communications to the Board of Trustees, provided that all such communications be transmitted to the Trustees through the Office of the President. In cases where the President is not in sympathy with the communication, he shall forward it to the Board with his statement

of disapproval, or he shall return it to the Senate with a written statement of his objections. If a communication is returned to the Senate, the Senate may . . . decide to resubmit the communication to the Trustees . . . Following such action, the President is under obligation to submit the communication . . . to the Trustees for a final determination.

Improvement in Faculty Morale

The two years of President Harshman's administration brought about a great inprovement in faculty morale. There were several reasons for this change. One of the most important was the realization, by the faculty, that the Board of Trustees was aware of and alarmed over the existing situation, and was trying to do something to bring about more pleasant and more efficient faculty-administration relations.

Another important factor was their confidence in President Harshman. They felt that through his years of service at Bowling Green State University, both as teacher and administrator, he understood the existing problems, and shared the faculty belief that the future development of the University required some decentralization of administration through the delegation of duties, responsibilities, and authority.

Although the final approval of the committee report by the trustees did not come during his administration, President Harshman started the process of decentralization by delegating more authority to the deans, and by inviting faculty cooperation in the selection of department chairmen and new deans for the Colleges of Liberal Arts and Education.

The Committee on Student Affairs

The second of the three important committees authorized by the trustees at their meeting of November 3, 1961, was the Committee on Student Affairs. This committee was composed of 16 members, six from the administrative staff, four from the teaching faculty, and six from the student body. The six students were all seniors. After a number of meetings of the whole committee, it was divided into six subcommittees, each of which investigated a particular aspect of student affairs. Each subcommittee included at least one student member. After completing their studies and discussions, the subcommittees reported to the committee as a whole. The final report was submitted to the trustees on May 15, 1962, and was approved by them (in general, not in detail) on January 10, 1964.

Reasons for Student Unrest

The Committee on Student Affairs was authorized by the trustees to study the entire field of student and University relationships, to attempt to determine the causes of student discontent, and to make recommendations for the betterment of student regulations and student-administration relationships. The committee was set up following the disturbances that occurred in the last year of President McDonald's administration, and after the trustees received the report of the Advisory Committee.

In order that the reader may better understand the existing situation and the recommendations of the Committee on Student Affairs, it seems advisable to summarize here some of the major causes for student discontent. This discontent did not begin during President McDonald's term in office. It had been gradually building up for some time, and had its origin in changing conditions and attitudes throughout the country and in northwestern Ohio.

Historically, two widely differing philosophies existed in America concerning the relationship of a college or university to its students. One of these may be summarized in the statement that the university should act in loco parentis. College students, the argument runs, are still immature, and need guidance and control. The other philosophy holds that college students of today are no longer children, and that they should, as part of their education, be permitted freedom to govern their own conduct, make their own decisions, and even make their own mistakes. All of this is a necessary part of the process of growing up.

The first of these two philosophies prevailed from the beginning of the institution. For many years, it was in agreement with the thinking of the parents of its students and with the students themselves, since most of the latter had grown up under rather strict discipline at home. In recent years, both home conditions and the attitudes of parents and the public have been rapidly changing. Young people of today have had more contact with life and are more mature than in the past. They are permitted more freedom at home, and both students and many parents believe that this freedom should be continued (and even increased) in college. The basic cause of students' discontent was their feeling that there should be fewer regulations governing student conduct, that the regulations should be less strict, and that the students themselves should participate both in their formulation and in their enforcement. It should again be noted, in passing, that this demand for greater freedom and participation was not confined to the Bowling Green campus, but was part of a national movement, as witnessed by the many demonstrations and disturbances on college campuses throughout the nation.

Committee On Student Affairs

In general, the report of the Committee on Student Affairs indicates that it felt that the organization and administration of student affairs on the Bowling Green campus were, in general, satisfactory and that no major changes were needed. This attitude may have been partly because the committee was heavily weighted with faculty members and administrative officers. There were 10 of these as compared to six student members. It is more probable, however, that their judgment was sound, and that student unrest rose largely from three causes: (1) the ever present (and often healthy) tendency of college students to criticize the existing order, (2) the lack of understanding of the part that students were actually taking in the administration of student activities, and, (3) their failure to take full advantage of the machinery provided for student participation.

The whole committee and the various subcommittees did, however, make some minor recommendations with respect to the machinery for student participation. Most of their recommendations had to do with the methods of obtaining more effective use of the existing machinery, and with the development of a better understanding of this machinery and the opportunities it afforded for student participation.

With respect to student government, the committee stated:

The Committee feels that the Grant of Powers for Student Participation in University Government is largely a cogently constructed and clearly stated document. It appears to the committee that if all individuals and groups involved . . . follow in good faith the spirit as well as the letter set forth in it, there is no need for change of the basic document.

The committee has found, likewise, that the Constitution of the Student Council and the Student Council Bills are fundamentally sound; however, a few . . . changes seem desirable.

Only a few of the specific recommendations of the committee need be considered here. At the time of the student disturbances in the spring of 1961, the *B-G News* was the target of considerable criticism. This was to the effect that it was a laboratory for the Journalism Department, rather than an organ for the expression of student views, and that it was subject to censorship by the faculty advisor and the administration of the University. The committee stated that the advisor had not acted, and did not act, as a censor. The committee felt that the *B-G News* currently was a free press. However, they suggested several changes to produce a better understanding on the part of both students and faculty. These included the creation of a Publications Committee in order that there would be no implication of Journalism Department control. This committee would assume final responsibility for the *B-G News*. They recommended that authority over the paper should be vested in the editor-in-chief with the cooperation of the editorial board, and that reviewing authority should be vested in the Publications Committee.

The three-man investigating committee appointed by the Board of Trustees specifically instructed the Student Affairs Committee to study the University Union, since there had been much criticism of its operation. This criticism was largely three-fold: (1) the students did not have enough part in planning its operations and activities, (2) the activities were too cultural and educational and did not consider the interests of the students, and (3) too many outside organizations were scheduled to use Union facilities. As a result of these criticisms, the committee suggested a number of changes. They recommended that the Union Activities Council (composed of students and faculty members and administrative personnel) should establish standards and policies to guide the Union activities program, and serve as an advisory group to the Director of the Student Union. They also recommended that student activities and other University activities should be given priority in the scheduling of University Union facilities, or that a quota should be established that limits the number of non-University activities held in the University Union.

The committee also emphasized that the enrollment at the University was rapidly outgrowing the facilities of the Union, and stated that expansion of the University Union facilities or substitute facilities for student activities and social life must be given primary consideration.

One of the major criticisms voiced by the students was to the effect that the regulations governing student conduct were too stringent; that the students had no voice in determining the regulations; and that their enforcement was too strict. The report of the sub-committee on discipline contains the following statement:

> We, as a committee, feel that student discipline cases by and large have been well handled by the various responsible administrative officers. However, the general attitude toward discipline might well be improved through a clearer statement in printing of disciplinary policy and by the creation of a student-faculty court on discipline or a university committee on student discipline.

The report of the committee emphasized the fact that the students already had a large part in carrying out the disciplinary functions of the University. It mentioned the Student Court, the Interfraternity Council, the Panhellenic Council, the Association of Women Students, and the judicial boards in the men's residences, all of which would exercise judicial functions.

The committee included a paragraph concerning the drinking regulations, which had, for years, been a major source of student discontent. They did not recommend any change in these regulations, but stated:

> The policies regarding drinking should be made clear to the entering student . . . from the catalogue or handbook. Policy implementation should parallel the rules as stated.

The subcommittee report ended by pointing out the need for continuing study of the desires and needs of the students regarding discipline. It enumerated three specific problems needing study:

> Extension of hours for women with regard to weekends and during exam week; keeping dormitory regulations at a minimum without jeopardizing study and rest hours; and emphasizing need for proper moral decorum on campus.

Improvement in Student Morale

The morale of the student body improved greatly during President Harshman's two years in office. Some changes were made in the regulations governing student conduct, but this was not the main cause of the improvement in the relations between the administration and the student body. The work of the Committee on Student Affairs was a factor, since it showed the student body that the trustees, administration, and faculty were interested in their problems and were making an effort to improve relationships. The presence of student members on this committee also gave the students some degree of the participation in determining policies and regulations which they so strongly desired. All of these helped, but they did not constitute the greatest reason for improved conditions. This was, without question, the confidence the students had in President Harshman. They knew that he had always been interested in the students and their activities, and they felt that he would consider their problems with understanding and sympathy. It was not the changes that were made in the regulations, or even the hope of further changes in the future, that brought about the improvement. It was rather the feeling of the students that the regulations were being enforced more reasonably. Perhaps the University was still acting in loco parentis, but, in the opinion of the students, it was a more understanding, benevolent, and liberal parent.

Campus and Buildings

The growth and improvement in the physical facilities of the University during President McDonald's administration continued without interruption and at an accelerated pace. Three new buildings and an addition to one old one were constructed during President Harshman's administration. These were McDonald Quadrangle, a domitory for women, completed in 1962; the new Administration Building (1963); a dining hall or Commons (1963); and a large addition to the Fine Arts Building (1962). Two other buildings were under construction, and completed in 1964. These were Harshman Quadrangle, a large dormitory named in honor of President Harshman, and an addition to Kohl Hall. Both were completed in 1964. Plans also were started during these two years for an addition to the central heating plant. This was necessary because of the increase in the number of University buildings, completed, under construction, and planned for the future.

For many years, it had been evident that the old Stadium was not only too small, but its location blocked the development of the academic area of the campus. To meet this situation, the University, in the fall of 1961, purchased 171 acres of land, east of the existing campus, to be used for a new stadium, and for the development of other athletic facilities. An architect was employed to develop preliminary plans for a stadium. Four additional acres (consisting of 17 lots) were purchased during President Harshman's administration, bringing the total acreage, as of August 31, 1963, to 906, including the airport. Thus, the campus in slightly over a half century grew from a little more than 80 acres to nearly 1,000.

Dr. Harshman Elected President

When President McDonald submitted his resignation to the Board of Trustees he suggested that Ralph G. Harshman be elected acting president. At the same time, he recommended that the office of Provost be revived, and that Paul F. Leedy, Director of the Library, be appointed to the post. He further recommended that Donnal V. Smith, Assistant to the President, be appointed Dean of Students to succeed Dr. Elden T. Smith, who had resigned to go to Ohio Wesleyan University, where he is now President. All these recommendations were followed by the trustees, with the result that the University was able to continue without any interruption in its progress.

Several other changes were made during these years. President Harshman's title was changed from Acting President to President, and made retroactive to September 1, 1961. A. Robert Rogers was appointed Acting Director of the Library to fill the vacancy caused by Dr. Leedy's becoming Provost. William E. Harrington became Acting Dean of the College of Education, and Archie H. Jones was appointed Dean of the College of Liberal Arts.

Two other changes were made, both of which will undoubtedly have much to do with the future development of Bowling Green State University. The first of these came in the fall of 1961, when the Board of Trustees was increased from five members (the number from the beginning) to seven. Then, by Act of the General Assembly in 1963, the number was again increased from seven to nine.

The other change was even more important, not only to Bowling Green State University, but to the whole system of higher education in Ohio. This was the creation by the General Assembly of the Board of Regents to coordinate and direct the state system of higher education. The influence of this board has already been great, and it will undoubtedly be even greater in the future.

Perhaps the greatest and most important change in internal administration was the fact that President Harshman delegated more responsibility and authority to other administrative officers and bodies than had ever been done in the previous history of the institution.

The Faculty

During this period, the teaching faculty grew at a slightly slower rate than the enrollment. In 1961-62 it numbered 252, and in 1963-64 it was 292. This was an increase of approximately 16 per cent as compared with over 18 per cent for the total enrollment. The proportion of doctorates represented on the faculty also decreased somewhat. In 1961-62, 61 per cent had doctorates, while in 1963-64 the corresponding figure was 51 per cent. This decline was due to the fact that most of the new appointments, during these years, were to the rank of instructor, and many of those appointed had completed all requirements for the doctorate except the dissertation, and were working on that.

A number of salary increases, for the academic year 1961-62, were made by President McDonald before his retirement from office. Relatively few additional increases were granted during President Harshman's two years in office, since only limited funds were available for this purpose. However, a number of adjustments were made to correct inconsistencies and injustices, which many members of the faculty believed to be present in the salary structure. Most of these changes were in the three lower ranks. For associate professors, the maximum salary increased by $1,000, and the minimum and the mean by $600 each. For assistant professors, the minimum increased by $500, and the maximum and mean both remained approximately the same. In the case of instructors, the maximum increased by $700, the minimum by $200, and the mean by $500.

The salary figures for 1963-64 are given below:

Rank	Maximum	Minimum	Mean
Professor	$15,000	$9,300	$12,807
Associate Professor	12,600	8,500	10,493
Assistant Professor	11,100	7,500	9,079
Instructor	9,400	5,000	7,257

It is interesting to compare these salaries with those paid in 1914 (the first year of classes) and see the change that occurred in a half century. In 1914 the faculty was not ranked and teachers of college classes received approximately $1,900 for the academic year.

The Academic Program

Few changes occurred in the academic program of the University during the two years of President Harshman's administration. No new colleges, schools, or departments, were created. Only minor changes were made in the course offerings. The only changes in the degrees offered occurred in the Graduate School, which dropped the Master of Science and Master of Science in Education degrees, and added Master of Business Administration and Master of Fine Arts. The Graduate School increased its offerings on the master's level by adding curricula in American studies, business administration and earth science. English remained the only major for the Ph.D. degree, but other fields of specialization were being developed. In general, the emphasis during this period was on the improvement of existing programs (especially in the Graduate School), rather than on expansion.

On-Campus Enrollments

On-campus enrollments were still limited, during these years, by the number of available living accommodations. The completion of Conklin Quadrangle in 1962 made it possible to increase the number of men from 3,239 for the first semester of 1960-61 to 3,813 in 1962-63. During the same period, the number of women enrolled increased from 2,990 to 3,691. The total on-campus enrollment during the first semester was 6,229 in 1960-61 and 7,504 in 1962-63.

The enrollment by colleges in 1960-61 was Education, 3,075; Business Administration, 1,221; Liberal Arts, 1,613; and Graduate School, 328. In 1962-63 the corresponding figures were Education, 3,854; Business Administration, 1,270; Liberal Arts, 1,842; and Graduate School, 524. The College of Education was still the largest, but the Graduate School showed the greatest rate of increase.

Off-Campus and Summer Enrollments

The number of students in the University branches and in extension classes changed little in these two years. During the first semester of 1960-61, 675 students were enrolled in the branches and 171 in extension classes, making a total of 846. During a corresponding time in 1962-63, the number was 779 in the branches and 118 in extension classes, for a total of 897. Neither funds nor faculty was available for a greater expansion at this time.

During this period, the number of students in the summer sessions, workshops, and special programs increased by over 70 per cent from 4,751 in 1961 to 8,401 in 1963. This growth was due to expanded offerings, and was possible because enrollments were not limited by dormitory facilities.

Fees and Expenses

The nonresident fee, which was $150 a semester in 1960-61, was raised to $175 in 1961-62, and remained at that level throughout President Harshman's administration. No other changes in fees were made during this period. The charges for board and room also remained the same and, as a result, the total necessary expense for a year at Bowling Green did not increase, except for nonresidents of Ohio.

Trustees

The first woman served on the Board of Trustees from 1928 to 1935, and the second from 1936 to 1941. After 1941 no woman was appointed for 20 years, or until 1961. This lack of female representation on the Board caused considerable criticism since, for many years, the majority of the students were women, and even today women constitute approximately half of the student body. This feeling led to the appointment of Anita S. Ward of

Columbus in 1961, and of Virginia S. Stranahan of Perrysburg in 1965.

For many years, the alumni of the University had been asking for representation on the Board of Trustees. Their hopes were finally satisfied when in 1961, Judge John W. Bronson of Gibsonburg, a graduate of the University, was appointed to the Board. Although Judge Bronson served only one year, since his appointment was not confirmed, he made significant contributions. Not the least of his contributions was the fact that he opened the door for other alumni. Sumner Canary, a former student, although not a graduate, was appointed to the Board in 1961; and, in 1963 another graduate, Robert E. Dorfmeyer of Rocky River, was added to the group.

Although there is no legal requirement, a precedent has been established, and it is hoped that the Board will always include both alumni and women.

Electing A New President

The trustees, at their meeting on November 3, 1961, authorized the appointment of a Committee to Screen Presidential Candidates. This committee, when appointed, represented a further improvement in the method employed in choosing a head for the University. The first three presidents, Dr. Williams, Dr. Offenbauer and Dr. Prout, were chosen by the Board of Trustees alone, but in the case of President McDonald, the trustees appointed a committee composed of members of the teaching faculty. The committee to find a successor to President Harshman went even further. It introduced two new elements by including the administration and the alumni of the University.

The committee was composed of three faculty members, President Harshman, a second administrative officer, two alumni, and three members of the Board of Trustees.

The work of this committee, which started at once, was completed on June 25, 1963, when Dr. William Travers Jerome III, Dean of the College of Business Administration, Syracuse University, was tendered the presidency of Bowling Green State University. Dr. Jerome accepted the appointment, and assumed office on September 1, 1963.

At the same meeting, President Harshman was granted the title of President Emeritus, with duties as administrative consultant to the Board of Trustees.

Other Events

During President Prout's administration, Bowling Green State University and its women graduates had been interested in obtaining approval of the American Association of University Women. Apparently, negotiations were nearing a successful conclusion at the time President McDonald assumed the presidency. However, the picture soon changed, and negotiations were dropped, since President McDonald felt that the AAUW should not act as an accrediting agency.

When President Harshman assumed office, the picture had changed again. The AAUW had ceased its accrediting activities, and had agreed to accept the accreditation of the regional agencies, in this case the North Central Association of Colleges and Secondary Schools. Application was renewed, and Bowling Green State University received approval early in President Jerome's administration. Although the final approval did not come during his term in office. President Harshman made the application and, even after his retirement, continued the negotiations with AAUW until a favorable conclusion was reached.

At their meeting of October 1, 1962, the trustees authorized the establishment of Channel 70, educational television and the inclusion, in the budget for 1962-63, of the cost of a building to house this station. In July, 1963, the President and other administrative officers moved into their new quarters in the recently completed Administration Building. On July 22 of the same year, the trustees met for the first time in the board room of the new building. One action taken was the giving of a new name to the old administration building: University Hall.

Summary of President Harshman's Administration

The contributions of Dr. Harshman as president were much greater than the length of his term in office would indicate. Since he was nearing retirement age, everyone knew that his administration would be short and, under such circumstances, the University might well have fallen into a period of stagnation. This did not occur. President Harshman, because of his long service as teacher, Dean of the College of Business Administration, Dean of Administration and Vice-President, was thoroughly familiar with the operations of the University, and was able to take over and continue without interruption, both the carrying out of existing operations and the planning for the future.

However, his ability to carry on without any break, important as it was, did not constitute his greatest contribution. He assumed office at a time of real crisis, when both faculty and student morale were at an all-time low. Only the confidence of all concerned in his ability, broadmindedness, and sense of justice enabled him to quiet the troubled waters and to turn the thoughts of the University community from the grievances of the past toward the promises of the future. Probably no other man on the staff could have done this so well. Certainly no stranger could have won the confidence of the faculty and students, and have accomplished so much in so short a time. He took over an institution torn by controversy, arguing about the mistakes of the past and doubtful about the future. He left it still aware of problems, but with a general spirit of willingness to cooperate in solving those of both the past and the future, and with faith in this future. Without President Harshman's administration, the new President's task would have been much greater, and his success would have been delayed and possibly endangered.

The University, in the first half-century of its history, faced four serious crises. The first of these was Ohio State University's claim that the new Bowling Green and Kent institutions had no legal right to do anything except offer two-year diploma courses for the training of elementary teachers. The second was the attempt to change the school into a mental hospital. The third was the serious threat of political interference and control which came at the time of the selection of a president to succeed President Williams. The fourth crisis was the unrest of the faculty and students at the end of President McDonald's administration which could have had very serious consequences for the future of the University.

President Harshman's two years in the presidency were a fitting culmination to his long years of loyal and devoted service to the University. The University was indeed fortunate that he was available at this time of crisis.

A Half-Century of Progress

Bowling Green State University has been fortunate in its presidents, as each was fitted for the particular task he had to perform. President Williams laid a solid foundation, and guided the institution from nothing to a university comprising a strong College of Education, a small College of Liberal Arts, a smaller College of Business Administration, and the beginnings of a graduate program. President Offenhauer, in his short administration, started to give the faculty a greater part in determining policies. President Prout guided the University through the difficult war and post-war years and left it with three fully organized undergraduate colleges and a growing Graduate School. President McDonald greatly strengthened the academic program, raised the faculty to high University qualifications and salaries, systematized and strengthened the administration in all areas, and greatly improved the physical facilities. President Harshman continued, without interruption, the progress started under his predecessors and, by greatly improving both student and faculty morale, made it possible for his successor to begin his administration under favorable conditions. Under the guidance of these four men, Bowling Green State University, in the short period of 53 years (49 of classroom instruction), grew from nothing to its present status as a strong state university.

Few institutions in the country (except its sister institution at Kent) have gone through all the stages from normal school to college to university in so short a time. The author considers himself uniquely fortunate in having been closely associated with, and to have participated in this development. The title of this history might well be *From Normal School to University*, or *A Half-Century of Progress*.

CHAPTER TWELVE

Trustees, Faculty, Administrative Officers, Alumni. A Brief Look Into The Future

IT HAS BEEN CONVENIENT to organize the history of Bowling Green State University's first half-century according to the administrations of its presidents. This does not mean that they alone were responsible for the progress made, as none would have been possible without the contributions of many other individuals. A number of these have been mentioned previously, but three groups deserve further consideration. These are the Board of Trustees, the faculty, administrative officers, and the alumni.

Board of Trustees

The trustees of Bowling Green State University have contributed greatly to its development. The fact that a few individuals have been mentioned previously does not mean that the contributions of the others were not substantial. A complete list of trustees together with their places of residence and terms of service follows:

John Begg	Columbus Grove	1911-1915
D. C. Brown	Napoleon	1911-1914; 1918-1936
J. E. Collins	Fremont, Lima	1911-1920
D. T. Davis	Findlay	1911-1914
J. D. McDonel	Fostoria	1911-1918
J. E. Shatzel	Bowling Green	1914-1924
William B. Guitteau	Toledo	1914-1916
E. H. Ganz	Fremont	1916-1928
F. E. Reynolds	Wapakoneta	1918-1920
Dr. H. J. Johnston	Tontogany	1920-1935; 1939-1944
E. L. Bowsher	Wauseon	1921-1926
E. T. Rodgers	Tiffin	1923-1928; 1943-1961

T. C. Mahon	Kenton	1926-1931
Myrtle B. Edwards	Leipsic	1928-1935
Judge Orville Smith	Cleveland	1928-1929
R. G. Snyder	Norwalk	1929-1934
A. L. Gebhard	Bryan	1932-1937
F. J. Prout	Sandusky	1934-1939
L. N. Montgomery	Tiffin	1935-1938
Dr. E. B. Pedlow	Lima	1935-1940
Bessie S. Dwyer	Montpelier	1936-1941
E. E. Coriell	Bowling Green	1937-1946
J. J. Urschel	Toledo	1938-1943
Dudley A. White, Sr.	Norwalk	1940-1945
Minor C. Kershner	Liberty Center	1941-1950
Alva W. Bachman	Bowling Green	1944-1964
Carl Schwyn	Cygnet	1945-1965
J. C. Donnell	Findlay	1946-1965
Frazier Reams, Sr.	Toledo	1951-1957
John F. Ernsthausen	Norwalk	1956-1966
John W. Bronson	Gibsonburg	1961-1962
Anita S. Ward	Columbus	1961-1967
Sumner Canary	Cleveland	1961-
Donald G. Simmons	Perrysburg	1963-
Dudley A. White, Jr.	Norwalk	1963-
Delmont D. Brown	North Baltimore	1963-
Robert E. Dorfmeyer	Cleveland	1964-
Virginia Secor Stranahan	Toledo	1965-

Faculty and Administrative Officers

Of the members of the first faculty, the contributions of Leon L. Winslow and Ernest G. Hesser have been considered in an earlier chapter. Although both left the University after a relatively short period of service, each left a lasting legacy—Hesser in music and Winslow in college traditions. Mr. Winslow's services were recognized in 1942, when the University conferred on him the honorary degree of Doctor of Pedagogy.

Although modesty makes the author reluctant to discuss his services, historical completeness makes it necessary for him to do so. Most of his contributions have been mentioned before and need only be summarized here. President Williams always told the author that he was the first faculty member employed, although he (President Williams) planned to offer positions to Rea McCain and Edwin Moseley, both of whom he had known for some time. The author was the only member of the Mathematics Department for many years, and teaching was always his primary interest. In spite of this, he was drawn into administration from the first. As we have already noted he served as librarian during the first year, shared the duties of a registrar with the President for some years, edited the catalog, was the first Dean of the College of Liberal Arts and guided it through its early years, served as Acting Dean of Men, was chairman of many important committees, and was the first Dean of Faculties. He has also conducted research on the transfer of training in arithmetic, and has written a number of textbooks on mathematics and the teaching of mathematics.

Dr. McCain made many contributions during her long years of service, from 1914 to 1953. First and foremost she was an enthusiastic lover of literature, and succeeded in arousing a similar enthusiasm in many of her students. In addition, her interests and contributions were many and varied. She sponsored several student literary magazines, and contributed numerous articles to professional journals. Before the Speech Department was organized, she gave courses in public speaking and drama, and produced and coached one or more student plays each year. Her interests were not confined to her profession, since she had many hobbies. These included painting and horseback riding. In addition to all this, she is a worldwide traveler, often to faraway places such as Iceland and South Africa. She is still, at the present writing, continuing her travels and her scholarly activities.

Whole books could be written about Edwin L. Moseley, who was probably the most widely known (and the most colorful) member of the original faculty. Although primarily a biologist and a naturalist, his scientific knowledge was wide and, in the early years, when he was the entire Science Department, he taught courses in hygiene, biology, chemistry, and physics. He was the author of numerous articles in the newspapers and in scientific journals and of two books, *Trees, Stars and Birds* and *Our Wild Animals*. Probably his best known scientific contributions were his discovery of the cause of milk sickness, which at one time was widely prevalent among the cattle of northwestern Ohio, and his studies of tree rings as a means of determining weather cycles.

In spite of his wide scientific qualifications, Mr. Moseley was primarily a naturalist, and his greatest contribution was the interest in nature which he stimulated in his students, the citizens of Bowling Green and of northwestern Ohio. He took his students on many field trips. Groups of students, with Mr. Moseley in the lead, were a familiar sight throughout the region. His walk was characteristic and famous. Apparently, his movements were slow and almost lazy, but they were deceiving and his long strides really covered the ground rapidly. Most students found it difficult to keep up, and many had to trot in order not to miss any of the running lecture. They knew they dared not miss a word, since they would later be quizzed about what they had seen and been told. The story is often related that a favorite type of question the next day, or on a test, was, "What bird did we see after we saw the squirrel?"

Mr. Mosley has become a legendary figure, and many stories are told concerning him. He was a bachelor and very frugal in the habits. His clothes were always clean, but usually inexpensive and shabby. The author recalls that on one occasion (at the request of the President), he called Mr. Moseley into his office, and suggested that he get a new overcoat, since the old one was a disgrace to the college. The professor agreed and in a few days created a minor sensation by appearing in a new coat. The author learned later that Mr. Mosley asked another faculty member to help him make the purchase, and that he wanted to keep the old coat to wear in bad weather.

Although Mr. Moseley never received a large salary, he was able to save money and to put it to good use. During his life, he was always helping one or more boys through college. At his death, he left a sizeable estate to the University to be used for scholarships and loans to worthy students. Mr. Moseley retired in 1936, but served as curator of the University museum until his death in 1948. His memory is preserved through the building bearing his name, his gift to the University, and the many legends concerning him.

George W. Beattie was the institution's first and only instructor in agriculture. Instruction in this subject was required by the Act of 1910, but the opposition of Ohio State University made it impossible to develop a strong department. Although the department died, Mr. Beattie made one lasting contribution. He was founder of and adviser to the Country Life Club and, with its cooperation, started the *Bee Gee News*.

Mary Turner Chapin was responsible for the early development of the Home Economics Department, but gave up this work to become Mrs. Beattie. Needless to say this faculty romance created great interest in the new and small institution.

Josephine Leach was a member of the faculty for only one year, when she supervised the practice teaching of the students in the Toledo branch. She later married William B. Guitteau, Superintendent of the Toledo schools, and an early member of the Bowling Green Board of Trustees.

Ernest G. Walker joined the staff as instructor in history and Director of Extension Teaching. He later taught psychology and, in 1916, became the college's first dean, when he was appointed Dean of the Faculty. He held this office until his resignation in 1920.

Dallas D. Johnson was Director of the Training School and teacher of education for one year. Although his term of service was short, it made a strong impression on both students and townspeople. He was not only an excellent teacher, but was a crusader, and set out to reform the town. In spite of this, he was popular with the citizens and started some movements which eventually led to changes for the better. His resignation was a loss to the new school.

Several individuals who were added to the faculty in 1915 made significant contributions. These included Frederick G. Beyermann, the first teacher of physical education, and the first athletic coach to be a regular member of the faculty. Mr. Beyermann was also the organizer of the Town and Gown Club which has done so much to promote friendly relations between faculty and citizens of Bowling Green. Calvin J. Biery had charge of the rural education program in the beginning, and later taught penmanship. He was well-known as a handwriting expert, and testified in numerous court trials. Harriet S. Hayward was supervisor of practice teachers in the Bowling Green schools, and was both loved and respected by the many students who came under her supervision and instruction. She was famous for the lesson plans she always required. William P. Holt, geography, also joined the faculty in 1915. He organized and conducted the first travel tours sponsored by the University. He was popular with his students, particularly at the end of the semester when he served ice cream in lieu of a final examination.

In 1915-16, John W. Zeller was added to the faculty as instructor in history, and held that position until his retirement in 1920. Mr. Zeller was a veteran of many years of service in Ohio schools, both as a teacher and as an administrator. He was state school commissioner for a number of years and, in that position, was influential in securing the establishment of the two new normal schools.

In 1918 and 1919, several new faculty members were employed who were destined to finish their long teaching careers at Bowling Green, and to play important roles in the development of the institution. These included Laura E. Heston, home economics; Caroline Nielsen, foreign language; Charles F. Reebs, education; and Maud F. Sharp, first Dean of Women. Two additions in 1919 deserve special mention. These were Daniel J. Crowley, in industrial arts, and James W. Carmichael, who first served as instructor in English, and later organized the Speech Department, when it was separated from English.

Richard M. Tunnicliffe succeeded Ernest Hesser in the Music Department in 1920, and was joined by Merrill C. McEwen in 1921. Mr. McEwen left Bowling Green after two years, but returned in 1928 and, on Mr. Tunnicliffe's retirement, became chairman of the department. These two men ably continued the work Mr. Hesser had started and built a strong Music Department.

Clayton C. Kohl was appointed professor of social science in 1920, and was the first member of the faculty to hold an earned Ph.D. degree. For a number of years he taught courses in economics, political science, and sociology, but later confined his teaching to sociology alone. Probably no other member of the early faculty had greater influence on students and public. He was a scholar, an inspiring teacher, and an effective public speaker. He was in great demand in the latter capacity. When graduate work was started in 1935, Dr. Kohl became chairman of the Graduate Committee and had a large part in the early development of the graduate program. His early death, in 1938, was mourned by faculty, students, alumni, and the citizens of northwestern Ohio. His memory is kept alive at the University by the dormitory named in his honor.

For many years, the faculty Class of 1923, as the group who joined the staff in that year were known, were famous on the campus. Many of them made significant contributions to the development of the institution. One of these was Clyde Hissong, whose services to the University and to the state of Ohio were both great and varied. He joined the staff as Director of the Training School and professor of education, was appointed Dean of Instruction in 1928, and Dean of the College of Education in 1929. After the death of Dr. Kohl in 1938, Dr. Hissong succeeded him as chairman of the Graduate Committee. His greatest services to the University were in the development of the College of Education and the graduate program. In 1945 Dr. Hissong took leave of absence from Bowling Green State University to become Ohio Director of Education and to serve the cause of education on a wider scale.

Another member of the Class of 1923 was Walter A. Zaugg, who was appointed professor of education in that year. He was a popular teacher, and served as chairman of the Graduate Committee, and numerous other committees. However, his greatest service to the University was probably in the field of public relations. Hs was an eloquent and popular speaker, and he was in constant demand at high school commencements and on many other occasions. He held the title of University Orator for a number of years. Dr. Zaugg was a diligent worker in church, the Red Cross, and other community activities. After his retirement, in 1954, he served as Director of Alumni Affairs for several years.

John Schwarz, professor of history from 1923 to 1948, was an outstanding and beloved teacher. For many years, he was the faculty adviser to the Emerson Literary Society, and trained its members in parliamentary procedure, oral expression, and habits of logical thinking. He was famous on campus, and throughout northwestern Ohio for his lectures on prominent figures in American history. He was also known for his voice, which could be heard throughout the third floor of the old Administration Building, and for his demanding prompt attendance from the students in his eight o'clock class. If they were not in the room before eight, sharp, they found the door locked. Mr. Schwarz took long daily walks from one end of Main Street to the other, and was a well-known figure to residents of that street.

Other members of the Class of 1923, all of whom made significant contributions to the college, were C. D. Perry, the first registrar; E. G. Knepper, first chairman of the Department of Commercial Education; C. S. Martin, first chairman of the Chemistry Department; E. C. Powell, of the Industrial Arts Department, who was famous as a teller of stories as well as a teacher; and Caroline Shaw who was for many years in charge of physical education for women.

In this discussion of the faculty, it has seemed advisable to include all of the members of the 1914 and 1915 faculties, and of the Class of 1923, since these constituted the group responsible for the development of the institution in the early days. None of these is now active. After 1923, the growth in enrollments, and the development from normal to college, and then to university status, brought many additions to both the teaching faculty and the administrative staff. These are so numerous as to preclude mention of even all of the outstanding individuals. It has seemed best to include only three groups: individuals who started new departments, those who assumed major administrative duties, and those for whom buildings or other University facilities have been named.

In view of the comparatively low salaries, it is really remarkable that the institution was able to attract and keep so many individuals of such high caliber. The faculty of the period from 1923 to 1951 not only developed a university, but they also furnished most of the administrators who were to guide it throughout the McDonald and Harshman administrations. The author deeply regrets that space does not permit special mention of more individuals whose contributions have been great.

In all that follows, when a date is given after the name, it is that of the first appointment. The contributions of Warren E. Steller (1924) as an instructor and coach have already been considered. William C. Jordan (1925) served first as Business Manager and later, was the first full-time Dean of Men. Still later, he was in charge of extension classes. He finished his long and varied career as professor of education.

Willard E. Singer (1927) was first an instructor in physical science and later, when a separate Physics Department was created in 1947, he became its first chairman. He continued to serve as chairman until 1967, and is now the oldest faculty member in point of service. Dr. Singer and Dr. Donald W. Bowman, who joined the staff in 1943, have built a strong department, and have both served on important committees and councils.

Frank C. Ogg joined the staff of the Mathematics Department in 1931, and later succeeded the author as its chairman. He also served as assistant to the author in the office of the Dean of the College of Liberal Arts, and as University librarian. During his long period of service, he has been a member of many important committees and chairman of several.

The career of President Harshman (1936) has already been fully discussed. He was successively Professor, Dean, Vice-President, and President. Although the author had retired before President Harshman assumed the presidency, he had the privilege of serving closely with him for many years. During most of that time, they occupied adjoining offices. President Harshman not only performed his own duties most efficiently, but also, was always ready to help others, and to take on other assignments when asked. The author cannot recall even one serious disagreement in their many years of association.

Waldo E. Steidtmann joined the staff of the Department of Biology in 1936, and became its chairman in 1948. The Steidtmann Wildlife Sanctuary is named in his honor. This 65-acre tract of swampland and woods, five miles south of the campus provides an undisturbed environment for field study and research.

Samuel M. Mayfield joined the staff of the Department of Geography and Geology in 1936, and later served as its chairman. When, in 1952, Geology became a separate department, he was its first chairman.

James Paul Kennedy also came to the University in 1936 as a member of the Music Department. He later became chairman, and the first Director of the School of Music when it was established.

An important addition was made to the administrative staff in 1937, when Ervin J. Kreischer (a 1930 graduate of Bowling Green) became Business Manager. His part in making possible the financing of income-producing buildings has already been mentioned. He served as financial administrator, and adviser to four presidents. He also played a prominent role in the organization and functioning of the Council of Presidents, which has played such an important role in higher education in Ohio. His long and outstanding services were recognized in 1965, when he became Vice President of Finance. Kreischer Quadrangle is named in his honor.

Two important additions were made to the staff in 1938. In that year, Paul F. Leedy joined the faculty as an extension instructor. Later, after completing his work for the doctorate in English, he returned to Bowling Green as professor of English, and later served as chairman of the department. He became interested in library work, earned the B.A. in Library Science, and became University librarian. In that capacity he did much to strengthen the library collection and services. He left the University Library to become Provost of the University in 1961, and Vice President for Academic Affairs and Provost in 1967.

Another future administrator joined the staff in 1938, when Lloyd A. Helms was appointed assistant professor of economics. He later became chairman of that department and, in 1954, was appointed first Secretary of the Faculty. In 1956 he became Dean of the Graduate School, and served until 1967. In addition, Dr. Helms has served on many important committees, and has been chairman of several.

In 1939, three more future administrators joined the staff. In that year, John W. Bunn came to Bowling Green as an extension instructor. Later, he served as Assistant Registrar, Registrar, Director of Admissions, assistant to the Dean of Admissions and Director of Residential and Plant Operations. In 1960, Mr. Bunn left Bowling Green State University to take a postion at her sister school in Kent, and is now Vice President of that institution. Even his long list of titles does not indicate the wide range of contributions that Mr. Bunn made to Bowling Green State University.

In the summer of 1939, Arch B. Conklin, then superintendent of the Bowling Green Schools, became Dean of Students. He rendered outstanding service in that capacity until his retirement in 1960. One of his most difficult tasks during much of this period was the finding of space and beds to accommodate the rapidly increasing number of students. Conklin Hall is named in his honor.

Benjamin L. Pierce (1939) came to Bowling Green as Director of

Teacher Training. After serving in that capacity for several years, he joined the staff of the Department of Business Administration as a teacher of business law. In 1951, when Dr. Harshman became Dean of Administration, Dr. Pierce succeeded him as Dean of the College of Business Administration. In that office, he ably continued the work of building and expanding the offerings of that college. He retired in 1960.

A few courses in political science were taught in the History Department almost from the beginning, but it was not until 1940 that the offerings were greatly expanded, and a full-time teacher of political science was added to the faculty. He was Charles A. Barrell. Later Dr. Barrell became chairman, when political science was separated from history.

For a number of years, two courses in journalism were offered in the English Department, but, in 1940, the Department of Journalism was created, and Jesse J. Currier joined the faculty as instructor and chairman of the department. Later, Mr. Currier became the first Director of the School of Journalism. Under the guidance of Mr. Currier, the department and school have developed rapidly, and have made many contributions to the University and to northwestern Ohio. In 1949, Mr. Currier's wife, Florence K. Currier became Dean of Women, and served in that capacity until 1963.

A few courses in drama were offered in the English Department from the earliest days of the school, and Dr. McCain directed one or more student plays each year. No major expansion was made in this field until after 1940. In January of that year, Elden T. Smith was employed as an instructor in speech. Under his supervision and direction, the offerings in the field of drama were greatly increased, and the dramatic productions of the students reached the highest quality. These productions became an important part of campus and community life. Dr. Smith also started the summer playhouse at Huron, Ohio. A number of outstanding actors were developed, the best known being Eva Marie Saint. Dr. Smith had always been interested in the larger problems of University administration, and had been a member of several important committees. In 1956 he became Director of Student Life and Services and, two years later, Dean of Students. He served in this capacity until 1961, when he went to Ohio Wesleyan University, where he is President.

F. Eugene Beatty began a long and varied career at the University in 1941. His ability to serve effectively in a wide range of activities has resulted in his holding at least as many positions as any member of the Bowling Green staff. He began as Assistant Registrar, and served in that position until he became Director of Services in 1947. After the close of World War II, he was successful in securing surplus equipment from the Federal Government. In 1952 his title was changed to Director of Special Services, and a year later he became Assistant to the President. He became Director of Extension in 1956, Capital Improvements Officer in 1957, and Director of Buildings and Facilities in 1960.

Prior to 1941, the University, except in times of crisis, did little to acquaint the people of northwestern Ohio with the operations and services of the institution. What little publicity there may have been was usually given out by the President. All this was changed in 1941, when Paul W. Jones was employed to teach courses in speech and to serve as Director of the News Bureau. Mr. Jones did much to acquaint the people of northwestern Ohio, state, and nation, with the University and the services it offered. Mr. Jones left the University in 1954 to become the editor of the Bowling Green *Sentinel-Tribune*.

In 1941 and 1942, two men who made athletic history joined the staff of the Physical Education Department. These were Robert H. Whittaker (1941) and W. Harold Anderson (1942). Their careers at Bowling Green have been discussed earlier.

Another future administrator joined the University faculty in 1941. Herschel Litherland first served as Director of Student Teaching. In 1947 he became Assistant Dean of the College of Education and, the next year, succeeded Dr. Hissong as Dean. Dr. Litherland made significant contributions to the College of Education and to the University as a whole.

In 1943, two men were added to the University faculty who were destined, with the author and Dr. Litherland, to guide the academic program of the University throughout the early years of President McDonald's administration. Emerson C. Shuck was employed as a teacher in English, and later was chairman of that department. From the beginning, he showed an interest in university administration, and served on many important committees. In 1947 Dr. Shuck was appointed Director of the Graduate School and, in 1951 this title was changed to Dean. In 1955 Dr. Shuck became Dean of the College of Liberal Arts and continued in that position until he resigned, in 1964, to accept the vice presidency of Ohio Wesleyan University. He is now President of Eastern Washington College at Cheney, Washington.

Kenneth H. McFall also joined the staff in 1943 as Dean of Freshmen. In 1945 he was given the additional title of Director of Guidance. While holding these positions, he devoted much of his time to visiting high schools and advising students with respect to their college plans. He rendered a great counseling service to high school students, even if they were not interested in coming to Bowling Green. In 1948 Dr. McFall became Assistant Dean of the College of Liberal Arts. A year later he succeeded the author as Dean. Following the author's resignation as Dean of Faculties, that position was discontinued. It was revived in 1955 under a new title of Provost, and Dr. McFall was appointed to this new office. He held it until 1960, when he became Vice President of the University.

At the time President McDonald assumed office, the author was appointed to the newly created office of Dean of Faculties, and, at the same time, the Academic Council was formd. The success of the author as Dean of Faculties and the success of the Academic Council were largely due to the cooperation, hard work, and loyalty of the academic deans—Kenneth McFall of the College of Liberal Arts, Herschel Litherland of the College of Education, Benjamin Pierce of the College of Business Administration, and Emerson Shuck of the Graduate School. The University owes much to this group of men.

Another future dean came to the University in 1946, when John E. Gee joined the faculty of the Department of Education. Dr. Gee, whose special field was school administration, worked effectively with the school principals and superintendents of northwestern Ohio. He was also interested in the administration of the University and served on several important committees. He succeeded Dr. Litherland as Dean of the College of Education in 1955, and held that position until he resigned to accept an appointment to go to Vietnam and help plan an educational program for that country.

In 1946 a separate Department of Philosophy was formed, and Tom H. Tuttle joined the University as its chairman. In the same year, Elton C. Ringer joined the staff of the business office and became comptroller in 1952. Later, on the retirement of Ervin J. Kreischer, he was made business manager and comptroller.

Glenn D. Van Wormer, a graduate of Bowling Green, returned to his alma mater in 1947 as Assistant Registrar. He also served as Alumni Secretary from 1951 until 1953, when Dr. Zaugg took over the duties of the office. Mr. Van Wormer, succeeded Mr. Bunn as Registrar in 1953, and still holds that office. He added Director of Admissions to his title in 1956, and performed the duties of that office until 1961.

William F. Schmeltz, the last of the academic deans to serve during the era of Presidents McDonald and Harshman, joined the faculty of the College of Business Administration in 1947. In 1955 he became the first chairman of the new Department of Accounting and, in 1960 succeeded Dr. Pierce as the Dean of the College of Business Administration. He resigned as dean in 1967.

With the influx of veterans after the close of World War II, Ralph H. Geer was appointed, in 1948, as assistant professor of education and Veterans and New Students Counselor. By 1951 the number of veterans entering college had diminished, and Mr. Geer became student counselor and Director of the Placement Bureau. Two years later, he became Director of Admissions, in addition to his other titles and duties. In 1956 he became Director of Off-Campus Programs and, since 1959, has served as Director of Summer and Off-Campus Programs.

Another famous coach joined the staff of the Physical Education Department in 1955. He was Doyt L. Perry. His outstanding record has already been discussed. When the new Student Union was opened in 1958, Farrar M. Cobb became its first Director. In the years that have followed,

Colonel Cobb and his wife have made the Union an asset to the life of the campus, and to the citizens of Bowling Green and northwestern Ohio. Colonel Cobb has also become well-known as a result of his great interest in Commodore Oliver Hazard Perry, about whom he has lectured frequently before many groups in the area.

In 1957 John H. Marsh became Director of the University Health Service. He played a major role in the development of this service and in planning the new Health Center, until his death in 1965. A prominent alumnus of Bowling Green State University returned to his alma mater in 1960 after a distinguished career elsewhere. He was Donnal V. Smith. His services to Bowling Green are discussed in a later section.

Many other individuals joined the faculty and administrative staff during the Prout, McDonald, and Harshman administrations, and many of these are now playing important roles in the development of the University. They are not included here for two reasons—lack of space and the fact that their contributions are continuing and belong to the future rather than the past.

Growing Alumni Body

The history of Bowling Green State University would be incomplete without some mention of its alumni, who have brought it prestige throughout the nation and even in foreign lands. Starting with a group of only 35 in 1915, the number of graduates has increased steadily and the total number is now about 25,000. Of these, approximately 4,000 were graduated from the two-year diploma course, and 2,000 have received graduate degrees.

The first class was composed entirely of women and women were in the majority throughout the early years. Many graduates, in the beginning, were from the two-year diploma course, and almost all were prepared for a career in education. Most were from northwestern Ohio and, upon graduation, took positions in that region. The picture gradually changed until, today, students are preparing for many different fields of service, and are widely distributed throughout the United States and foreign countries. Although the largest number for whom information is available are engaged in education, the remainder is distributed through 44 different occupations. The largest number are still located in Ohio, but Bowling Green graduates can be found in every state, and in a number of foreign countries.

Many Bowling Green State University graduates have had, or still have, distinguished careers. Several have made significant contributions to their alma mater. Donnal V. Smith received a bachelor's degree from Bowling Green in 1924. He was prominent as an undergraduate, was a member of the football team, president of the senior class, and sales manager of the first *Key*. After leaving Bowling Green, he received his master's degree, and doctorate from the University of Chicago. He joined the history faculty of New York State Teachers College in 1929, and in 1943 was appointed president of the New York State Teachers College at Cortland. He was the first Bowling Green

Graduate to become a college president. In 1960 Dr. Smith returned to his alma mater as Assistant to the President, and the following year was appointed Dean of Students. His services, while in this office, have made lasting contributions to the future of the University.

Ervin J. Kreischer, of the class of 1939, was prominent as an undergraduate, manager of the football team, actor in school plays, and business manager of the *Key*. After graduation, he taught for several years in the Bowling Green High School, before joining the staff of the college. Since most of his career has been at Bowling Green State University, it is discussed elsewhere. Mr. Kreischer is a cousin of Donnal V. Smith. The services of F. Eugene Beatty, Glenn D. Van Wormer, and Doyt L. Perry to their alma mater have been discussed in a previous section.

Space permits discussion of only a few of the many other alumni who have won more than local fame. Those included below have been selected to show the wide range covered by the careers of Bowling Green graduates. The date following the name shows the year of graduation.

Paul Woodring (1930). Educator, Writer and Editor. While in college, Paul was a member of the cross-country team, and started his editorial career by serving as assistant literary editor of *The Key*. He has a Ph.D. degree from Ohio State University, and has an honorary Doctor of Humanities degree from Bowling Green. He was also the recipient of the Distinguished Alumnus award in 1960. Dr. Woodring has had a distinguished career in psychology and education. After teaching at Ohio State, San Jose College, and Carleton College, he joined the staff of the Fund for the Advancement of Education. He has acted as consultant on several studies of educational institutions and programs, and has served as education editor of the *Saturday Review*. Dr. Woodring is the author of four books and numerous articles and reviews.

Isabelle Wagner Taylor (1930). Psychologist. After graduation from Bowling Green, she taught in Sandusky, Ohio; later she entered Ohio State University, and earned the Ph.D. degree in psychology. She is professor of psychology at Russell Sage College. She has written two books, and numerous pamphlets and articles on the education of physically handicapped children. She is well known for her research in that field. Dr. Taylor is a member of the World Commission on Special Education of the International Society for Rehabilitation of the Disabled.

William F. Gernert (1938). Brigadier General, U. S. Air Force. During his student days Bill was a member of Five Brothers Fraternity, vice-president of Aeropagus, and was active in intramural sports. He was assigned to the Armed Forces Special Weapons Project at Sandia Base, N.M. in 1941, served a year in London, and then established the first operations center for SHAPE in Paris. In addition to his Bowling Green degree, he holds the B.S. degree from West Point, and the master's degree in business administration from Ohio State University. He is a graduate of the Armed Forces Staff College and the Industrial College of the Armed Forces. He is director of safety for the Air Force nuclear weapon systems, worldwide. Although his organization is a Pentagon-level unit, it is located in Albuquerque, N.M., the center of nuclear research and development. Gen. Gernert holds the Legion of Merit, the nation's second highest peacetime decoration, for his accomplishments in the fields of atomic weapons and vulnerability. In addition, he has been awarded the Distinguished Flying Cross, Purple Heart, and five air medals.

Kermit Long (1939). Minister. While an undergraduate, Kermit was a member of the men's glee club and quartet, and took part in many other activities. He was president of the fraternity for Methodist men, and president of his senior class. After receiving his bachelor's degree, he earned a Bachelor of Divinity degree at Garrett Theological Seminary, and a Master of Arts degree at Northwestern University. In 1951 Bowling Green State University named him the Alumnus of the Year, in 1955 awarded him an honorary Doctor of Divinity degree and in 1961 gave him the Distinguished Alumnus Award. After serving in several churches in Ohio and Illinois, he became pastor of Trinity Church, the largest Methodist congregation in Chicago. He left Chicago to become pastor of the Central Methodist church, Phoenix, Arizona, with a congregation of over 4,000. In 1965 he was elected general secretary of the General Board of Evangelism of the Methodist Church.

Darwin Mayfield (1941). Chemist. While a student at Bowling Green, Darwin was active in numerous organizations including the band, YMCA, *B-G News,* and Student Council. After graduating, he received his master's degree from the University of Chicago, and the Ph.D. degree from the University of Wisconsin. He worked on the Manhattan Project (atomic bomb) of World War II, and later performed research for the U. S. Office of Scientific Research and the U. S. Rubber Reserve Board. He joined the faculty of the Long Beach State College in 1956, and has since received many research grants. Collaborating with an associate at Long Beach, Dr. Mayfield performed the first successful experiment in isolating a plant hormone which controls blooming. In 1962 he received Bowling Green's Distinguished Alumnus Award.

Eva Marie Saint (1946). Actress. Moviegoers all over the nation are familiar with the name of Eva Marie Saint. She received her early dramatic training at Bowling Green, played many leading roles in college plays and, when she did not have a part, was often seen behind the scenes sewing on costumes or painting scenery. She was also active in many other ways, including women's glee club, modern dance club, debate, student council, and Panhellenic Council. In addition, she was Pi Kappa Alpha Dream Girl, Skol Sweater Swing Queen, and was twice elected *Key* Beauty Queen. After leaving Bowling Green, Eva Marie played numerous roles on radio and television. Her first great success in a movie was in *On the Waterfront,* in which she co-starred with Marlon Brando. Her outstanding performance in this movie won her an *Oscar* as the Best Supporting Actress of 1954. This first success has been followed by many others. Miss Saint received the Distinguished Alumnus Award in 1960.

Charles Kurfess (1951). Lawyer and Legislator. Charles had his first legal experience while an undergraduate, when he served as the chief justice of the student court. In 1957, while only 26 years old and still a student in the Law School at Ohio State University, he entered a three-way contest for the Republican nomination for Wood County representative to the General Assembly, and surprised everyone by winning by a wide margin. During his first term, Mr. Kurfess was selected by State House newsmen as the outstanding freshman representative. He has made an outstanding record, and has served on many committees. He is probably best known in the areas of education and finance. In 1967, Mr. Kurfess became Speaker of the House, and the University gave him the Distinguished Alumnus Award in 1967.

Tim Conway (1956). Actor. Like Eva Marie Saint, Bowling Green's other well-known personality in the dramatic field. Tim (changed from Tom) gained much experience while an undergraduate. He had his own radio show on WBGU, served as master of ceremonies at various campus functions, and gave comedy routines in shows. In addition, he found time for other activities, and was president of his sophomore class. After graduation, he worked for radio station KYW in Cleveland. His work there led to several guest appearances with Steve Allen. This was followed by a role in the TV show *McHale's Navy*, in which he starred for several years. He has also appeared on several TV specials and on the *Hollywood Palace*. He was nominated for a *TV Emmy Award* in 1963 as *Best Supporting Star*. In addition to his work as an actor, he has written numerous scripts for radio and television shows. He received the Distinguished Alumnus Award in 1966.

Bernard T. Casey (1961). Artist and Athlete. As an undergraduate, Bernard Casey, was an outstanding star in both football and track. He won All-Mid-American halfback honors in 1959; Little-All-American honors in 1960. He won the Mid-American high hurdles three times, finished fourth in the NCAA's 110-meter high hurdles, and tied for fourth place in the finals of the Olympic trials. After graduation, Mr. Casey became a member of the San Francisco team of the National Football League. At the end of every professional football season, for several years, he returned to Bowling Green as a graduate assistant in the Art Department, and received the Master of Fine Arts degree in 1966. In addition to his fame as a football star, Mr. Casey is gaining national recognition as an artist. He was selected as one of the Outstanding Young Men of America in 1966.

A Brief Look Into the Future

Although they did not take place until after the close of the period covered by the history, several important developments of 1963 and 1965 affected the future of Bowling Green State University, higher education in Ohio, and throughout the nation. Early in his administration, Governor James A. Rhodes proposed that Ohio issue bonds for capital plant improvements at state institutions and, in 1963, the voters of Ohio approved an amendment to the State Constitution authorizing the borrowing of $250 million for this purpose. Of this amount, $175 million were earmarked for higher educational institutions. A second bond issue for $290 million was authorized in 1965. To date, Bowling Green State University has received appropriations of almost $15 million from these bond issues.

Following proposals of President Johnson, the Congress of the United States passed two measures to provide aid to higher education. The first of these was the Higher Education Facilities Act of 1963, and the second was the Higher Education Act of 1965. The first, as the name indicates, provided federal aid for the construction of new buildings. The second authorized a five-year program of assistance in improving undergraduate instruction. To date, Bowling Green State University has received grants totaling approximately $3.5 million under the provisions of these two laws.

It is fitting that this history end with the spring of 1963. In many ways, President Harshman's administration completed the first era of the institution's history, and President Jerome's starts the second. The first period was one of building. It ended with a strong undergraduate University and the beginnings of a graduate program. The new period promises to be one of expansion in enrollments, in physical facilities, in educational programs, and in national prestige.

At the time of this writing, the enrollment is over 12,000. A few years ago, it would have been considered large, but now is considered relatively small. The plans of the regents call for an institution of 15,000 students, and this figure will soon be reached at the present rate of growth. The Regents also have suggested that the University make tentative plans to provide for 30,000 students, if this should become necessary.

The expansion of the physical facilities is now well under way. At the time of this writing, many new buildings and other facilities are under construction, and some are nearing completion. Most of these have been financed with the aid of money appropriated from the state bond issues mentioned above, and from grants received from the federal government. It is evident, however, that, even with continuing and increased support from the state and federal governments, other sources of income must be obtained to prevent student fees from rising to prohibitive levels. Apparently, the only other source will be increased gifts from the alumni of the University and from the public.

As early as 1939, there was a faculty Committee on Gifts, Endowments, and Memorials, but its activities were largely confined to the administration of the money received, and little or no effort was made to encourage gifts. The only major exceptions were the efforts of President Prout, which resulted in substantial gifts from Sidney Frohman. In 1951 the name of the committee was changed to Research and Development, but there were few changes in its activities.

In 1956 the Research and Development Committee was succeeded by the Bowling Green State University Foundation, Inc. The articles of incorporation state:

> The corporation shall seek and receive money, property, works of arts, historical papers and documents, museum specimens and relics, and other resources and facilities of monetary or educational value or significance from sources other than those from which the state of Ohio ordinarily makes appropriations to Bowling Green State University.

Following the incorporation of the Foundation, efforts were made to secure gifts from alumni and other sources, but with disappointing results. The idea was too new. It met with opposition from the alumni and little interest from others. After a few years, however, most people realized the need, and the major effort now under way to secure increased gifts from the alumni of the University and from the general public is meeting with success.

Some research was carried on by faculty members from the beginning, and efforts were made, from time to time, to increase the amount. However, throughout the first period, emphasis was on good teaching, rather than research. Paralleling this was the fact that Bowling Green was primarily an undergraduate institution, with only the beginnings of a small graduate program. Overshadowing everything else, throughout much of this period, Bowling Green's financial support was inadequate.

All this will undoubtedly be changed in the second era; in fact, the changes are already taking place. New sources of revenue give promise of more adequate financial support, which should bring even better facilities and staff. In the future the great expansion in the academic program will undoubtedly be in the graduate field, and research will become a primary, rather than a secondary objective and activity. It is hoped that these changes can be accomplished without serious damage to the undergraduate program and without any diminishing of the emphasis on good teaching.

One needs only look back on the developments of the first half-century, most of which were unforeseen in the beginning, to realize that no one can foretell the future with any great degree of certainty. However, the author is sure of one thing—Bowling Green State University will continue to develop into one of the strong state universities of the nation. The author hopes that this history of the first half-century will be a challenge to all now concerned with the University's operations to write some new and exciting chapters to the Bowling Green story.

Epilogue

I T IS FORTUNATE that Dean Emeritus James Robert Overman has undertaken this history. More than any other individual, he is qualified to write from total experience, from personal involvement in developments, and from research into national and state educational movements and Ohio politics at the beginning of the century. He speaks with the authority of one who was there and who influenced the course of events.

Throughout his career Robert Overman demonstrated such qualities as solid academic background, broad cultural interests, high academic standards, belief in the liberal arts tradition, and respect for scholarship, in combination with such characteristics as persistence bordering on stubbornness and a kind of patience willing to progress when possible and to await the propitious moment when necessary. He was also close-lipped and knew when to keep his own counsel. As a result of this combination of personal traits, Robert Overman as faculty man and administrator succeeded in exerting a positive influence on the academic growth of the institution. This influence is apparent throughout the present history.

During approximately its first half century, Bowling Green was headed by presidents and governed by boards who adhered closely to the authoritarian concept of administration. The winds of change blew somewhat faintly from the late 1930's on. Evidence of this is found in the establishment of a chapter of AAUP, the early Policies Commission, the first and second Tenure Statements, the growth of the Faculty Senate in its several forms, student riots, and faculty petitions and protests.

225

The winds of change blew vigorously from 1961. The Faculty Study Report began the process of regularizing faculty participation in administration and resulted in the revised Charter of the University Faculty. Under President Harshman the process of delegation of authority began in limited fashion. This process and resulting decentralization of decision-making have gone on with increased rapidity under the present administration.

In selecting William T. Jerome III, the trustees brought to the presidency a man of New England, New York, and Ivy League background. Dr. Jerome has his roots clearly in the liberal arts and in professional business. He is not an Ohioan; he is not a professional educator. His experience as professor and administrator is in the milieu of the large, multi-purpose, graduate-professional university.

It is too early to assess the administration of President Jerome. Regardless of the outcome, he has brought a new vocabulary to the administration of the University. He recognized immediately that this is a *developing university.* That like other former teachers' colleges and state colleges, this institution is struggling to become a university in the full sense of the term. Faculty research, which for years was not regarded as essential, has become top priority. Doctoral programs which were little more than plans on paper are in various stages of realization as degree programs.

In his first address to the faculty, President Jerome clearly indicated a desire to encourage a climate in which faculty and students can develop a kind of educational institution to meet the needs of the present and the future. He has stated repeatedly that his job is to provide resources to enable the faculty to get on with creative teaching and research. He has encouraged new ideas and new programs. Some interesting new programs are under way, such as the Center for Research on Social Behavior, an Honors Program, and the Anderson Center for Personal Development. An experimental college is under discussion. A residential college is planned.

It is too early to know where these thrusts will lead. It is also hazardous to generalize about the future of the University. I am willing, however, to make one sweeping generalization. When the history of the next 50 years of Bowling Green is written, the unit of measure will not be the presidency. Bowling Green has rapidly become the kind of institution in which the measure of success will relate to the various disciplines, centers and institutes, and experimental educational programs.

This is not to say that the President will not be important. But increasingly the President's attention will be directed to extra-mural matters, hence the significance of delegating much of the operation of the University to other officials. The President's success will be measured increasingly by his capacity to provide resources for the exploding academic and research programs of the University, for faculty salaries, for fringe benefits for faculty, for a sabbatical-leaves system, and the like. The University itself will be measured by the quality of its faculty, by the students—both graduate and undergraduate—

which it turns out, by the prestige developed by its strong departments, and by the significance of the books and articles published by its faculty members.

The second half century of Bowling Green will be very different from the first. The University is on the threshold of achieving genuine distinction in limited areas. Whether or not it does so will depend on a number of variables. The most important of these relates to governance. Can faculty, students, and administration—working separately and together—provide the freedom and resources needed for the development of all aspects of the University and yet have the wisdom to select and strengthen most those aspects of the University which promise genuine superiority? Can the needs of the many disciplines be reconciled with development of some to the level of academic eminence? Can the University avoid mediocrity and become really first-rate in selected areas? These are several ways of stating the basic issue confronting the University as it looks to the future.

Paul F. Leedy
Provost

Bowling Green, Ohio
1967

Index

228